Narrative and Becoming

Plateaus – New Directions in Deleuze Studies

'It's not a matter of bringing all sorts of things together under a single concept but
rather of relating each concept to variables that explain its mutations.'
Gilles Deleuze, *Negotiations*

Series Editors

Ian Buchanan, University of Wollongong
Claire Colebrook, Penn State University

Editorial Advisory Board

Keith Ansell Pearson
Ronald Bogue
Constantin V. Boundas
Rosi Braidotti
Eugene Holland
Gregg Lambert
Dorothea Olkowski
Paul Patton
Daniel Smith
James Williams

Titles available in the series

Christian Kerslake, *Immanence and the Vertigo of Philosophy: From Kant to Deleuze*
Jean-Clet Martin, *Variations: The Philosophy of Gilles Deleuze*, translated by
Constantin V. Boundas and Susan Dyrkton
Simone Bignall, *Postcolonial Agency: Critique and Constructivism*
Miguel de Beistegui, *Immanence – Deleuze and Philosophy*
Jean-Jacques Lecercle, *Badiou and Deleuze Read Literature*
Ronald Bogue, *Deleuzian Fabulation and the Scars of History*
Sean Bowden, *The Priority of Events: Deleuze's Logic of Sense*
Craig Lundy, *History and Becoming: Deleuze's Philosophy of Creativity*
Aidan Tynan, *Deleuze's Literary Clinic: Criticism and the Politics of Symptoms*
Thomas Nail, *Returning to Revolution: Deleuze, Guattari and Zapatismo*
François Zourabichvili, *Deleuze: A Philosophy of the Event* with *The Vocabulary of
Deleuze* edited by Gregg Lambert and Daniel W. Smith, translated by Kieran Aarons
Frida Beckman, *Between Desire and Pleasure: A Deleuzian Theory of Sexuality*
Nadine Boljkovac, *Untimely Affects: Gilles Deleuze and an Ethics of Cinema*
Daniela Voss, *Conditions of Thought: Deleuze and Transcendental Ideas*
Daniel Barber, *Deleuze and the Naming of God: Post-Secularism and the Future of
Immanence*
F. LeRon Shults, *Iconoclastic Theology: Gilles Deleuze and the Secretion of Atheism*
Janae Sholtz, *The Invention of a People: Heidegger and Deleuze on Art and the Political*
Marco Altamirano, *Time, Technology and Environment: An Essay on the Philosophy
of Nature*
Sean McQueen, *Deleuze and Baudrillard: From Cyberpunk to Biopunk*
Ridvan Askin, *Narrative and Becoming*
Marc Rölli, *Gilles Deleuze's Transcendental Empiricism: From Tradition to Difference*
translated by Peter Hertz-Ohmes
Guillaume Collett, *The Psychoanalysis of Sense: Deleuze and the Lacanian School*
Ryan Johnson, *The Deleuze–Lucretius Encounter*

Forthcoming volumes

Cheri Carr, *Deleuze's Kantian Ethos: Critique as a Way of Life*
Alex Tissandier, *Affirming Divergence: Deleuze's Reading of Leibniz*

Visit the Plateaus website at edinburghuniversitypress.com/series/plat

NARRATIVE AND BECOMING

Ridvan Askin

EDINBURGH
University Press

Edinburgh University Press is one of the leading university presses in the UK. We publish academic books and journals in our selected subject areas across the humanities and social sciences, combining cutting-edge scholarship with high editorial and production values to produce academic works of lasting importance. For more information visit our website: edinburghuniversitypress.com

© Ridvan Askin, 2016

Edinburgh University Press Ltd
The Tun – Holyrood Road
12(2f) Jackson's Entry
Edinburgh EH8 8PJ

Typeset in Sabon by
Servis Filmsetting Ltd, Stockport, Cheshire,

A CIP record for this book is available from the British Library

ISBN 978 1 4744 1456 2 (hardback)
ISBN 978 1 4744 1457 9 (webready PDF)
ISBN 978 1 4744 1458 6 (epub)

The right of Ridvan Askin to be identified as the author of this work has been asserted in accordance with the Copyright, Designs and Patents Act 1988, and the Copyright and Related Rights Regulations 2003 (SI No. 2498).

Contents

Acknowledgements	vi
Abbreviations	viii
Introduction: Differential Narratology	1
1 Intensive Narration: Ana Castillo's *The Mixquiahuala Letters*	41
2 Narrating Sensation: Michael Ondaatje's *The Collected Works of Billy the Kid*	77
3 Sensational Realism: Colson Whitehead's *The Intuitionist*	118
4 Real Folds: Mark Z. Danielewski's *House of Leaves*	153
Conclusion: From the Becoming of Narrative to the Narrativity of Becoming	180
Works Cited	190
Index	204

Acknowledgements

They come first always and everywhere: Rania, Nila, and Tara – thank you for everything.

I owe my deepest gratitude to the following people, who have all contributed to the accomplishment of this project in one way or another:

Wolfgang Hochbruck and Oliver Scheiding for gently pushing me on to the path to academia while I was still a student at the University of Freiburg, and once again Wolfgang for his tireless encouragement and support ever since; the Freiburg Deleuze Reading Group, particularly Vega Damm, Moritz Gansen, and Martin Dornberg, for the many insightful discussions and the great breakfasts; Sergey Sistiaga for helping me out with Spinoza, for offering me a copy of Roy Bhaskar's *A Realist Theory of Science*, and for agreeing to drink beer any time anywhere; Paul J. Ennis for all things speculative; N. Katherine Hayles for her kind words and encouragement; Jan Alber and Johannes Fehrle for the many joint coffees and lunches, and their unnatural willingness to engage with my verbose smartassery; Andreas Hägler for his friendship and for enduring my Deleuze lingo over all these years (though Adorno isn't much better!); Derek Gottlieb for the extensive email discussions on cognitive literary studies and an expert indexing job; Matija Jelača for disagreeing about Deleuze; Jon Cogburn for his enthusiasm; the many philosophy blog writers for distracting me at the right time; all the faculty and staff at the University of Basel's Department of English for making it such a great place to work and be; Claire Colebrook for inviting me to Penn State, for reading and commenting on the manuscript, and for encouraging me to submit it to Edinburgh University Press's Plateaus series; and the series editors, as well as Carol Macdonald and the staff at EUP, for all their help and a thoroughly enjoyable publication process. Finally, Philipp Schweighauser deserves extra-special thanks for his unflinching support, his incisive advice, his patience, his hard-hitting critical interventions, for taking apart every single chapter of earlier versions of the manuscript, for making me

Acknowledgements

believe in my capacities, for pushing me ever further, and for his friendship – thank you.

This book is a revised version of my dissertation defended at the University of Basel in January 2014 and supervised by Philipp Schweighauser and Wolfgang Hochbruck. The research that went into this project was generously funded by the University of Basel, the Conférence Universitaire de Suisse Occidentale, and the Swiss National Science Foundation.

Parts and earlier versions of chapters and chapter sections of this book have previously appeared in the following venues:

(2015), 'Prolegomenon to a Differential Theory of Narrative', *SubStance* 44.3, pp. 155–70. © 2015 by the Board of Regents of the University of Wisconsin System. Reprinted by permission of the University of Wisconsin Press. All rights reserved.
(2014), 'Sweet Dreams Are Made of This: Speculation', in Caoimhe Doyle (ed.), *Weaponising Speculation*, New York: Punctum Books, pp. 61–8.
(2012), '"Folding, Unfolding, Refolding": Mark Z. Danielewski's Differential Novel *House of Leaves*', in Sascha Pöhlmann (ed.), *Revolutionary Leaves: The Fiction of Mark Z. Danielewski*, Newcastle: Cambridge Scholars, pp. 99–121. Published with the permission of Cambridge Scholars Publishing.

Abbreviations

ATP   Deleuze, Gilles and Félix Guattari (2007) [1980], *A Thousand Plateaus*, vol. 2 of *Capitalism and Schizophrenia*, trans. Brian Massumi, London: Continuum.

D II   Deleuze, Gilles and Claire Parnet (2006) [1977], *Dialogues II*, trans. Hugh Tomlinson and Barbara Habberjam, London: Continuum.

DR   Deleuze, Gilles (2004) [1968], *Difference and Repetition*, trans. Paul Patton, London: Continuum.

FB   Deleuze, Gilles (2003) [1981], *Francis Bacon: The Logic of Sensation*, trans. Daniel W. Smith, Minneapolis: University of Minnesota Press.

LS   Deleuze, Gilles (2004) [1969], *Logic of Sense*, trans. Mark Lester, London: Continuum.

NP   Deleuze, Gilles (2006) [1962], *Nietzsche and Philosophy*, trans. Hugh Tomlinson, New York: Columbia University Press.

TF   Deleuze, Gilles (2006) [1988], *The Fold: Leibniz and the Baroque*, trans. Tom Conley, London: Continuum.

WIP   Deleuze, Gilles and Félix Guattari (1994) [1991], *What Is Philosophy?*, trans. Hugh Tomlinson and Graham Burchell, New York: Columbia University Press.

Mir kommts so vor, als wär ich ganz aus Gefühlen gebaut.
Nila Darwish

Introduction:
Differential Narratology

> Everywhere, the depth of difference is primary.
> Gilles Deleuze, *Difference and Repetition*

> Es gibt Wiederholungen.
> Attwenger, 'Es gibt Wiederholungen'

This book proposes a differential theory of narrative. In doing so, it goes against the most basic fundamentals of narratology. These fundamentals seem so self-evident that they are generally assumed as granted and only rarely voiced explicitly. They are exemplarily set out in this covert manner in the following programmatic statement from Roland Barthes's 'Introduction to the Structural Analysis of Narratives':

> It may be that men ceaselessly re-inject into narrative what they have known, what they have experienced; but if they do, it is at least in a form which has vanquished repetition and instituted the model of a process of becoming. Narrative does not show, does not imitate. (Barthes 1978: 124)

While the statement's thrust seems to go against a mimetic and thus traditional understanding of narrative, it in fact leaves intact the most basic parameters that all theories of narrative have endorsed in one way or another before and ever since Barthes. These parameters are: (1) narrative is a specifically human business (both in the sense that all humans tell stories – storytelling as a pan-cultural phenomenon; and in the sense that humans tell stories whereas apes, trees, stars, and stones do not); (2) narrative is limited to the field of knowledge (as either its acquisition, storage, or expression, or any combination of these); and (3) narrative is based in experientiality (either as a means of communication or as a way of making experience intelligible in the first place, or both). In short, narrative is taken to be *anthropocentric, epistemological*, and *experiential*.

I cannot possibly go through the entire history of narratology here to substantiate this point: namely, that the richness and diversity of narratology rest on these three more or less tacit assumptions. Instead, I will have recourse to exemplary discussions of pertinent conceptualisations and theorisations throughout the book. But let me briefly point to three recent essays on the history of narratology that corroborate my claims. Jan Christoph Meister's entry on 'Narratology' in *The Living Handbook of Narratology* sketches the history of both the discipline and the term. Already its very first sentence makes clear that narratology concerns 'the study of the logic, principles, and practices of narrative *representation*', taking narrative's representational character for granted (Meister 2011/2014: n. p.; my emphasis). Meister then ends his second paragraph, which also concludes his definition of narratology, by asserting that the discipline is concerned with the 'exploration and modeling of *our ability* to produce and process narratives in a multitude of forms, media, contexts, and *communicative practices*' (n. p.; my emphases): that is, narrative is taken to be intrinsically related to *human* capacities, capacities to produce and receive stories, narrative thus being understood as a particular kind of information transmission, as essentially caught up with human communication. Similarly, in their mapping of the theoretical diversity and methodological richness of narratology, the historical surveys by David Herman and Monika Fludernik in *A Companion to Narrative Theory* never question that narratives are 'representations' or some form of 'mimesis' (Herman 2005: 32; Fludernik 2005: 43, 50). In addition, both Herman and Fludernik highlight the rootedness of modern narratology in questions of epistemology and cognition (Herman 2005: 23; Fludernik 2005: 48).

The *locus classicus* of conceptualising narrative on grounds of experientiality, in turn, is Fludernik's *Towards a 'Natural' Narratology*, where she famously defines narrative as the 'quasi-mimetic evocation of "real-life experience"' (1996: 12), but the single most important work in this respect is Paul Ricœur's massive three-volume *Time and Narrative*, the major thrust of which is to provide an argument for storytelling as making experience intelligible, both to oneself and to others. Narrative thus assumes an ethical role. *Narrative and Becoming*'s impetus derives in large parts from what I perceive to be an unjustified ethicisation of narrative. Ricœur's work thus provides, to some extent, the foil against which this book is developed.

The differential narratology presented here grants that narrative can and frequently does play out within the categories of human world, knowledge, and experience, but it denies that these categories

Introduction

present a *necessary*, let alone *sufficient* reason for theorising narrative. On the contrary, *Narrative and Becoming* argues that the ground from which to extract a coherent concept of narrative has to be trans-experiential, unconscious, and non-human. Differential narratology thus agrees with Barthes's basic anti-mimeticism. If narrative goes beyond human knowledge and experience, it cannot be representational. Indeed, as its title suggests, this study also joins Barthes in holding that narrative is invested in the 'process of becoming' (Barthes 1978: 124). Everything here hinges on the understanding of the notion of becoming, however. For Barthes, the relation between narrative and becoming boils down to this: in being told, experiences become other. This is the reason why, for Barthes, narrative vanquishes repetition. It does not just repeat prior experience and knowledge but produces new experiences and new knowledge. Thus, against narrative as the static reproduction of experience and knowledge, Barthes pits it as a process of their dynamic creation. It is only in this very restricted sense that Barthes's notion of narrative is anti-mimetic or non-representational. It is, however, very much representational in so far as it plays out entirely *within* the realm of experience and knowledge. In Barthes, becoming merely comes to mark change on the epistemological and experiential level. This is why Barthes, in due structuralist fashion, focuses so much on language and meaning:

> [T]he passion which may excite us in reading a novel is not that of a 'vision' (in actual fact, we do not 'see' anything). Rather it is that of meaning [. . .]; 'what happens' is language alone, the adventure of language, the unceasing celebration of its coming. (124)

In contrast, this book holds that narrative precisely goes beyond the grip of language and meaning. Against the all-pervasive restrictions of narrative to a narrow epistemological and experiential framework, *Narrative and Becoming* seeks to inscribe narrative within a much wider *metaphysical* horizon. Rather than being the Barthesian synonym of experiential and epistemological change, becoming here is taken up in the sense of a *philosophy of becoming* where it names the fundamental metaphysical processes of onto- and morphogenesis. As such, becoming does not merely encompass human concerns. The human just happens to be one mode of being among innumerable others (anything from entire galaxies to the Higgs boson) determined by becoming. Becoming itself simply unfolds: an unconscious, non-human, and non-experiential process. This realm of unconscious and non-human becoming is precisely the realm of Deleuzian difference, and it is in this realm that this book situates narrative.[1]

This is not to deny narrative any experiential and epistemological value, however. It is merely to relegate experience and epistemology from foundational matrices within which to understand narrative to secondary problems, cutting them down to size. As it turns out, and as I hope to show in the following chapters, it is precisely narratives that are apt to provide insight into the interstices of the realm of becoming, something the concepts of pure reason fall short of. While being caught up with the ontogenetic processes of becoming, narrative is thus also the very means of accessing the realm of becoming. In this sense, and against Barthes, narrative is indeed visionary.

Narrative as it is theorised here thus assumes a double function: on the one hand, it pertains to the *metaphysical processes* of onto- and morphogenesis; on the other hand, it provides *aesthetic knowledge* of these processes. Directly inscribed into the primary constituents of being, narrative is metaphysical. Probing the metaphysical depths of these constituents, narrative is speculative. Already Viktor Shklovsky emphasised this latter aspect when he insisted that literary[2] narrative is primarily a matter of sensation, that it is a means to encounter *things themselves*, a means 'to make a stone feel stony':

> [I]n order to return sensation to our limbs, in order to make us feel objects, to make a stone feel stony, man has been given the tool of art. The purpose of art, then, is to lead us to a knowledge of a thing through the organ of sight instead of recognition. By 'enstranging' objects and complicating form, the device of art makes perception long and 'laborious.' The perceptual process in art has a purpose all its own and ought to be extended to the fullest. *Art is a means of experiencing the process of creativity. The artifact itself is quite unimportant.* (Shklovsky 1998: 6)

This passage from his 'Art as Device' renders Shklovsky's programme in a nutshell: art, particularly literary art, by means of its form, makes us aware of both our perceptual process and the essential qualities of the object we perceive. It thus functions as a corrective to conceptual thought, as conceptual thought merely gives us objects in general but never the particularity of the objects we encounter, like, for example, the stoniness of stones. This is needed, according to Shklovsky, because in everyday life we are much more aware of our thoughts and our capacity to think than of our senses and our capacity to feel (5). Basically, the importance of art lies in the fact that it affords aesthetic experience, with aesthetic understood in its original sense

Introduction

here, as *aisthesis*: that is, a sensual taking in, intuition, perception. Ultimately, Shklovsky presents us with a riff on Immanuel Kant's famous dictum that '[t]houghts without content are empty, intuitions without concepts are blind' (A/51, B/75). It is just that for Shklovsky we clearly think too much and do not feel enough. The function of art is to give us back the content, the richness of things that we lose with pure thought. This is also why works of art are tools and why they themselves are 'quite unimportant'. What is important is the experience they afford, the richness of the world they disclose. Shklovsky thus pits the perception of creativity and the creativity of perception against sclerotic thought. This means that, for Shklovsky, intuitions without concept are not blind at all. On the contrary, it is intuition, aesthetic experience, which gives us the concrete world as it is rather than just its mere abstract representation. Instead of a state of blindness, intuitions provide true 'visions'.

While Shklovsky's essay is entitled 'Art as Device' and thus aims at the function of art in general, his concrete discussions of artworks are limited to literary works of art, and even to literary narratives. Thus, the devices of form he scrutinises and lists as tools of enstrangement all pertain to the domains of linguistics, rhetoric, and narrative structure. This explains the essay's canonical status within literary theory in general and narrative theory in particular.

I am very much in line with Shklovsky's insistence on sensation. But his insistence is still of a strictly epistemological and experiential kind as it concerns our access to things and their essential qualities. Differential narratology, however, pushes narrative theory to where epistemology capsizes and reverts into ontology, to where narrative ceases merely to be a form of human access to things (while also being that) and becomes expressive of being as such. What this study proposes, then, is that any epistemological understanding of narrative needs ontological grounding, that narrative's ontological make-up determines its epistemological value. Taking into account that narratology hitherto has focused on narrative exclusively in terms of epistemology – whenever it deals with it in terms of ontology it is always *within* a larger framework of epistemology: what is at stake is always the question of knowledge – *narrative has, in a strange way, never been the focus of narratology*. In other words, narrative has always been and still is viewed as being limited to issues of knowledge (in relation to the fictional or factual world it depicts and its very act of depicting) and never as something in its own right.[3]

While I do not deny that narrative always is about something,

I wish to emphasise that before being *about* something it simply *is* something itself and that this *is* determines its aboutness. This book thus tackles the fundamental question, 'What is narrative?' – a question that still awaits an adequate answer. In fact, the history of twentieth-century narrative theory can be viewed as a progressive move away from this fundamental question. While Shklovsky still upheld that the essence of (literary) narrative was to be found in its capacity to access things themselves, the focus has subsequently shifted from things as the end of cognition to language and meaning taking the place of things to the very processes of cognition itself. Narrative is thus reduced to nothing but a cognitive process. The history of modern narratology is a history of increasing recoil away from ontological questions to epistemological ones, from things vis-à-vis the human to the very interstices of the human mind itself, from an emphasis on things in our accessing them to the workings of this very access itself. Seen this way, it seems that narrative is nothing but human, the epitome of humanity's narcissistic self-indulgence: narrative as the playground of human self-concern. Indeed, this diagnosis is confirmed in an essay by Fludernik, where she asserts that 'the revived concern for narrative in history, legal studies, and economics may indicate the incipient or ongoing *rehumanization* of the social sciences. Profiting from these trends, narratology finds itself again flourishing' (Fludernik 2010: 925; my emphasis). According to Fludernik, such a 'revived concern for narrative' amounts to a 'rehumanization of the social sciences' precisely due to the 'renewed emphasis on consciousness' (926) which narratology shares and actively promotes. This is the reason why narratology is flourishing. It is in this vein that Fludernik maintains that 'a coming together of all language- and consciousness-related areas of literary studies promises fair to provide convincing explanations for the aesthetic status of the literary or of art' (927). Thus, by means of narrative, the aesthetic status of literature and art is invariably bound to the human mind. Across the disciplines, from literary studies to the social sciences, consciousness is taken to reign supreme and the study of narrative is singled out as apt to provide the shared ground for all these diverse enquiries. The questionable accuracy of Fludernik's diagnosis concerning rehumanisation aside – it seems much more the case that the order of the day is a sweeping post- or dehumanisation, from eliminative neuroscience to the digital humanities, from actor-network-theory to the new materialisms – narrative thus understood seems to fall under the verdict of what Quentin Meillassoux termed

Introduction

'correlationism' (Meillassoux 2009: 5), the very means by which things are turned into the correlate of thought, the way any in-itself turns out to be always already for us. Such a characterisation is indeed to the point if one considers Meillassoux's diagnosis that '[d]uring the twentieth century, the two principal "media" of the correlation were consciousness and language' (6). These are precisely the two media in which narrative is unanimously believed to play out. In contrast, one of the principal tasks of this book will be to show that narrative cannot be reduced to the workings of consciousness and language, and neither can literature and artworks. Such a task entails going back to Shklovsky's insistence on sensation and taking it up in its ontological connotations.

There is thus a fundamental bifurcation located at the roots of modern narratology: one path is the path narratology has taken leading up to the current cognitive paradigm; the other path is untrodden and leads down into metaphysical depths. *Narrative and Becoming* initiates a voyage off this beaten track of narratology uncovering a subterranean alliance between metaphysics, aesthetics, and narratology. This voyage begins with a subtle but decisive shift with regard to Shklovsky's employment of sensation: rather than seeing narrative merely as a means of human access to things, to the stoniness of the stone, via sensation as the very human mode of accessing the essence of things, sensation is here understood in its Deleuzian sense as an autonomous mode of being. Narratives are 'beings of sensation' (WIP: 165, 169, 175) expressive of being as such. Like Shklovsky, Deleuze opposes sensation to recognition, positing the 'fundamental *encounter*' (DR: 176) before any use of cognition – we encounter things before we start processing them cognitively.

> What is encountered [Deleuze continues] may be grasped in a range of affective tones: wonder, love, hatred, suffering. In whichever tone, its primary characteristic is that it can only be sensed. In this sense it is opposed to recognition. In recognition, the sensible is not at all that which can only be sensed, but that which bears directly upon the senses in an object which can be recalled, imagined or conceived. (DR: 176)

The distinction Deleuze draws is between something that can *only* be sensed – the object of encounter – and something that is sensed *and* processed differently – the object of recognition. This means that that which can only be sensed is, in fact, impossible to be sensed 'from the point of view of recognition': that is, 'from the point of view of an empirical exercise of the senses' (DR: 176). In other words, what is encountered is not a mere 'sensible being but the being *of* the sensible. It is not the given but that by which the given is given' (DR: 176). Since the given is, of course, the domain of representation – the given is given to us; that is, it *is* our representation: namely, of that by which the given is given – it follows that that by which the given is given, the being of the sensible, is sub-representational. It is the domain our representations both cannot reach and in which they are generated (they are given by it).[4] The Deleuzian encounter thus solicits the *transcendental* use of our senses, what Deleuze refers to as the method of transcendental empiricism. This is the speculative aspect of his philosophy. And that which is encountered, the being of the sensible, what Deleuze also calls 'the *sentiendum*' (DR: 176), the very sensation of the 'beings of sensation' referred to above, pertains to the heart of his metaphysics (Deleuze is thus indeed a speculative metaphysician). Sensations are '*beings* whose validity lies in themselves' and as such they can 'exist in the absence of man' (WIP: 168). To put it simply: sensations and their relations constitute the basic fabric of reality. It is thus that sensation achieves genuine ontological status. Such a Deleuzian shift of emphasis necessarily results in the problematisation of the primacy of consciousness in narrative theory.

The source of this primacy, in turn, can be traced back to Kant's critical project. It all starts with Kant's limitation of the field of reason's legitimate inquiry to reason itself inaugurated by his (in)famous Copernican Revolution: in Kant, everything plays out within the human mind. This is true of both the *empirical*, the realm of experience, and the *transcendental*, the realm of the conditions of experience. Kant conceives of both realms as immanent to consciousness and thus relegates things in themselves to an inaccessible outside. With Kant, even though things in themselves are thinkable, they remain unknowable. Kant's transcendental idealism fundamentally constrains the powers of thought, limiting its legitimate field of enquiry to itself; for thought, there is no outside of thought. While Kant himself does not demolish the realm of the in-itself, he exorcises it; ever since Kant, any in-itself turns out to be always already for-us. Kant achieves the all-pervasiveness of consciousness. In fact, he effectively facilitates the reign of *experience* and of *representation* – despite, or, as we will shortly see, because of his transcendental.

It is not hard to see how this philosophical programme underpins narratology's explanatory frameworks, which cast narrative precisely as representational and experiential with no purchase on any

Introduction

mind-independent reality whatsoever.[5] This is exemplarily manifest in the current paradigm of cognitive narratology. This exemplarity of cognitive narratology with respect to Kant's critical project is no coincidence since Kant basically 'founds cognitive science as we know it today' (Dunham et al. 2011: 98). In this vein, narrative is taken to be fundamentally grounded in human experience and consciousness dealing in mental representations only. It is this 'nexus of narrative and mind' (Herman 2009: 137; Herman 2012) that is deeply troublesome and unsatisfactory. There are two reasons for this: one has to do with Kantianism's intrinsic deficiency, the other with actual literary narratives' palpable anti-Kantian performance. As to Kantianism's intrinsic deficiency, it is precisely what Meillassoux's coinage 'correlationism' (Meillassoux 2009: 5) so aptly captures.[6] Correlationism names the quintessentially Kantian operation of turning things into the correlate of thought. In a recent essay, Ray Brassier formulates an exceptionally clear characterisation of the correlationist argument. Correlationism is

> that form of argumentation that slides from the true claim that we need a concept of mind-independent reality in order to make claims about the latter to the false claim that the very concept of mind-independent reality suffices to convert the latter into a concept, which is by definition mind-dependent. This is the fatal non-sequitur at the root of every variant of correlationism. (Brassier 2011: 64)

With respect to narrative, we could then say that while a concept of narrative is necessarily mind-dependent, narrative in-itself is not. The question, of course, is whether there is any good reason to think that narrative is extra-mental. Indeed, such a claim seems to be absurd. How could human consciousness not be decisive for the being of narrative? In narratives, surely, some consciousness is telling something to some other consciousness. How not to speak of consciousness? Yet my claim is precisely that narrative is a mind-independent reality on its own terms.

Before developing this claim, however, some further qualifications concerning narratology's pervasive representationalism need to be provided. While it is certainly uncontroversial to argue that *most* theories of narrative are representational and experiential, it might be less so to claim that such a characterisation holds true for *all* theories of narrative. Such a claim needs to be further substantiated if it is not to be discarded on the grounds of unsound scholarship. This task becomes even more pressing in face of narratologies which explicitly insist on their opposition to representational accounts of narrative. In what follows, I will thus deal with two such allegedly non-representational theories and show how they ultimately fail to break out of a representational understanding of narrative. This brief foray into recent discussions within narratology serves not only to underscore once more the fact that representation reigns supreme in narrative theory, but also to emphasise that a non-representational theory of narrative is very much needed, and that this need has in fact already been registered by narratologists.

The first of these allegedly non-representational theories is pragmatic narrative theory as expounded by David Rudrum in an article and the subsequent discussion with Marie-Laure Ryan published in the journal *Narrative* in 2005 and 2006. Rudrum begins his article precisely with the observation that narratology is thoroughly representational and provides an extensive list of quotations from several major contributors to the field, such as Gérard Genette, Robert Scholes, Gerald Prince, and Mieke Bal to make this point (Rudrum 2005: 195). Indeed, he identifies representation as 'one of the few methodological constants of narratology' (196). Rudrum bluntly 'disagree[s] with the narratologists' and proposes a pragmatic take on narrative instead. However, even though the pragmatic narrative theory Rudrum envisions does not seek to explain narrative primarily on representational grounds, representation nevertheless remains a precondition as pragmatic narratology plays out entirely within the realm of representation. This becomes immediately evident in Rudrum's article when he quotes this passage from Wittgenstein's *Philosophical Investigations*:

> Imagine a picture *representing* a boxer in a particular stance. Now, this picture can be used to tell someone how he should stand, should hold himself; or how he should not hold himself; or how a particular man did stand in such-and-such a place; and so on. (Wittgenstein 1981: 11; qtd in Rudrum 2005: 199; my emphasis)

Wittgenstein indeed emphasises language use, but there is no doubt that this use plays out within the domain of representation: the picture of the boxer Wittgenstein refers to is taken to represent a boxer. Accordingly, Rudrum's pragmatic account does not challenge representation per se. Its claim is much more modest. Rudrum merely suggests that representation alone is not a sufficient enough category for conceiving narrative and needs to be expanded according to its particular uses. In fact, Rudrum explicitly states that while repre-

Introduction

sentation might be a *necessary* condition of narrative (he remains agnostic as to whether this is the case or not), it is not a *sufficient* one (198). According to Rudrum, in order to be a sufficient condition of narrative the theory of representation needs to be supplemented with the category of use; narrative amounts to a particular, historically and culturally contingent, use of representation. Rudrum's account, rather than challenging representation, is thus an attempt at refining the classical representational take on narrative. His reorientation does not really concern the *theory* of narrative but rather a shift in terms of *method*. What Rudrum advocates is precisely a '*methodological* re-orientation in the way we go about conceiving narrative, and hence narratology' (Rudrum 2006: 201; my emphasis). However, a mere methodological reorientation does not do the trick. As long as this new method plays out within the limits of a correlationist and representational anti-metaphysics, it will change very little.

Ultimately, it is difficult to assess whether Rudrum really intends to break out of the representational framework. However, taking into account his agnosticism concerning the representational nature of narrative and given the title of his article – 'From Narrative Representation to Narrative Use' – his essay does seem to gesture towards a beyond of representation. At the very least, as Ryan points out in her rather fierce response, it aims to invert the hierarchy between semantics and pragmatics by positing pragmatics as primary (Ryan 2006: 189). Even if in light of the presupposition of a thoroughly representational framework, how such a reversal should be possible remains to be answered, and even if Rudrum's conceptualisation of narrative does ultimately not oppose representation per se, it does constitute an attempt at overthrowing representation's unconstrained reign, cutting it down to size. That this rather modest operation needs to be employed as an exemplar of an anti-representationalist narrative theory is quite telling, as it serves to emphasise how thoroughly representational a discipline narratology in fact is. This impression is further enhanced by Ryan's immediate response to Rudrum warding off his attack, and firmly cementing the representationality of narrative. This indicates two things: there seem to be hardly any non-representational theories of narrative, and those which threaten to be such have a hard time holding their stance.

Another such allegedly non-representational theory of narrative, which has gained traction recently, is that of unnatural narratology.[7] Unnatural narratology's explicit aim is to counter narratology's pervasive 'mimetic reductionism' (Alber et al. 2010: 115), as it perceives this reductionism to be a major limiting factor when it comes to conceptualising narrative. In formulating this programme, unnatural narratology seems to be a strong ally of differential narratology and thus deserves close scrutiny. According to unnatural narratology, by taking natural or mimetic narratives as its default model, traditional narratology risks losing 'sight of the specific features and forms of narrative' (115). Unnatural narratology thus sets out to detect anomalies in narratives which precisely defy representation. Unnatural narratologists have been very successful in this effort, discriminating and describing a host of narrative strategies and techniques which pose serious problems for representational theories of narrative. More importantly still, unnatural narratology shows us *why* and *how* these strategies and techniques pose the problems they pose – why representational theories of narrative are incapable of accounting for these techniques and how these strategies work to crack open the representational frame. Unnatural narratology proves to be a veritable treasure chest in this respect. Unfortunately, it also just stops short at this point. When it comes to answering the question of what to do with these anti-representational features, unnatural narratology knows only two options: either actively naturalise the anomaly – that is, translate it back into representational categories and thus undo it (Alber 2009: 82), or be content with pointing out these anomalies just for the sake of pointing them out – creating a list of deviant narrative strategies – without trying to address the implications of such anomaly (Richardson 2006). While in the first case unnatural narratology actively works to rein in deviant behaviour and tries to reinscribe it within the established representational paradigm, in the second case it gives these anomalies some leeway just to parade them before our eyes in a kind of freak show.[8] While in the first case unnatural narratology acts as both police and parole officer, in the second it assumes the role of voyeur. Thus, it is no surprise that it claims just two possible options for coping with such narratives: either actively naturalise them or passively accept them in a Zen-like meditative mind set (Alber et al. 2012: 376–7).[9] But this is only the case because its metaphysical assumptions are precisely representational to the core. While naturalisation is already explicitly representational, the second option of meditative acceptance likewise only enters the picture when one assumes that these deviations are actually *representations* of the deviant. Faced with such representations, indeed either one works to integrate these deviations into a workable framework (epistemology police) or one opts for a sort of

Introduction

detached *Gelassenheit* in face of the spectacle (theological voyeur).[10] All this becomes tellingly evident in the use of the term 'real-world' in Alber, Iversen, Nielsen, and Richardson's joint articles (Alber et al. 2010: passim; Alber et al. 2012: passim) where they apply this term to the *phenomenal* world, thereby equating the merely phenomenal with the real: the real is what appears real to us. What is real are thus precisely our representations. Unnatural narratology, like all narratology, thus clearly operates within a correlationist and even outright idealist framework.[11] In addition, Alber and his colleagues restrict mimesis to the relation a given narrative has to the phenomenal world. Thus, every narrative that does not conform to such a relation is deemed non- or even anti-mimetic and unnatural. In short, every narrative that does not conform to the logic and physics of 'our' world becomes automatically non-representational (Alber 2009: 80; Alber et al. 2010: 116). Such an argument is deeply flawed, however. Just because a given narrative is not mimetic with respect to our phenomenal world does not entail that it is non-representational *tout court*. Indeed, these narratives can still be understood as representational in so far as they are seen to represent possible or even impossible worlds. This is exactly the formula according to which unnatural narratology proceeds: 'An unnatural storyworld contains physical or logical impossibilities that concern the *represented* world's temporal or spatial organization' (Alber et al. 2010: 116; my emphasis). The key word here is 'represented', giving away unnatural narratology's thoroughly representational bias. Contrary to the four authors' assertions, everything is representational in unnatural narratology. All that unnatural narratology achieves is an extension of the representational stranglehold on narrative. This is made possible by two distinct moves. First, unnatural narratology firmly inscribes narrative within a Kantian anti-metaphysics of the primacy of consciousness by reducing the real to the phenomenal. Second, it makes sure that nothing escapes the reign of mentality by reinscribing all narrative deviations, particularly those it detects as non-representational, into a mimetic relation. Interestingly, the four authors have been taken up on their understanding of mimesis by Fludernik and asked to clarify their employment of the term (Fludernik 2012: 366–7). In their response to Fludernik's challenge, the unnaturalists admit that their usage of the terms anti- and non-mimetic merely applies to Platonic mimesis and that they fully endorse mimesis in its Aristotelian sense (Alber et al. 2012: 378). This obviously begs the question as to how far unnatural narratology then deviates from traditional understandings of narrative, as Aristotelian mimesis is precisely the version to which almost all accounts of narrative default. There is hardly anything more traditional and conventional than the conceptualisation of narrative in terms of Aristotelian mimesis. This is only half the story, though, as narratology's Aristotelianism actually comes refracted through Kant. While Aristotle merely insisted on mimesis as the representation of 'people in action' (Aristotle 1987: 32) without specifying where this representation takes place, Kant establishes the *human mind* as the only playground of representation. Kant irrevocably interiorises Aristotle.[12] It is this interiorised, Kantian notion of representation to which unnatural narratologists adhere. This becomes particularly evident in Alber's definition of the unnatural as impossible according to the laws of either physics or logic. Distinguishing between the natural and unnatural thus depends on our cognitive capacities and the respective state of our knowledge (physics), or else the demarcation process plays out entirely within the space of reason (logic). In addition, in the first case we are basically told to check whether any given narrative world and its events and existents adequately *represent* the empirical reality of our world – that is, whether they adequately trace the way our world is for us at the given moment in history in which we are running the check. In the second case, we are told to check whether the given narration adheres to the rules of rational thought *tout court*. In both cases the question of (un)naturalness is decided within the space of reason – the distinction is a mere cognitive issue, not an ontological one. Unnaturalists' notion of representation is neither Platonic nor Aristotelian but thoroughly Kantian.

Overall, unnatural narratologists' aim to articulate a narratology capable of addressing what they term anti-mimetic and unnatural is flawed from the outset since their framework for doing so remains utterly representational. Unnatural narratology turns out to be thoroughly natural, all too natural. Or rather, from the point of view of a Deleuzian realist philosophy of nature endorsed here, both natural and unnatural narratology are thoroughly unnatural. This is so because their respective agendas conform to Kantian transcendentalism with its firm cementing of the nature–culture divide and the subsequent implementation of second nature as foundational everywhere. As Iain Hamilton Grant, referencing Schelling, puts it:

> Kant and Fichte at the very least invented a new terrain for philosophical activity, but did not exploit it sufficiently; and Fichte, especially, showed

Introduction

a considerable grasp of the powers of abstraction. Such powers, since they are demonstrably actuable, require therefore a physical grounding to remove them from the 'unnature' the transcendentalists have established as taking the place, in 'all branches of culture and education' of nature (VII, 80). (Grant 2008: 158)

To undo this reign of unnature, only a thoroughly *naturalised* and thus *non-representational* transcendental will do.

A characterisation of narrative which rests on such a naturalised transcendental and thus avoids the correlationist fallacy can be directly drawn from Deleuze's critique of the Kantian project. Unsurprisingly, this critique hinges on the Kantian conception of the transcendental. Deleuze criticises Kant for conceiving of the transcendental as a mere copy of the empirical, for building his transcendental in the image of consciousness. The Kantian relation between the empirical and the transcendental is thus one of resemblance. This resemblance effectively establishes the primacy of the empirical since the empirical is thus transplanted into the heart of the transcendental, precisely the realm which is supposed to account for the very conditions of the empirical. Against this circular and subjectivist conception of the transcendental, Deleuze pits his own processual and speculative conception. Against the transcendental situated firmly *within* the human mind, Deleuze proposes a truly metaphysical transcendental operating *outside* the human mind. In addition, Deleuze's transcendental is generative since it brings about the empirical – it is ontogenetic and morphogenetic. In short, the Deleuzian transcendental realm of Ideas is productive of the empirical realm of experience. Both realms together constitute the Deleuzian real. With Kant, the transcendental, lacking a genetic relation to the empirical, turns out to be transcendent. An unsurpassable gap divides the two realms of the transcendental and the empirical, and in contrast to Deleuze's all-encompassing realism, this gap introduces a division between the real and the possible. Kant's tracing of the transcendental from the empirical thus ultimately results in the positing of a transcendent subject. His Copernican Revolution places the human subject in the position of God and makes the experiential immanent to a transcendent consciousness. Deleuze, in contrast, establishes a pure immanence since his transcendental and empirical play out on the same plane. Even though they are firmly differentiated, and even though the transcendental produces the empirical, the transcendental does not exist apart from the empirical. Rather it 'insists and persists' (DR: 203) in the empirical. In Deleuze, the place of God has thus been evacuated and flattened out. In place of Kant's vertical and hierarchic regime of subjectivity, Deleuze proposes a fundamentally flat and anarchic ontology.[13]

By following Bergson and employing the notions of the virtual and the actual in place of the transcendental and the empirical, Deleuze makes his deviation from and reworking of Kant also apparent on the terminological level. Taking this into account, we can then say that the Deleuzian real is constituted by virtual Ideas productive of actual experience. It is important to emphasise that Deleuzian Ideas are ontological and not merely mental. In this respect, they are closer to Platonic Forms than the empiricists' ideas on which Kant draws.[14] Deleuze thus effectively re-ontologises what Kant de-ontologised, reinscribing the noumenal at the heart of philosophy. To sum up, we could say that against Kant's transcendental as transcendent consciousness, Deleuze posits his transcendental as immanent unconscious. And while Kant's empirical amounts to the representational realisation of a possibility with the real merely resembling the possible, Deleuze's is the processual actualisation of virtuality with the virtual really becoming the actual. While Kant's conception of the transcendental is thoroughly anthropocentric and anti-metaphysical, Deleuze's is fundamentally non-human and speculative. While Kant cannot remedy the gap in his account of the relation between the empirical and the transcendental, Deleuze makes this relation an ontogenetic and morphogenetic one. In short, Kant's system is thoroughly *representational* while Deleuze's is *expressive*. While narratology has hitherto conceived of narrative as Kantian mind-dependent, ideal representation, it should be conceived of as mind-independent, expressive reality. *Narrative and Becoming* thus aims at a vast tectonic upheaval; its goal is to shift the narratological grounds from a Kantian anti-metaphysics to a Deleuzian metaphysics. It is important to emphasise that this upheaval and shift by no means result in the ruin of narratology and its categories; on the contrary, they are tantamount to their proper grounding.

Apart from the centrality of consciousness in narratology, such grounding needs to tackle a second problem: narratology has never been abstract enough. This, too, is a direct result of its Kantian legacy. In all its elaborate theoretical architectonics it has always been concerned with what Deleuze terms the actual, even when seemingly being engaged with the abstract idea of narrative as such. Conceiving the abstract in the image of the concrete, the transcendental in the

Introduction

image of the empirical, the unconscious in the image of consciousness – in what amounts to its inherent Kantianism – narratology has ceaselessly conceived the general idea of narrative in the image of particular narratives. It has never gone far enough in its efforts at abstraction. It has never attained narrative as an intransitive, supra-historical, universal idea. Admittedly, this is not a very original diagnosis. In fact, this problem is at the very heart of one of the central debates within narratology: namely, that concerning narrativity, the question of what makes a narrative a narrative.[15] Thus, Meir Sternberg lambasts narratology precisely for not having been able 'to establish narrative differentials' (Sternberg 2001: 116), thus failing to formulate universals of narrative and, concomitantly, lacking a suitable notion of narrativity. Sternberg's own work is a continuous effort to elaborate such narrative universals, most recently in two long essays (Sternberg 2003a; Sternberg 2003b). It also serves to point out why narratology continuously fails to provide a satisfactory account of narrativity. Sternberg's universals – suspense, curiosity, surprise – play out entirely within what Deleuze would term actuality, an explicitly mental actuality at that (that is, representation), and thus are susceptible to the critique of narratology mounted here. In their actualism Sternberg's universals 'explain nothing and must themselves be explained' (WIP: 7). Sternberg's particular efforts concerning narrativity highlight a very general problem of narratology: the discipline incessantly tries to formulate empirical answers to a metaphysical question and thus cannot but fail in its task.

Accordingly, in order to answer the question 'What is narrative?' adequately, a *metaphysical* notion of narrativity needs to be formulated. In alignment with Deleuze's philosophy, the task will thus be to elaborate the Idea of narrative. Since, in the Deleuzian framework, this Idea is only to be found in its concrete expressions, the task necessarily warrants concrete analyses of such expressions: that is, actual narratives. The task of such analysis in turn is to trace the genesis of these actual narratives from their underlying virtual narrative structure (Idea, narrativity). The means to do so is to investigate *how* this structure is implicated in the respective narrative in question. This procedure is apt to give us an adequate *concept* of narrative, a concept that captures the Idea of narrative without sacrificing the particularity of its expressions for the sake of generalisation. Before we can concern ourselves with the actual analysis of narratives in light of Deleuze's virtual–actual relation, however, two propaedeutic questions need to be dealt with.

For one, it has still not become quite clear why exactly we should overhaul the most basic convictions of narratology. Even if one were to grant that the discipline grapples with a host of fundamental problems, and, further, that these problems are of a distinctly philosophical kind, it is not at all clear – in view of the highly contentious character of the issues involved – on which grounds to base one's decision in solving these problems. In short, is it really necessary to introduce such a radical shift of framework? In addition, the position I propose is far from expressing anything like the philosophical mainstream view, which in fact is still very much Kantian. And even if one were to grant that Kantianism is a prevailing problem in need of being resolved, it still does not follow that the solution has to be Deleuzianism. The second question, then, is: why exactly Deleuze?

As to the first question, one part of the answer obviously needs to be given on the argumentative battleground, which we already find ourselves in the midst of; the other lies in the object of analysis itself. It is narrative itself, particularly in its literary guise, which incessantly counteracts the limits imposed by Kantianism, as literary narratives often explicitly enquire into their very own conditions qua narrative, their essence or narrativity. In short, narrative turns out to be a question not only of aesthetics but also of ontology. This tripartite relation between narrative, aesthetics, and ontology is made more than explicit in much of postmodernist and contemporary literature. Again, this is a fact that has already been observed by narratology as voiced in Brian McHale's now canonical take on postmodernist fiction as predominantly grappling with problems of ontology rather than epistemology. And again, narratology failed to provide a satisfactory account. McHale's book is another instructive illustration of narratology's shortcomings precisely because it relies on an unacknowledged Kantian fundament for its argument. In his account, McHale relegates the ontological concerns the texts display to the field of thematics and then goes on to analyse what he considers to be postmodernist poetics proper (McHale 1987: 27). He is only interested in form at the expense of content. There are two major problems with this move. First, it dissociates thematics – what a text says – and poetics – how it says what it says; and second, McHale's analysis of postmodernist poetics rests entirely on an identitarian notion of ontology, precisely the kind of ontology that is explicitly contested in the postmodernist texts he analyses. The first problem, the separation of thematics and poetics, makes it possible for McHale to focus solely on the how, the narrative strategies these narratives

Introduction

employ. But by focusing on poetics only and discarding thematics, he, according to his own account of the implication of ontology, evades accounting for the ontological concerns of these texts, concerns that are *irreducibly entangled with the very narrative strategies they employ*. He thus misses out on the ontological import of these strategies themselves. The second problem only reinforces the first, since relying on an identitarian notion of ontology is inadequate for capturing what is explicitly designed to elude such an apparatus: 'the largest fish pass through' (DR: 81). In short, McHale does not take seriously what he himself diagnoses: namely, the ontological dominant inherent in postmodernist fiction. Or, rather, the ontological dimension of these narratives remains unexplored, as they are made to fit well-established categories, categories they actively work to undo. This deconstructive activity of narratives has remained under the radar of narratology. Thus, the relation between narrative, aesthetics, and ontology that these narratives display – and let me repeat that this relation is by no means restricted to, but only made particularly explicit by, postmodernist and contemporary fiction[16] – is still in need of exploration. But this is a task which traditional narratology,[17] due to its predominantly epistemological outlook and inherent Kantian limitations, cannot adequately address. It simply does not possess the adequate metaphysics for such an undertaking.

That the major source for such a metaphysics is Gilles Deleuze, and this is the answer to the second question posed above, has heuristic and pragmatic as well as properly metaphysical reasons. It is well known that the twentieth century was, by and large, an era of the *critique* of metaphysics and thus at heart an extension of the Kantian project. The very beginning of Raphaël Millière's extremely rich survey, 'Metaphysics Today and Tomorrow', sums the situation up nicely:

> Throughout the twentieth century, numerous philosophers sounded the death knell of metaphysics. Ludwig Wittgenstein, Rudolf Carnap, Martin Heidegger, Gilbert Ryle, J. L. Austin, Jacques Derrida, Jürgen Habermas, Richard Rorty, and, henceforth, Hilary Putnam: a great many tutelary figures have extolled the rejection, the exceeding, the elimination, or the deconstruction of first philosophy. All these necrological chronicles do not have the same radiance, the same seriousness, nor the same motivations, but they all agree to dismiss the discipline, which in the past was considered 'the queen of the sciences', with a violence at times comparable to the prestige it commanded at the time of its impunity. Even today, certain philosophers hastily spread the tragic news with contempt for

philosophical inquiry, as if its grave solemnity bestowed upon it some obviousness. Thus, Franco Volpi writes: '"Grand metaphysics is dead!" is the slogan which applies to *the majority of contemporary philosophers, whether continentals or of analytic profession*. They *all* treat metaphysics as a dead dog.' (Millière 2011: 1)

One result of the ubiquity of the metaphysics-bashing that is characteristic of the twentieth century is that there simply are not that many contemporary metaphysical systems from which to choose. While the analytic tradition has arguably produced more works of a metaphysical nature (metaphysics *of*) than its continental counterpart, not many of its proponents have ventured to build a whole metaphysical *system* (metaphysics *simpliciter*). This is without doubt partly due to the very nature of analytic philosophy, which tends to favour the intricately crafted small job over the ambitiously sweeping strokes involved in painting the big picture.[18] As to continentalists, Louis Morelle in a recent assessment only lists 'Bergson, Whitehead, and Deleuze' (Morelle 2012: 248) as serious contenders for the label of twentieth-century metaphysician. While metaphysics thus was the twentieth century's most beloved philosophical whipping boy with only very few unflinching proponents located at the very margins of the philosophical discourse, it seems as if it has now returned with a fervour only matched by the previous attempts at denial. The first few years of the twenty-first century brought not only a plethora of commentaries on and works inspired by the three continental figures mentioned above but also a rekindled interest and powerful return to metaphysics in general, both on the analytic and continental sides of the divide. The most notable foray in this respect on the continental side of things, at least in terms of impact, is without doubt the philosophical movement known as speculative realism, a movement characterised more by its dismissal of the Kantian Copernican Revolution than any shared positive doctrine.[19] The differing entryways into the realm of metaphysics that speculative realism provides range from dynamic process philosophy (Grant 2008) to object-oriented ontology (Harman 2011c; Bryant 2011; Garcia 2014; Morton 2013a),[20] from speculative aesthetics (Negarestani 2008; Shaviro 2009; Shaviro 2014; Askin et al. 2014) to speculative scientism and mathematicism (Brassier 2007; Meillassoux 2009). Neither by themselves nor in their totality do these diverse strands come anywhere close to the consistent systematicity of Gilles Deleuze's œuvre, however.[21] Quite on the contrary: they have spawned, and continue to do so, a multitude of closely related but irreducible new concepts impossible to

Introduction

integrate without too much technicality and interpretative work into a coherent formulation of a metaphysical concept of narrative. These are essentially philosophies in the making, to appropriate Graham Harman's characterisation of Meillassoux's project for all strands of speculative realism (Harman 2011b). These recent developments in metaphysical thought nevertheless provide important points of reference, particularly since some versions of this movement build heavily on Deleuze's philosophy. In fact, the programme of differential narratology as it is sketched here could easily be subsumed within this recent shift towards speculation and realism within the continental tradition, as it basically proposes a Deleuzian *speculative narratology*.

In short, Deleuze has the double advantage of being contemporary enough *and* of providing a worked-out, consistent metaphysics. In addition and as we have already seen, Deleuze's starting point is precisely Kant. He detects a delirious moment in Kant himself, takes up that particular moment and builds his philosophy of difference from there.[22] Deleuze's metaphysics amounts to a sort of anti-Kantian Kantianism, the *Verwindung* of Kant rather than his *Überwindung*, as Gianni Vattimo might put it (Vattimo 1987). Another way to express this would be to say that Deleuze's metaphysics constitutes a veritable working through of the Kantian legacy in contrast to the deadening repetitiveness of much of contemporary philosophy. Since this repetition compulsion is narratology's major driving force, it seems more than fitting to propose a Deleuzian cure.[23]

It is about time, then, that a few fundamentals of differential narratology are mentioned. *Theoretically*, differential narratology casts narrative as expressive rather than representational; or, what amounts to the same thing, representation is reformulated in terms of expression rather than resemblance, analogy, or verisimilitude. Differential narratology thus entails the expression of the virtual Idea of Narrative made up of differential elements and relations in actual, numerically differentiable narratives. Expression here is synonymous with neither emanation nor participation. Deleuzian Ideas do not exist in a transcendent realm from which they would have to descend in order to be embodied in actuality (emanation) or which would have to be somehow tapped in order to guarantee and validate the assignment of rightful positions (participation). Rather, virtuality and actuality constitute a plane of immanence with virtuality explicating (unfolding) actuality and actuality implicating (infolding) virtuality. It is precisely this implication of virtuality which can be traced in actual narratives, and which some literary narratives make explicit. They do this by way of a host of narrative strategies which fracture and break up, and thereby render inconsistent, their representational surface. These strategies range from the employment of inconsistent narrative voices to the mixing of incongruent narrative levels, from the projection of impossible perspectives to the interweaving of incompossible storylines. It is in these inconsistencies that the virtual manifests itself. To be clear, it is not the virtual itself which is thus made explicit – such a claim would be oxymoronic – but the implication of the virtual in the actual.

It is with respect to both the implication of the virtual and the making explicit of this implication that the third term in Deleuze's tripartite ontology – intensity – is of utmost relevance, since the virtual is implicated in the actual precisely by way of the intensive. Intensity connects virtuality with actuality; virtual differential elements and relations have to pass through the intensive in order to become actualised. Intensity selects those virtualities that will be made actual and thus marks the threshold between actuality and virtuality. It constitutes a sort of membrane or filter inserted between the two, with one side immersed in virtuality and the other side in actuality. Alluding to the ubiquity of interdimensional portals and gateways in science fiction, one could say that intensity constitutes just such a gateway if one keeps in mind, first, that the two dimensions of the virtual and the actual belong to one and the same world, and second, that the relation is asymmetrical[24]: the passage through the gateway works in only one direction – namely, from the virtual to the actual. The virtual incessantly erupts into the actual by way of the intensive, with this eruption bringing about the actual in the first place. Eruption here means production. The virtual is transformed into the actual by passing through the gateway of the intensive. This transformation is exactly what the term expression denotes. The virtual is expressed in the actual and remains implicated in it precisely as this transformative and expressive power: intensity. Again, it is important to keep in mind that the virtual–actual relation is one of immanence, as the virtual does not exist apart from the actual. If that were the case, the virtual would be transcendent and not transcendental. The virtual–actual relation is thus topological; it folds in on itself. The virtual produces the actual while never existing apart from it. In terms of narrative, one could then say that virtual Narrative, made up of differential elements and relations, produces and remains implicated in actual, numerically differentiable narra-

Introduction

tives by way of passing through a zone of narrative intensity. Such narrative strategies as mentioned above, and their correlative devices like metalepsis and paralepsis, as well as specific uses of tropes and schemes – from metaphor to the sentence fragment, from ellipsis to congeries – are precisely the markers of these zones. In this vein, Narrative with a capital N denotes the virtual Idea or multiplicity, whereas narrative with a lower case n refers to the actualised state. What needs to be distinguished from these instances of narrative is precisely the concept of narrative as expression denoting the entire virtual–intensive–actual compound. We thus have four different uses of narrative: virtual Narrative, actual narratives, narrative intensity, and the expressivist concept of narrative.

Overall, the Deleuzian stance adopted here can be described as a strange sort of formalism: philosophically, if formal means universal and necessary, what turns out to be universal and necessary in such a Deleuzian formalism is precisely difference; literarily, if formal refers to a given work's specific form, its formal features, then from a Deleuzian point of view everything turns out to be always already torn asunder, cracked open, fractalised precisely because being is difference – differen*t*iated and differen*c*iated at once.[25] Thus, the ground on which this theoretical edifice rests is an unground, an incessant ungrounding: the continuous differen*t*iation and differen*c*iation of difference. This differential character of Deleuze's pure immanence feeds into his postulation of the univocity of being according to which '[b]eing is said in a single and same sense of everything of which it is said, but that of which it is said differs: it is said of difference itself' (DR: 45). The pure immanence of the ceaseless differen*t*iation and differen*c*iation of univocal being: this is what Deleuze ultimately terms becoming.

Narrative as virtual unground, then, amounts to the abyssal swarming of differential elements and their relations. Narrative intensity captures a selection of differential elements and relations and turns them into properties of fully actualised narratives – the respective set of events and existents and their configuration: that is, the actual narrative's plot. Actual narratives in turn constitute narratives as we encounter them in novels, films, paintings, philosophy, history, everyday life – in short, in experience. In the context of narrative, becoming then names the incessant movement of swarming Narrative out of which experiential narrative is constituted.

But there is a second kind of becoming, one which goes back from the actual to the virtual: while becoming in the first sense is onto- and morphogenetic, becoming in the second sense is speculative. While out of the depths of ontogenetic becoming actual narratives are drawn, speculative becoming denotes the movement by which actual narratives dive back into these depths. This speculative trajectory is not to be confused with ontogenetic becoming but rather constitutes a means of probing its depth. As such, it is nevertheless caught up with becoming in the ontogenetic sense since the starting point of these speculative forays of narrative lies precisely in those moments in representational and experiential narrative, which crack open the representational and experiential framework and thus reveal becoming in its circulation without cessation.[26] These moments of breakage are those narrative traits unnatural narratology discriminates and emphasises. Generally, one could say that such instances of breakage constitute what Shklovsky termed *enstrangement*, albeit with a Deleuzian twist: they open up to the strange realm of becoming underlying the experiential and representational. It is in these often microscopic interstices of actual narrative that the zones of narrative intensity are located, gesturing towards the underlying vast depths of narrative virtuality.

Methodologically, differential narratology therefore operates with a kind of close reading sensitive to the work's aesthetic autonomy in so far as this autonomy is always already conceived as torn open and turned inside out. It is a highly textual practice but only in so far as it uncovers the *beyond* of mere textuality, a beyond inherent in the text. It is a method complicit with narrative's very own speculative lines of flight. In this vein, the method of close reading promoted here is attentive to narrative intensities and directed towards unearthing virtual multiplicities; it is sensitive to the inner workings of narratives while being ever attentive to the fact that these inner workings never comprise a mere closed interiority since it is precisely this interiority which comes from elsewhere. Thus, the guiding questions of differential narratology no longer are 'What does a text mean? What is its aesthetic value? What are its formal properties?' but rather, 'How does it work? What does it do? Which forces does it harbour?' Narratives are 'little machine[s]' (ATP: 4), not sphinx-like icons. Accordingly, differential narratology does not attempt to solve riddles; rather, it is interested in how these little machines work, how they can be plugged into, and what other machines they can connect with.

In compliance with both Deleuze's philosophy of expression, which warrants concrete, rather than abstract universals, and the sin-

Introduction

gularity of any given narrative irreducible to general categories, I will now proceed by providing two short exemplary readings in order to showcase such narratological 'mechatronics'. My first tutor text will be a passage from Richard Powers's novel, *The Echo Maker*.[27]

> A flock of birds, each one burning. Stars swoop down to bullets. Hot red specks take flesh, nest there, a body part, part body.
> Lasts forever: no change to measure.
> Flock of fiery cinders. When gray pain of them thins, then always water. Flattest width so slow it fails as liquid. Nothing in the end but flow. Nextless stream, lowest thing above knowing. A thing itself the cold and so can't feel it.
> Body flat water, falling an inch a mile. Torso long as the world. Frozen run all the way from open to close. Great oxbows, age bends, lazy delayed S, switch current to still as long as possible the one long drop it already finishes.
> Not even river, not even *wet brown slow west*, no now or then except in now or then rising. Face forcing up into soundless scream. White column, lit in a river of light. Then pure terror, pealing into air, flipping and falling, anything but hit target.
> One sound gets not a word but still says: *come*. Come with.
> Try death.
> At last only water. Flat water spreading to its level. Water that is nothing but into nothing falls. (Powers 2007: 12–13)

This is a fairly poetic passage in an otherwise extremely diegetic and discursive novel. In terms of representation, it recounts the unfolding of a car accident in which the novel's protagonist is involved. The car leaves the road and crashes through a flock of birds, flipping over several times until it comes to rest next to a shallow river. It seems reasonable to assume that the accident is refracted through the point of view of the driver, with whose disjointed experience of having the accident we are being presented. However, in the passage's narrative discourse, this representational and experiential coherence is thoroughly shattered to the point of being barely recoverable. This is so because the passage foregrounds the liminal state of narrative intensity as the threshold between subjective representation and personal experience on the one side and objective[28] expressivity and impersonal becoming on the other. It is this 'other side', the realm of becoming, which is thus made tangible by way of intensity. In fact, what narrative makes clear in passages such as this one is that what it primarily deals with are precisely not representations – no conscious images, or images of consciousness – nothing subjective and human at all, but what Deleuze terms percepts and affects, the populace of the realm of becoming: impersonal and non-human sensations. Linguistically, affects and percepts register in infinitives, partitives, and indefinite forms. With respect to our example one could thus enumerate: to burn, to go fast, to flow, to freeze, to go slowly, to panic, to die as examples of affect; a river, a flock of birds, some fire, a thing, a flatness as examples of percept. Affects and percepts in turn capture forces such as pressure, tension, velocity, gravitation, friction, and elasticity, just to mention a few relevant to our example. Forces and sensations are impersonal and non-human; in short, they are ontologically objective. Affects and percepts as objective sensations register as affections and perceptions only once they have become subjective: *my* pain, *this* river, *I* panic. Passages such as this one thus unveil the non-human *within* the human, the objective *within* the subjective, the virtual *within* the actual. And this is achieved precisely by means of style. In this particular example, we immediately notice that, even though presumably focalised through Mark, the novel's protagonist, there is not a single linguistic feature indexing Mark. Overall, there is a lack of personal pronouns. This becomes especially clear towards the end of the passage when we read 'come with' instead of come with *me*. In addition, many of the sentences are mere fragments that highlight what could be called the eventness, the thisness of the event – namely, the unfolding of the accident – at the expense of actants performing acts; something happens, not someone does something. Rhetorically, sentence fragments function as figures of isolation.[29] Here, they precisely work towards isolating both the account of the accident from the narrative flow of the novel, and distinct moments within the accident, thus breaking it apart into a series of such distinct moments. As Deleuze points out in *The Logic of Sensation*, isolation is the first step in Francis Bacon's means of cracking up the representational surface of his paintings in a trajectory that goes from isolation to deformation to dissipation (FB: 53) – a trajectory I want to refer to as *disfiguration*. What then becomes tangible in this movement of disfiguration is precisely the realm of affects, percepts, and forces. This is why there are no personal pronouns: there are no persons involved in this realm of events, only forces and sensations. Sensation does not have a 'me'. This is also why the passage cannot quite be said to be focalised through Mark after all, as it makes tangible the Deleuzian unconscious, transcendental domain of forces and sensations rather than navigating the Kantian domain of human consciousness, whether empirical or transcendental.

Introduction

These Deleuzian transcendental forces and sensations are the stuff narratives are made of. They are precisely the differential elements (affects and percepts) and relations (forces) constitutive of actual narratives. If this is the case, then the Idea of Narrative has to be conceived in these unconscious and non-human terms rather than any features of anthropocentric consciousness. Consciousness is thus by no means the foundation of narrative but only a derivative of the expression of the antecedent virtual realm of forces and sensations in actual narratives. The passage from Powers's novel precisely emphasises this 'antecedence criterion' (Grant 2011: 69).

While my first example thus highlights both the *constituents* (sensations, forces) and the *heterogeneity* (elements, relations) of this antecedent realm, my second example shows that it is nevertheless *continuous* (one realm). Together, the two examples emphasise the three pillars on which Deleuze's system rests: difference (heterogeneity), immanence (topological folding of virtual and actual), and univocity of being (one realm, one voice). Both examples have in common that they dissolve the organisation and orderliness of the empirical in order to reach the sub-representative domain of the transcendental. And in both examples this shattering of empirical, experiential, and representational coherence also registers in the shattering of the coherence of narrative discourse. Thus, in the Powers passage, the shattering of coherence with respect to the character-as-subject goes hand in hand with the shattering and fragmentation of syntax. In fact, the latter *generates* the former. While in Powers the shattering of coherence thus primarily pertains to the narratological categories of character and event, in my second example, Rick Moody's short story, 'The Grid', it concerns the categories of voice and mood. Apart from the fact that Moody's text is extremely amenable to serve as an example, it comes with the added value of having been the focus of attention of unnatural narratologists. Given my discussion of unnatural narratology above, a reading in the light of differential narratology vis-à-vis the unnaturalists' practice should prove doubly enlightening as to both the *methodology* and the *explanatory power* of differential narratology. Let me begin with the very beginning of Moody's short story:

> Inside, in the warm light of contemporary domesticity, her roommate is talking long-distance to the first boy she ever kissed. She's talking while vengefully chasing their cats, the cordless phone cradled like a papoose at an interstice of ear and hand and shoulder. We can just make out the melody of her joy. We are standing outside under the window, on the

front step. There's not much more to the tableau than this. (Moody 2002: 29)

There is something strange about this passage. As Rüdiger Heinze has pointed out, 'The Grid' starts off with an epistemological impossibility, as it features internal focalisation but provides more information than the focaliser could possibly have access to. How does the focaliser know that the roommate is talking to 'the first boy she ever kissed', even though he (it becomes clear later on that the focaliser and homodiegetic narrator is indeed a he) can 'just make out the melody of her joy'? Such an epistemological breach is what Genette calls *paralepsis* and paralepses proliferate throughout the story as the narrator incessantly recounts events and other characters' thoughts of which he cannot possibly have knowledge. Thus, shortly after the beginning, which is told in the present tense and which builds up to the moment just *before* the narrator kisses Susan – as her name will turn out to be – for the first time, the narrative switches to future tense and relates incidents in the future in quite declarative fashion. For example, the narrator tells us that Susan 'will believe that her lips yielded too easily' (30), that Nina, a financial analyst, will move into Susan's place after she herself 'will have moved elsewhere' (31), and that a guy called Joe will rob the apartment (32). As it turns out in the end, the whole narrative constitutes an act of memory and thus a recounting of *past events* that the narrator, for whichever reasons, decided to tell proleptically. The deployment of the future tense is epistemologically consistent with a homodiegetic narrator and internal focalisation after all, even if it makes for a quite complex and elaborate narrative architecture. What cannot be explained, though, are the numerous instances of the narrator's access to other minds and his knowledge of events he cannot possibly have knowledge of, such as when the narrator knows exactly what Nina feels when she kisses a man in a bar, or when he tells us about incidents in Joe's personal life (32).

How do we account for this predominance of paralepsis in 'The Grid'? One possibility is to interpret this as the manifestation of the all too human wish for transcending one's self, one's own human standpoint – and indeed this is the take suggested by both Heinze and Alber in their respective treatments of Moody's short story (Heinze 2008: 293; Alber 2009: 91). However, this explanation is very unsatisfying for two related reasons. First, transcending the human standpoint can be and has been identified as a crucial feature of literature in general. Such an assessment is simply too general an assertion, as it does not tell us anything about the specificity of the text at hand. Second, there is no hint whatsoever in the story itself that would suggest such a reading. Transcending one's self is not what the story is about. Instead, if we look at its content, between the narrator's and Susan's first kiss at the beginning of the story and the disclosure of the recounting as an act of memory at the end, what the story presents us with is an ever accelerating succession of couples exchanging first kisses. Over the course of just nine pages, the story invokes more than twenty first kisses. This makes it safe to say that kissing for the first time has to be taken into account when interpreting this story. In order to account for the specificity of this story its paralepses have to be read in conjunction with all these kisses. Thus, instead of correlating paralepsis with an alleged human wish for transcendence, a suggestion the narrative itself provides no grounds for, let me propose the following way of accounting for the story's paraleptic set-up.

Paralepsis here is the marker for the narrative's impersonal forces at work. The paraleptic moments in the course of the narrative should not be correlated with the protagonist's point of view, but attributed to the workings of actualisation, the process whereby virtual Narrative turns into actual narrative. The paralepses of 'The Grid' are delimitations of the narrative's zones of intensity. As such, they embody the point of view of impersonal and pre-individual sensations and forces, or what Deleuze, quoting Lawrence Ferlinghetti, also calls '"the fourth-person singular"' (LS: 118). More precisely, paralepsis here marks the point where the fourth-person singular makes itself felt in the narrative's first person.

Two questions need to be immediately tackled: what does this strange expression – fourth-person singular – denote? And what does it mean to say that it makes itself felt in the first person? With the notion of the singular, we are already moving within Deleuze's realm of the virtual since the virtual is populated by what Deleuze calls singularities or singular points. Singularities denote the determining points in a given system; they are special or *remarkable* differential elements. Thus, a triangle has three singular points alongside an indefinite number of ordinary points. Add another singular point and the system changes in kind; in our case, the triangle becomes a quadrangle. Note that singularities qua differential elements belong to the virtual. As such, they have no extensity – they have no extension in space; rather, they inhere in and produce the extensive. In short, they are intensities. As intensities, singularities are the determinants of any extensive – that is, actual – entity or state of affairs to come. The following passage from 'The Grid' perfectly exemplifies this determining character of intensive singularities:

> We are going to kiss one another for the first time. The arrangement of our faces and noses, whether there is a complete mutuality to our kiss, whether particles are trapped between our teeth, whether she will action-paint me with lipstick – these are some of the variables of the instant. Do I let my palm rest lightly on her shoulder, on the right angle of her black pullover sweater? Do I pull her to me, gently? Do I let her pull me closer? (29–30)

Those 'variables of the instant' are precisely the differential elements which the intensity of the moment will or will not select to actualise. Some of the elements which will be selected will have been the singularities determining the actuality that is about to be produced. It is thus that virtual and intensive singularities are turned into the extensive particulars of actual experience.

There are at least two such singular points with respect to Moody's story: first, the sensations involved in bringing about the narrator's first kiss with Susan; second, those pertaining to his memory of this kiss. These two instances determine both the narrator qua character, the emotional and mental set-up of the character as he appears in the story and the story as such. How so? With respect to the narrator, his first kiss with Susan apparently constitutes such an intensive moment that he repeatedly returns to it in memory. Thus, the memory of this kiss still determines his love life to some extent. This kiss carries such an immense affective power that he still feels its repercussions. What the narrative unfolds between these two singular points in the life of the narrator – kissing Susan and remembering this kiss – is precisely an account of the affective powers of a first kiss: to kiss for the first time. *The singularity of a first kiss.* In *What Is Philosophy?*, Deleuze and Guattari say that all artworks are monuments made of sensations (WIP: 164, 168, 176–7). 'The Grid' is just such a monument, a monument made of the sensation 'to kiss for the first time'. This sensational monumentality is what the ever-accelerating succession of couples exchanging first kisses constructs. And this is how the fourth-person singular inheres in the first person: it denotes a crack in the 'I' of the first person. Deleuze repeatedly cites Rimbaud's dictum that 'I is an other' since this phrase makes palpable the crack within the 'I'. It is in this crack that the fourth-person singular resides; it is

Introduction

this crack that opens up to the virtual realm of pre-individual and impersonal differential elements and relations. In Moody's short story, paralepsis marks precisely this crack, this breach in the first person. Thus, when the narrator states that the 'implications of the practice [of kissing] expand around us, like the spirits of our baptised ancestors, like airborne pollutants' (30) and subsequently goes on to invoke numerous first kisses he possibly cannot have knowledge of, the narrative opens up to the great unconscious of the virtual plane. What 'The Grid' unfolds between the two singular points of first kiss and memory of this first kiss is its plane of immanence populated by the differential elements and relations of the joys, anxieties, trepidations, frictions, tensions: in short, the infinite catalogue of sensations of first kisses, Deleuzian affects, percepts, and forces. And this is precisely what the story's title denotes. 'The Grid' *is* the gridding, the diagramming[30] of the differential network of affects and percepts, of pre-individual and impersonal forces of *a body and a body to kiss*. This grid at the same time *generates* particular moments of kissing such as those between the narrator and Susan, Nina and the guy in the bar, and numerous others, and is implicated, folded into these particular acts of kisses. Moody's short story thus makes tangible that there is no first-person singular without the fourth-person singular since the fourth-person singular is precisely *the impersonal voice of univocal being*; it is *perspectivity itself*.

In this context, one should not forget that Henrik Skov Nielsen had already proposed his concept of the impersonal voice, now recognised to be a staple feature of unnatural narratives, well before becoming known as one of the foremost theorists of unnatural narratology (Nielsen 2004). His essay is an important point of reference in the genealogy of unnatural narratology also because it triggered Heinze's 'Violations of Mimetic Epistemology in First-Person Narrative Fiction', the article that contains his discussion of 'The Grid', and that was, at least in part, conceived as a response to Nielsen. In his article, Heinze takes issue with Nielsen's suggestion of an impersonal voice permeating all of first-person narrative fiction, as, according to Heinze, Nielsen's distinction between narrator and character function that is supposed to map on to the distinction between impersonal and personal voice in some cases 'amount[s] to proclaiming the narrative schizophrenic in the clinical sense of the term: hearing voices' (Heinze 2008: 288). This is one of the reasons that prompt Heinze to propose an entire typology of paralepses instead. Indeed, Heinze's aim is to ensure that 'one of the most prominent effects of first-person narrative (and indeed of all fictional narrative) is exactly the projection of a human consciousness' (281). With his introduction of the impersonal voice Nielsen admittedly and explicitly posits 'the presence of two voices in first-person narrative' (Nielsen 2004: 138; qtd in Heinze 2008: 287) and thus renders inconsistent the projection of such consciousness. Nielsen's dualism, however, can be remedied and the impersonal voice rescued (and made pervasive) if we substitute Nielsen's narrator function as the source of impersonality with Deleuze's metaphysical function. All of narrative displays an impersonal voice and this voice is *thoroughly metaphysical*, not grammatical.[31]

'The Grid' thus makes palpable the virtual dimension of narrative: it expresses the impersonal, virtual dimension of narrative, which inheres in every actual narrative and generates it. There is no narrative situation that is not governed by the fourth-person singular. There is no actual narrative without its virtual dimension. There is no conscious narrative without its unconscious. And this is what Moody's narrative ultimately does: quite contrary to presenting us with the human wish for *transcendence*, this story shows the workings of *immanence*; it makes tangible the virtuality of narrative, its differential relations, impersonal affects and percepts, singularities and intensities constituting individuals, both in terms of characters and in terms of this particular narrative qua narrative.

There is a beyond of cognition, and the wager of this book is that the anti-representational features of narrative make this palpable – they provide an *aesthetic knowledge* of this beyond. If we really want to take these narratives seriously – and as literary scholars we should – we need to break out of our cosy little Kantian world of cognition. We have become so used to our Kantian world that we have almost forgotten that there are indeed other options available. In addition to those rogue philosophers that have already been mentioned – Schelling, Whitehead, Bergson, Deleuze, the speculative realists – we could also turn to a sub-field of contemporary logic, dialetheism, a paraconsistent logic that postulates true contradictions, in order to equip us with the respective tools. It is telling that Graham Priest, one of dialetheism's best-known advocates, whose most famous book is tellingly called *Beyond the Limits of Thought*, wrote up a short story about a box that is absolutely empty but also contains something – an impossible object – to make a case for his paraconsistent logic. This short story was originally published in the *Notre Dame Journal of Formal Logic*. It is a wonderful example of an appeal to *aesthet-*

Introduction

ics to make palpable something that is hard to settle in the space of pure *reason*. That this appeal was made in a journal of formal logic makes it all the more stunning. In the text framing his story, Priest explicitly says that 'anyone who misapplied the principle of charity to interpret the story in a consistent way, would have entirely misunderstood it' (Priest 1997: 580). In my readings of Ana Castillo's *The Mixquiahuala Letters*, Michael Ondaatje's *The Collected Works of Billy the Kid*, Colson Whitehead's *The Intuitionist*, and Mark Z. Danielewski's *House of Leaves* that follow, I have thus attempted to be as uncharitable as possible in order to revel in the splendour of their inconsistencies and to follow them in their speculative flights into the realm beyond the limits of thought.

Notes

1. I should state at the outset that I take Deleuze's self-description as 'pure metaphysician' seriously (Deleuze 2007a: 42). Before anything else, Deleuze was a profoundly metaphysical thinker and his entire œuvre is dedicated to what A. W. Moore glosses as his attempt 'to make sense of things at the highest level of generality', which, for Moore, makes Deleuze's attempt even 'a *paradigmatically* metaphysical project' (Moore 2012: 554; my emphasis).

    In line with such a metaphysical outlook, my employment of the term unconscious builds on the metaphysical rather than the psychoanalytical tradition. Deleuze's transcendental unconscious falls squarely within this metaphysical tradition. For a recent and poignant treatment of the metaphysical unconscious and for further references, see Austin 2011. For an extensive treatment, both historical and systematic, of the notion of the unconscious in Deleuze's work, albeit from a Kantian perspective, see Kerslake 2007.

2. The question of literariness, alongside those of fiction and fictionality in relation to narrative and narrativity, constitutes a strong undercurrent throughout this book. In all brevity let me already point out here that I see narrativity as the most fundamental term grounding both literariness and fictionality. While literariness is a question of degree, however, fictionality is one of kind. The verdict of literariness correlates with the quantitative and qualitative employment of linguistic, rhetorical, and narratological devices and their achieved effect. Fictionality simply marks possible and impossible worlds in contradistinction to the actual world we inhabit. Fiction in turn assumes an admittedly idiosyncratic role as it names the construction work underlying any kind of narrative, fictional or factual, and thus does not correlate with fictionality. Richard Walsh's already classic *The Rhetoric of Fictionality*

operates according to a similar distinction – in fact, it only gets off the ground precisely due to the observation that narrative and fiction have both come to mark constructedness and thus do not designate distinctive qualities any longer: hence the need to theorise fictionality anew. The big difference, however, is that Walsh's distinction is based on discursive grounds whereas my distinction is ontological: the difference between factual and fictional is an existential question. Factuality marks existence, fictionality marks non-existence.

3. The most important and influential philosophical account of narrative as essentially entangled with questions of knowledge to surface in the past few decades is, of course, Jean-François Lyotard's *The Postmodern Condition*. It is no coincidence that its subtitle reads *A Report on Knowledge* (my emphasis). Lyotard's book is particularly interesting with respect to speculative metaphysics, as one of his prime examples of a grand or metanarrative – the kind of totalising explanatory account postmodernism is said to reject – is precisely Hegel's speculative philosophy. I will come back to this conundrum in my Conclusion.

4. This is the trajectory of Deleuze's geneticism – the form his account of the genesis of representation takes. Henry Somers-Hall makes it clear that the genesis of representation is tantamount to the genesis of the subject as Deleuze presents us with 'a theory of the transcendental that maintains the differentiated structure of the [Kantian] transcendental field while removing the subject as the synthesizing agent' (Somers-Hall 2012: 11) with 'the synthesis of the world' now happening 'outside of the subject' (12). One should note that while *Difference and Repetition* indeed focuses on the genesis of representation and, concomitantly, of the subject, the subject's genesis is just one particular case of onto- and morphogenesis in general. The 'synthesis of the world' is an incessant process, the continuous becoming in which all entities are swept up – see, for example, Deleuze and Guattari's famous discussions of the encounter between the orchid and the wasp (ATP: 11, 263), or that between the tick and the mammal (ATP: 57, 283).

5. To corroborate this point once more, let me briefly return to Fludernik's introduction to *Towards a 'Natural' Narratology* where she makes narratology's representational and experiential bias unmistakably clear:

> Unlike the traditional models of narratology, narrativity [. . .] is here constituted by what I call experientiality, namely the quasi-mimetic evocation of 'real-life experience'. Experientiality can be aligned with actantial frames, but it also correlates with the evocation of consciousness or with the representation of a speaker role. Experientiality, as everything else in narrative, reflects a cognitive schema of embodiedness that relates to human existence and human concerns. The anthropomorphic bias of narratives and its correlation with the fundamental story parameters of personhood, identity, actionality, etc., have long been noted by theoreticians of narrative and have

Introduction

been recognized as constituting the rock-bottom level of story matter [...] Where the current proposal supersedes this setup is in the redefinition of narrativity qua experientiality *without* the necessity of any actantial groundwork. In my model, there can therefore be narratives without plot, but there cannot be any narratives without a human (anthropomorphic) experiencer of some sort at some narrative level. (Fludernik 1996: 12–13)

Suffice to say here that what I propose constitutes in some sense the inverse of Fludernik's stance: human experiencers are merely contingent and derivative whereas there cannot be any narrative without at least a virtual plot, or, rather, virtual emplotment. This book contests precisely what, according to Fludernik, narratology takes to be 'the rock-bottom level of story matter'.

6. It should be noted that Meillassoux himself, while presenting correlationism as one of the most fundamental problems to be tackled, does not believe it is a deficiency *sensu stricto*. Far from it; he actually thinks that correlationism constitutes an irrefutable argument – hence his painstaking efforts at overcoming correlationism from within rather than simply dismissing it.
7. That unnatural narratology has caught on despite its apparent anti-representationalism may be accounted for by several reasons: first, it is a group venture involving several well-known scholars and institutions; second, it rhetorically posits itself as a complement, not an alternative, to representational theories of narrative – a complement that is predominantly (although not exclusively) interested in experimental and deviant narratives at that, narratives deemed to be marginal rather than central by the discipline as a whole; third, the venture is primarily descriptive rather than theoretical; fourth, one 'wing' of unnatural narratology is, in fact, interested in how experimental and deviant narratives can be naturalised (in the narratological sense) and thus accommodated within a representational framework; in what follows, these last two points will be elaborated on.
8. While Brian Richardson's book restricts itself to anomalies of voice, the first of the two joint articles by Jan Alber, Stefan Iversen, Henrik Skov Nielsen, and Richardson is broader in scope and constitutes a cursory inventory of deviant narrative strategies, from antinomic temporality to incompossible events, from discontinuous minds to impersonal narration. For Richardson's updated and expanded take on these issues, see Richardson 2015.
9. The Zen comparison is the unnaturalists'. It should be noted that Jan Alber has slightly modified his terminology: while he initially referred to all sense-making cognitive strategies in the face of unnatural narratives as naturalisation, he now reserves the term for one specific strategy among others. For the sake of simplicity, my employment of naturalisation reflects his earlier, more general use of it. For a recent

synoptic overview of his version of unnatural narratology and his expanded list of reading strategies, see Alber 2013; for the detailed and systematic presentation of his programme, see his *Unnatural Narrative: Impossible Worlds in Fiction and Drama* (Alber 2016). Overall, the project of unnatural narratology produces a steady flow of publications, and it has become quite difficult to keep abreast of them. Apart from the publications already mentioned, two essay collections serve as good starting points: the more recent *A Poetics of Unnatural Narrative* (Alber et al. 2013) and the earlier *Unnatural Narratives – Unnatural Narratology* (Alber and Heinze 2011).

10. There might even be a hidden bond between these two kinds of approach within unnatural narratology: one can only safely watch the freak show when the police make sure that the freaks will do no harm.

11. This is also more than evident in their endorsement and extension of Käte Hamburger's position: 'Hamburger argues that if there *is* a statement subject, then it will narrate something that exists prior to its narration. On the other hand, if there is no statement subject, then the sentences of fiction will produce the world they describe' (Alber et al. 2010: 125). Unnatural narratology takes up Hamburger's assertion concerning fictions without explicit enunciators and makes it pervasive for *all* narratives:

> In fact, we find that we can eliminate Hamburger's distinction between narratives with and those without a statement subject. Both third-person and first-person narratives are thus characterized by not having a narrator who speaks *about* something, but rather a narrative world created by the reference. (125)

This concept of narrative is utterly idealist since it presupposes a narrative consciousness capable of bringing about what it narrates (some mind doing the referencing). It is even an absolute idealism since all the individual narrating minds (whether explicitly enunciating or not) are thus posited as mere manifestations of an all-pervasive narrative consciousness, a sort of narrative spirit embodied (represented) by local manifestations.

12. This is particularly evident in his adaptation of Aristotle's *ontological* categories as categories of *thought*.

13. Deleuze develops this account throughout *Difference and Repetition*, but see particularly the passages on the *sentiendum* I quoted further above, as well as pages 67–8 (pitting transcendental empiricism against representationalism), 70–1 (positing that the starting point has to be within Kantianism, rather than pre- or post-Kantianism), 90–114 (his account of the three passive – as against Kant's active – syntheses of time, with 109 directly attacking the transcendence of the Kantian subject), and 171 (on Kant tracing the transcendental from the empiri-

Introduction

cal), as well as the final two chapters, which mostly flesh out Deleuze's own expressivist and genetic programme, especially pages 220–32 (on the differential nature of Ideas and Ideas as multiplicities), 235–44 (on the metaphysical status and expressivism of Ideas), 260–74 (on the real productivity of the transcendental), and 334–9 (on the transcendental illusions of representation).

There is a burgeoning and quickly increasing literature on the relation between Kant and Deleuze with Beth Lord's and Daniela Voss's recent monographs constituting the latest forays into this emerging territory (Lord 2011; Voss 2013). Apart from Lord and Voss, Bryant 2008, Kerslake 2009, Rölli 2003, Shaviro 2009, Smith 2006, and Somers-Hall 2012 (11–40, 179–86) are particularly recommendable. See also the first four contributions to Lundy and Voss 2015 (25–102).

14. While Kant's ideas are archetypal and could thus be legitimately viewed as Platonic too, it is crucial that these archetypes are innate to the human mind and by no means constitute the fundamental fabric of reality, which, in contrast, is the case in Deleuze's metaphysics.

15. In his rich entry on 'Narrativity' in *The Living Handbook of Narratology* H. Porter Abbott points out that narrativity has indeed gradually become a focal interest within the discipline, with a plethora of suggestions as to its proper conceptualisation (including alternative terms such a narrativehood and narrativeness) being presented 'over the last three decades' (Abbott 2011/2014: n. p.).

16. This is very much in accordance with McHale's employment of the Russian formalist term 'dominant', which merely denotes a dominance of something, not its absolute prevalence. For an analysis of a nineteenth-century realist text along the lines suggested here, see my reading of Charlotte Perkins Gilman's 'The Yellow Wall-Paper' (Askin 2015: 164–7).

17. The notion of traditional narratology is not to be taken as the counterpart to Herman's term, postclassical narratology (Herman 1997; Herman 1999: 2). While the latter distinguishes the plethora of recent trends in narrative theory in contradistinction to classical, structuralist narratology, my employment of traditional narratology comprises all these approaches on grounds of the essentially Kantian framework they consciously or unconsciously endorse. For a recent survey on postclassical narratology, see Alber and Fludernik 2010.

18. This is obviously a very crude simplification and names but a general tendency. The point is that, as its name already indicates, analytic philosophy is *analytic* rather than *systematic* in nature. Let me defer again to Millière's text, as it is an ideal starting point for anyone interested in the current state of metaphysics, particularly in its analytic guise. With respect to this latter point, see also Timothy Williamson's somewhat personal (but no less illuminating) account of the shift from

'anti-metaphysics' to 'the growth and flourishing of boldly speculative metaphysics' (Williamson 2014: 7–8) that occurred within the analytic tradition over the course of the last few decades.

That Millière, despite his generalist impetus, favours analytic metaphysics becomes evident if one considers that, astonishingly, Gilles Deleuze is not even mentioned once by him. To be fair, Millière himself acknowledges that while his survey is 'resolutely conciliatory' it is also 'necessarily partisan' (2011: 1). In such a conciliatory spirit from a partisan point of view, let me point here to the work undertaken in analytic process philosophy, particularly that of Johanna Seibt (not mentioned by Millière), whose General Process Theory promises to be an extremely fruitful interlocutor for Deleuze's philosophy of becoming and vice versa – in fact, Seibt herself briefly references Deleuze in her entry on 'Process Philosophy' in the *Stanford Encyclopedia of Philosophy* (Seibt 2012). Since, for obvious reasons, this book is not the place for such an undertaking, an exploration of this potential dialogue has to remain a task for the future. For a crisp introduction to General Process Theory, see Seibt 2009.

19. While Millière's long paper provides an extremely informative overview on the contemporary status of metaphysics in general, Morelle's essay constitutes an excellent survey of the substantive internal differences within speculative realism in particular. In addition, issue 4 of the journal *Speculations* is entirely dedicated to the assessment of the status quo in speculative realist thought on the one hand and its potential future orientations on the other. Finally, with the publication of Peter Gratton's *Speculative Realism: Problems and Prospects* in 2014, there is now also a first book-length introduction and overview.

20. I would like to extend my gratitude to Jon Cogburn and Mark Allan Ohm, who were so generous as to share their translation in progress of Garcia's book with me.

21. It needs to be acknowledged that there is a debate within Deleuze scholarship as to this consistency. Peter Wolfendale's and Alistair Welchman's recent contributions serve as two excellent contrastive examples in this respect (Wolfendale 2012; Welchman 2009). I firmly side with Wolfendale and the consistency camp.

22. His oft-quoted appropriation of Rimbaud's dictum that 'I is an other' derives directly from his reading of Kant:

> Rather than being concerned with what happens before and after Kant (which amounts to the same thing), we should be concerned with a precise moment within Kantianism [...] For when Kant puts rational theology into question, *in the same stroke* he introduces a kind of disequilibrium, a fissure or crack in the pure Self of the 'I think', an alienation in principle, insurmountable in principle [...] A cogito for a dissolved Self: the Self of 'I think' includes in its essence a receptivity of intuition in relation to which *I* is

Introduction

already an other. [. . .] [F]or a brief moment we enter into that schizophrenia in principle which characterises the highest power of thought, and opens Being directly on to difference. (DR: 70)

23. 'All cure is a voyage to the bottom of repetition' (DR: 20), as Deleuze points out. As we will see, the bottom of repetition turns out to be the abyssal ungrounding of becoming.
24. Hence the title of *Difference and Repetition*'s final chapter, which presents Deleuze's account of intensity and its role in the actualisation of virtualities: 'Asymmetrical Synthesis of the Sensible' (DR: 280–329).
25. On Deleuze's distinction between differen*t*iation and differen*c*iation, see DR: 258–63. In its entirety, the notion of different/ciation names the movements of difference *in-itself* and *towards* actuality. On Deleuze's formalism, see Buchanan 2001b and Tynan 2012: 1–24; 55–87. One should note that, in contrast to my focus on *Difference and Repetition*, Buchanan's and Tynan's discussions are mostly informed by Deleuze and Guattari's *Capitalism and Schizophrenia*, as well as Deleuze's *Critical and Clinical* projects, and framed in terms of a Jamesonian Marxism in Buchanan's case and psychoanalysis in Tynan's, both being too dialectic (that is, Hegelian) for my taste. Fredric Jameson himself, in turn, partly draws on Deleuze in his recent elaboration of literary realism when he identifies affect as one of its antinomic 'twin sources', the other precisely being narrative (Jameson 2013: 1–44). Ultimately, however, Jameson subscribes to a Kantian notion of affect where affects are 'bodily feelings' and the 'very chromaticism of the body itself' (32; 42). Positing narrative and affect as contradictory instances, Jameson identifies realism as the literary form that emerges from their dialectic synthetisation. In contrast, employing Deleuze's genuinely metaphysical notion of affect, *Narrative and Becoming* shows how narrativity intrinsically correlates with affect (and sensation in general) and how this fact comes to be expressed most explicitly in literary works that undo their formal coherence: that is, works that do not adhere to realist conventions.
26. On these two notions of becoming, see Deleuze and Guattari's own distinction between conceptual and sensory becoming in *What Is Philosophy?*: 'Conceptual becoming is heterogeneity grasped in an absolute form [speculative becoming]; sensory becoming is otherness caught in a matter of expression [ontogenetic becoming]' (WIP: 177). These two senses of becoming are already at stake in one of Deleuze's earliest writings, a comment on Bergson:

[W]e can already say that there will not be in Bergson's works anything like a distinction between two worlds, one sensible, the other intelligible, but only two movements, or even just two directions of one and the same movement: the one is such that the movement tends to congeal in its product, in its result, that which interrupts it; and the other turns back and retraces its steps, rediscovers in the product the movement from which it resulted. (Deleuze 2004a: 23–4)

This passage articulates in a nutshell what I take narrative to be doing. The project of this book is precisely to show that narrative in fact is doing this.

27. An earlier version of the following analysis is presented in my essay on Powers's novel (Askin 2012).
28. My use of objective and object in the context of Deleuze's notion of becoming needs to be understood as de-correlated: this is precisely *not* the object as correlated to the subject. Rather, the reference is to the in-itself of objects and of reality at large.
29. I am indebted to Matthew Clark for making this explicit to me in both his talk at the 2012 International Conference on Narrative and our personal conversation afterwards (Clark 2012).
30. The use of the term diagram here is not coincidental. 'Diagram' and 'diagrammatic' are technical terms in Deleuze's philosophy, evoked to render art's capacity to capture sensations and forces. The notion is elaborated on in Chapter 2.
31. Grammar here needs to be understood in the extensive sense of a Derridean *grammatology*: namely, as denoting any kind of sign-system. Obviously, this comes with a Deleuzian inflection where sign-systems, whether properly discursive or natural (any system of products), are always actual and precisely in need of virtual grounding (system of production). All produced grammar rests on metaphysical production.

1

Intensive Narration:
Ana Castillo's *The Mixquiahuala Letters*

> Exit light
> Enter night
> Take my hand
> We're off to Never Never Land
>   Metallica, 'Enter Sandman'

Difference and Hybridity

Ana Castillo's œuvre is generally taken to be descriptive of Chicana culture and thus predominantly received in terms of ethnicity, feminism, and politics. As a result and as befits Chicana literary studies' received tradition, Castillo scholarship is strongly thematic, with the themes of ethnic, sexual, and cultural identity taking centre-stage. Accordingly, the conceptual tools used for these thematic explorations are predominantly derived from postcolonial, feminist, and cultural studies with those of hybridity – or *mestizaje* as its specific Chicano/a variant – and difference ranging foremost among them. In this vein, and in accordance with the general bent of Chicana literary criticism, Castillo's work is read as representing the particular cultural, political, and economic situation of Chicanas and as articulating and affirming a resistant politics of hybridity and difference. The often unusual formal aspects of her work, if considered at all, are subsumed within this framework and relegated to the role of servant to these presumably primary political concerns. In short, in both Chicana literary scholarship in general and Castillo scholarship in particular, politics rules over poetics.[1] This relationship needs to be reversed, however, as otherwise the critic runs the risk of effacing the poetic work's being qua literary art; no matter how explicitly political Chicana literature may be, it is always political *as* literature and warrants being treated as such. First and foremost, these works are works of literature and their respective politics is always channelled by means of literature. Scrutinising these means is the primary task of literary criticism. Thus, with respect to literature, rather than poetics (and, more broadly, aesthetics) being a question of politics, politics in fact is a question of poetics (or aesthetics).[2] This is the case precisely because poetics itself is in turn a question of ontology: it is the poetics of a given literary work, which tells us what it *is*. In other words, literary artefacts are poetic objects. This is hardly a revolutionary diagnosis; nor should it generate much antagonism. In fact, this observation borders on the trivial. It is astonishing, however, that this trivial fact seems to have been forgotten or disavowed in much of the work done in literary criticism and theory in the course of the past three decades, with Chicano/a literary studies constituting a particularly salient example of this trend.[3] The politicisation of literary scholarship over this period has resulted in works of literature being treated as political works with certain poetic features rather than poetic works that (might) advocate certain political commitments. The most forceful project in this vein that explicitly zooms in on the question of narrative is certainly Jameson's *The Political Unconscious*, which leaves no doubt about its objective from the very start, as the first chapter's very first paragraph reads:

> This book will argue the priority of the political interpretation of literary texts. It conceives of the political perspective not as some supplementary method, not as an optional auxiliary to other interpretive methods current today – the psychoanalytic or the myth-critical, the stylistic, the ethical, the structural – but rather as the absolute horizon of all reading and all interpretation. (Jameson 1981: 17)

And, a few pages further on, Jameson adds that 'everything is "in the last analysis" political' (20), thus firmly establishing the pervasiveness and primacy of the political vis-à-vis all other discourses. Accordingly, Jameson reduces narrative to a 'socially symbolic act', as the subtitle of his book has it: an act that, in the specific forms it plays out in – for example, that of the novel – primarily transports what Jameson calls ideologemes, 'the smallest intelligible unit of the essentially antagonistic collective discourses of social classes' (76). Hence, the critic's task becomes to hunt down and identify a given text's operative ideologeme(s), and politics always and invariably trumps poetics.

With respect to Chicano/a literary studies and Castillo scholarship, instead of jumping right on to the thematics the works display and reading them in the framework of a ready-made politics of hybridity and difference, thus reducing the poetic to the political, the guiding question, then, should be *whether and how such a politics is expressed poetically and aesthetically.* In short, rather than grounding hybridity and difference in politics, these concepts need to be grounded in poetics. But, in line with the ontological argument, if it is the case that these works manifest a differential and hybrid poetics, this is tantamount to saying that they are differential and hybrid objects. We would then need *ontological* concepts of difference and hybridity rather than the current *cultural* concepts in order to talk about these strange objects.[4] This is indeed my argument: namely, that first, talk of difference and hybridity in relation to literary works needs to be of a metaphysical nature; and second, that this metaphysical difference and hybridity need to be traced via the particular work's poetics and aesthetics. Only in a third step can we determine how difference and hybridity play out on the thematic level.

This relation between a metaphysics, a poetics, and a politics of hybridity and difference becomes more than apparent in Ana Castillo's debut novel, *The Mixquiahuala Letters*. Accordingly, this chapter traces how the novel's poetics comes to determine its political thrust. On these grounds and against the hitherto unchallenged consensus view, I argue that *The Mixquiahuala Letters* stages neither a search for Chicana identity, nor an attempt at Chicana self-definition; nor does it represent the struggle of its protagonists to attain an independent subject position.[5] On the contrary, the novel in fact promotes the labour of *de*personalisation and affirms the utter *loss* of identity. Against any attempt at self-definition, it pits the active *dissolution* of the self. The novel does not simply indulge in affirming good, self-defined hybridity and difference over against bad, heteronomous purity and identity. It problematises *all* acts of definition and identification. Subjectivity, identity, and selfhood constitute the *starting* rather than the end points of the novel and are the conditions which it wants to leave behind rather than strive for.

The dissolution of self, the disintegration of identity, and the journey towards the zero point of subjectivity are precisely enacted on the level of poetics. They are most tangibly on display in the novel's monologic epistolary form, its hypertextuality, and its appropriation and valuation of dreams in conjunction with and for the purposes of narration. All these features not only emphasise the narrative's non-integrality but also successfully differentiate it; while the novel's epistolarity as such already produces a fractured narrative rather than an organic whole, its monologic character further emphasises this feature. By denying us the voice of the letters' addressee, it makes unmistakably clear that an entire dimension to the narrative is, in fact, missing, thus making incompleteness a fundamental feature of the novel. This is still further radicalised by the novel's hypertextual form. The novel is not content with merely showcasing non-integrality but actively disintegrates its narrative through its hypertextual structure. This is not one single, coherent, complete narrative; rather, we as readers are confronted with a (virtually infinite) disjunctive series of fragmented stories. Finally, *The Mixquiahuala Letters* not only contains frequent references to dreams and dreaming and a number of visionary dream sequences but also, as will be shown, casts literary narrative as such as a kind of dreaming. If we take into account that dreams, according to Freud, constitute a 'distorted substitute for something else, something unconscious' (Freud 1977: 114) and that they are 'the product of the dream-work – that is to say, the form into which the latent thoughts have been transmuted by the dream-work' (183), then every fully formed narrative qua dream is indicative of some withdrawn, unconscious, prior realm conditioning it. In its three major features – monologic epistolarity, hypertextuality, dream character – *The Mixquiahuala Letters* is concerned not merely with the problematics of subjectivity and selfhood (its epistolary aspect), the different possibilities of casting its story matter (its hypertextual aspect), and the invocation of the powers of unconscious imagination (its dream aspect), but also, more fundamentally, with the relation between poetics and ontology. The novel amounts to an exploration of narrative as such via narratively insinuating a hidden and foundational (unconscious dream-work), fractured (epistolarity), and disjunctive (hypertext) realm located beyond its apparently orderly surface. It is in the novel's evocation of a subterranean realm of narrative that we need to look for hybridity and difference at work. Ultimately, rather than narratively representing a search for identity (in whichever sense: ethnic, sexual, cultural, personal), *The Mixquiahuala Letters* constitutes a poetic voyage into difference itself.

Gilles Deleuze is without doubt the philosopher who has most thoroughly and systematically elaborated a metaphysics of difference and will thus be the guiding light in retracing this voyage.[6] Let us briefly review the most important points of his philosophy. Difference in-itself, as Gilles Deleuze points out in his *Difference and Repetition*, comes to be expressed by means of intensive processes. Intensity in turn occupies a liminal position in Deleuze's tripartite ontology of virtuality–intensity–actuality. The intensive forms the threshold between the virtual and the actual, with one side immersed in virtuality and the other in actuality. Virtual and actual are Deleuze's names for the more common philosophical notions of the transcendental and the empirical, and his position is that of a transcendental empiricism. What sounds contradictory and counterintuitive indeed comprises Deleuze's philosophy in a nutshell: according to Deleuze, the empirical has a transcendental dimension from which it emerges. The transcendental is thus generative of the empirical. At the same time, the transcendental only exists as implicated in the empirical; it is an aspect of the empirical itself. The relation between the transcendental and the empirical is thus topological and immanent. In this topological ontology of immanence, difference is the transcendental principle generative of and implicated in empirical differences: that is, differing identities. Empirical identity, then, is the product of transcendental difference. Intensity names that zone (space) and process (time) in-between where and through which transcendental difference reverts to empirical identities. While any narrative is always and needs always to be an actual, empirical object of encounter, Castillo's *The Mixquiahuala Letters* makes clear that there is also another, virtual dimension to narrative. It does this by *intensifying* narration, by making narration intensive. Through opening up its zones of intensity and unveiling its spatiotemporal dynamics, the novel intimates its constitutive virtual dimension. It is this unconscious, impersonal, and non-human realm of virtuality which accounts for the novel's utopian political thrust. This realm of the virtual, which the novel opens up by means of narrative, *is* the locus of utopia. It is here, in the virtual, the novel insinuates, that the respective connections and alliances for actual change to take place need to be forged. The novel's name for this site of utopia is precisely 'Mixquiahuala'. It is thus that 'Mixquiahuala' emerges as the narrative's insurrectionary feminist anti-Aztlán, its differential counter-figure to male Chicano identitarian mythography. Let us now turn to the novel's three most salient poetic devices complicit in intensifying narration in order to work out how it goes about achieving this.

Hypertextual Epistles

The Mixquiahuala Letters is both a novel written in letters and a hypertextual novel. Hypertextual as it is used here refers to a concrete textual practice, a practice, however, which does not have to be embodied in electronic media. It nevertheless follows the definition initially proposed by Theodor H. Nelson, who coined the term in the

1960s, according to whom hypertext means 'nonsequential writing – text that branches and allows choices to the reader [. . .] a series of text chunks connected by links which offer the reader different pathways' (Nelson qtd in Landow 2006: 2). Hypertext fiction thus allows for the simultaneous coexistence of variations of its story matter, the sum total of its events and existents. Every repeated reading, depending on the links one follows, constitutes a different actualisation of this matter. While the epistolarity of *The Mixquiahuala Letters* is obvious (since it consists of forty letters), its hypertextuality will need additional explanation. In Espen Aarseth's now classic terms, Castillo's novel is ergodic and hypertextual because it adds the explorative function – making choices – to non-ergodic literature's sole interpretative function (the only user function every literary text has by default). It is not properly cybertextual, however, since it lacks the configurative and textonic functions, functions that allow the reader to actively intervene in and make changes to the story matter (Aarseth 1997: 64).[7] Apart from their cybertextual potential, digital media, due to medium specificity, also provide a more suitable environment for literary hypertexts. Obviously, electronic literature is both able to integrate a much vaster array of possible choices, and thus divergent actualisations, and is also capable of processing this amount more easily by effortlessly providing the respective connecting links. The print book in turn needs to be cleverly designed in order to yield at least a couple of different possible choices and pathways and to resolve the problem of linking these appropriately.[8] *The Mixquiahuala Letters* offers exactly three pathways (I am discounting the fourth option proposed by the author, that of reading all letters as distinct short fiction pieces since one does not follow any path in the sense of a series of letters in this case). These pathways consist of a certain arrangement of a certain number of the novel's letters. Since the letters are numbered, it is possible to provide the necessary links in the table of contents, which lists three series of letter numbers with correlating page numbers. Not all letters appear in all three series; nor are those that appear more than once arranged in the same order in each of the series. Having consulted the table of contents and having made their decision, readers know when to read which letter. In comparison to the seemingly infinite possibilities of electronic literature, it is clear that *The Mixquiahuala Letters'* hypertextuality is extremely constrained. It offers a mere three choices, and the decision has to be made at the outset. In addition, once the decision is made, the reader is firmly set on their path with no further

Intensive Narration

branching off of text and no further decision-making waiting ahead. Despite these differences, both electronic and print hypertexts nevertheless operate according to the same principles: non-sequentiality, seriality, branching, and linking. How do these principles play out? Non-sequentiality and seriality fundamentally go together, as hypertexts provide mere series of events and existents with no dominant underlying sequential organisation. The organising – the sequencing or emplotment – only happens during the reading process, dependent on the links the reader decides to follow. These links function as the crossroads on the narrative pathway and thus mark the points of divergence and branching. Despite electronic texts' seemingly infinite possibilities, these principles are brought to bear on finite matter in both print *and* electronic works: however greater the quantity of existents and events and their increased flexibility with respect to emplotment in electronic environments, this quantity and flexibility always remain distinctly finite. As Eskelinen points out, '[electronic] hypertext fiction just complicates the reading process without rendering impossible the conventional goal of reading it all' (Eskelinen 2012: 81). While it is thus true that electronic hypertext fiction is prone to provide a much vaster field of story matter variations, it is also true that *The Mixquiahuala Letters* is no different from its electronic relatives in terms of underlying structure. This structure precisely consists in providing a finite amount of divergent and often mutually exclusive story variants that coexist simultaneously (let me already point out that this also means that the reader's choice is not a structural necessity). While this simultaneous coexistence is necessarily marked by *actual finitude* and *experiential sequentiality* (empirically, there are just so many variants which can only be experienced one after the other), it makes tangible *virtual infinity* within this actual finitude (transcendentally, there is infinite variation unfolding at once and on the same plane). In terms of possible worlds theory, hypertext fictions allow for so many (however slightly varied) possible worlds. But by allowing for these divergent (and, to repeat, often contradictory) possible worlds, they precisely affirm one infinite virtual world of possibles *and* incomposibles. Let me illustrate this point with an example. The following excerpt is from Robert Coover's *Spanking the Maid*:

> She enters, deliberately, gravely, without affectation, circumspect in her motions (as she's been taught), not stamping too loud, nor dragging her legs after her, but advancing sedately, discreetly, glancing briefly

at the empty rumpled bed, the cast-off nightclothes. She hesitates. No. Again. She enters. Deliberately and gravely, without affectation, not stamping too loud, nor dragging her legs after her, not marching as if leading a dance, nor keeping time with her head and hands, nor staring or turning her head either one way or the other, but advancing sedately and discreetly through the door, across the polished floor, past the empty rumpled bed and cast-off nightclothes (not glancing, that's better), to the tall curtains along the far wall. As she's been taught. [. . .] And she enters. Deliberately and gravely, as though once and for all, without affectation, somewhat encumbered by the vital paraphernalia of her office, yet radiant with that clear-browed self-assurance achieved only by long and generous devotion to duty. [. . .] She enters once and for all encumbered with her paraphernalia which she deposits by the wall near the door, thinking: it should be easier than this. Indeed, why bother at all when it always seems to turn out the same? (Coover 1982: 9; 17; 21)

Making tangible virtual infinity (an infinite number of potential actualisations of the maid entering the room) by means of divergent actual finitude (a finite series of mutually exclusive actualisations), *Spanking the Maid* is an excellent example of hypertext fiction. This is the case, even though it lacks explicit reader involvement. In fact, Coover's novella is such an excellent example precisely *because* it shows that explicit reader involvement is not a decisive feature of hypertextuality. This claim, of course, goes against the grain of established hypertext theory, which views reader interaction as crucial. This not only is apparent in Nelson's original definition of the term, but also is the case in Aarseth's theorisation – a theorisation that, to a large extent, still determines the discussion today – where, out of the seven variables that comprise his typology of textual communication, only the variable of user-function determines whether a text is ergodic or non-ergodic, a point that Eskelinen explicitly draws attention to (Eskelinen 2012: 88). What *Spanking the Maid* shows, however, is that the ergodic and the hypertextual (and, by extension, cybertextual) do not *necessarily* go together. *Spanking the Maid* is both non-ergodic and hypertextual, an impossibility in Aarseth's scheme. It is only impossible, however, because in Aarseth's account everything hinges on the reader. Indeed, hypertext theory in general is exclusively focused on the reader's experience of hypertext rather than the hypertext form as such. In other words, it never moves from an elaboration of hypertext as it is for-us to a theorisation of hypertext in-itself. No wonder that reader interaction turns out to be *the* decisive feature.[9]

Intensive Narration

In Nelson's definition above, then, non-sequentiality, seriality, branching, and linking need to be extracted as the decisive terms marking the qualities of hypertext. These characteristics have to be viewed as genuinely ontological rather than ontic, or, in Deleuzian terms, virtual rather than actual qualities. Thus, hypertext fictions are determined by the virtual coexistence of an infinite number of disjunctive series, and it is this virtual build-up and constitution which they make explicit in their actual form. It is here, in their actual form, that they often adopt a strategy of reader involvement since reader involvement is an excellent tool for expressing the intensive work of linking disjunctive series. More precisely, repeated decision-making on the part of the reader, with its concomitant conversion of a not yet ordered series of events and existents into a particular sequence and order by linking them appropriately, essentially simulates the intensive process of actualisation, the movement whereby virtual elements become actual.[10] This is in fact the most salient function of the hypertext form, that it makes explicit the implicit *intensive process of actualisation*, the movement of emplotment, of ordering the not yet ordered. And it is in this sense that hypertext fiction is a paradigmatic case of intensive narration. Reader choice is just one possible strategy of achieving this, a strategy that is on display in Castillo's novel. Coover's *Spanking the Maid* in turn foregrounds the intensive process of actualisation without any explicit reader interaction simply by never getting off the ground. By repetitively retelling variants of the maid entering her master's bedroom and invariably ending up being spanked it provides a finite amount of divergent actualisations and thus emphasises the very process of actualisation, the bringing together and ordering of divergent series of elements. This is precisely hypertext as intensive narration. What hypertext ultimately emphasises, then, is the intensive process of actualisation germane to *narrative as such*. In its actual, finite form, hypertext intimates the virtual realm of infinite variation (unlimited emplotment potential) that is narrative in-itself. *The Mixquiahuala Letters* cashes in on this function of the hypertext form. While its epistolarity and hypertextuality differentiate it as narrative, this movement of differentiation and disintegration is repeated with respect to the protagonist's personal identity. *The Mixquiahuala Letters* narratively takes apart its own integrity as narrative and, concomitantly, that of its protagonist within that narrative. It is a narrative dismantling of identity and a speculative probing into difference on all levels.

One might be tempted to argue that the novel's epistolarity

contradicts this diagnosis since epistolary fiction is traditionally taken to be *the* narrative form of the transparent self, a diagnosis that much epistolary writing seems to confirm explicitly. In this vein, Jane Talbot, the heroine of Charles Brockden Brown's eponymous epistolary novel, states in one of her letters: 'I have always found an unaccountable pleasure in dissecting, as it were, my heart; uncovering, one by one, its many folds, and laying it before you, as a country is shewn in a map' (Brown 1986: 255). In letters, it is assumed, one gets the closest to characters' minds and the otherwise hidden crevices and folds of their hearts, in just the way Brown's heroine suggests. How does this go together with the dissolution and differentiation of identity, subjectivity, and self that *The Mixquiahuala Letters* performs? First, the last decade and a half has seen the rise of a new trend in scholarship on the epistolary form that mounts a general critique targeted at the traditional correlation of epistolarity with self-transparency. Second, more specifically and more interestingly from the point of view of narrative, Joe Bray has pointed out that, qua recording of past events and act of memory, '[e]pistolary writing' in fact 'oscillates between unity and disintegration of self' (Bray 2003: 16). Bray's diagnosis of oscillation rests on the irrevocable narratological splitting of the letter's 'I' – a splitting characteristic of all homodiegetic accounts – into a narrating and experiencing 'I', a present and a past self that, due to the temporal lag between them, do not coincide. Contrary to the traditional assumption, in epistolary writing the self's unity is thus split from the outset and constantly threatened by dissolution. This threat of dissolution is realised in *The Mixquiahuala Letters*. In a first instance, Castillo's novel multiplies the fissure of the self through its hypertextual structure, producing at least three narrating 'I's and three experiencing 'I's. To appropriate Deleuze and Guattari's self-characterisation as multiplied, fractalised selves from the very beginning of *A Thousand Plateaus*, this, indeed, is 'already quite a crowd' (ATP: 3). These fissures, however, constitute but the first step in the novel's movement of dissolution and disintegration. These fissures still belong to the realm of representation and are mere indicators of much deeper crevices. Indeed, the narratological split between narrating 'I' and experiencing 'I' can be correlated to Deleuze's philosophical account of the active synthesis of memory in *Difference and Repetition*. This synthesis consists in the reproduction of a former present and the simultaneous reflection of the present present:

Intensive Narration

> [T]he former present cannot be represented in the present one without the present one itself being represented in that representation. [...] The present present is treated not as the future object of a memory but as that which reflects itself at the same time as it forms the memory of the former present. (DR: 102)

Thus, in Castillo's narrative, the narrating 'I' forms the memory of the former experiencing 'I' precisely by representing the latter's experiences *and* by representing itself representing. Otherwise, we would not be able to distinguish the two different 'I's in the first place. The active synthesis of memory thus belongs entirely to the realm of representation. But, says Deleuze, this synthesis is grounded on another synthesis, the passive synthesis of memory – and this passive synthesis is 'sub-representative' (DR: 106). It is not a conscious act of recollection but an unconscious temporal process. This second synthesis becomes necessary in order to account for the passing of the present, in order to answer the question of how the present passes and where it goes. For Teresa, *The Mixquiahuala Letters*' protagonist, to be able to represent her former present, this former present needs to have passed and still be 'somewhere'. When, as narrating 'I', Teresa calls up her memories of travels through Mexico, where does she call them up from? Obviously, from the past. This cannot be a particular past, however, since the particular past is precisely that which is being called up by memory, but has to be the past in general where this particular past resides. The particular past is the former present; the past in general is what Deleuze terms 'pure past' (DR: 102), the past as such or in-itself. It is the past as such which is constituted by the passive synthesis of memory, and this pure past houses *all* presents, both former and present. What sounds counterintuitive follows from the fact that

> [i]f a new present were required for the past to be constituted as past, then the former present would never pass and the new one would never arrive. No present would ever pass were it not past 'at the same time' as it is present; no past would ever be constituted unless it were first constituted 'at the same time' as it was present. (DR: 103)

The past cannot be constituted by the present; it must have been there all along. From this 'contemporaneity of the past with the present that it *was*' (DR: 103), Deleuze further deduces the coexistence *and* pre-existence of the past in relation to the present: coexistence, because if, to paraphrase Deleuze, every former present is contemporaneous with the present that it was, then all former presents must coexist with the new present to which they are anterior. But this essentially means that anteriority, that pastness in-itself, does not exist; it 'neither passes nor comes forth' (DR: 103). This is why Deleuze says that the past as such 'insists' and 'consists' rather than exists (DR: 103). The insistence and consistence of the pure past account for the way the past *pre-exists* the present; the past as such is 'presupposed by the passing present' (DR: 104) – it is the *condition* of any present. To sum up, 'each past is contemporaneous with the present it was, the whole past coexists with the present in relation to which it is past, but the pure element of the past in general pre-exists the passing present' (DR: 104). It is the past in general which is transcendental and sub-representative – it can never be captured by representation but always insists in and consists with representation. The past in-itself thus understood is what Deleuze, following Bergson, calls the virtual.

While the Deleuzian active synthesis of memory accounts for the split between the novel's narrating 'I' and experiencing 'I', the present present and the former present, the passive synthesis of memory, the past that was never present, provides the insistent ground upon which this representational game plays out. Any actual present is the actualisation of the differentiating variations of the virtual pure past. This is exactly what the novel's hypertextual form, with its three equally possible but mutually exclusive variants, expresses – that they are mutually exclusive only *empirically*. These three variants with their respective present present narrating 'I' representing its former present experiencing 'I' rest on the transcendental ground of their virtual contemporaneity and coexistence, which thus pre-exists each variant-as-actualisation. The infinity of the virtual relations involving 'Mixquiahuala', 'Teresa', and 'Alicia', the letters' addressee, grounds any finite actualisation of them. The external difference between the different actualisations (which the author titles 'For the Conformist', 'For the Cynic', and 'For the Quixotic', respectively) is thus built on internal difference *productive* of these differences.

'Mixquiahuala' is not merely the empirical small 'Pre-Conquest village of obscurity' (Castillo 1992: 25) that gives the novel its name and which Teresa and her friend Alicia visit on their travels to Mexico (and which is introduced in letter 3, one of the first two letters in each variant). More importantly, it is the novel's most salient figure of the virtual, of the past that was never present, of internal difference. Even empirically, the village seems to present the coexistence of past and present, with the visit providing an 'experience' that 'took us back at least to the time of colonial repression of peons and women' (25), as Teresa writes. In the course of the novel, Mixquiahuala comes to stand for the virtual pure past, the 'splendour which was never lived' (DR: 107), that force which incessantly propels and pushes Teresa forwards, that 'imperative to search, to respond, to resolve' (DR: 107), that 'insistence in all [her] existence' (DR: 107). In this sense, one has to take seriously Alicia's tongue-in-cheek remark that Mixquiahuala explains the 'undiscernible origin of [Teresa's] being' (Castillo 1992: 26). While Mixquiahuala by no means constitutes Teresa's origin in actuality, virtually it determines her in her entire being. It is thus no wonder that every actual place Teresa visits – her travels bearing witness to the urge and insistence of 'Mixquiahuala' – invariably turns out to be a deception vis-à-vis this imperative.

In letter 15, Teresa states that '[t]here was a definite call to find a place to satisfy my yearning spirit [...]; a need for the sapling woman for the fertile earth that nurtured her growth', making clear that she in fact did 'search [...] for [her] home' and that for this home she 'chose Mexico' (52). But none of the Mexican places – from Acapulco to Oaxaca to Yucatán to Mexico City to nameless 'quaint Mexican town[s]' (53) – satisfies this yearning and search. On the contrary, the novel forcefully drives home that settling down and making a home is no viable option at all; it invariably results in caving in to 'the slavery to a pattern', as the Anaïs Nin epigraph to the novel has it, being subjected to man and succumbing to his rule. This is precisely the outcome of both variants one and two. In 'For the Conformist', Teresa finally goes back to her husband, has a child and 'settle[s] back to the even pace of [a] quiet life' in which her 'husband [is] gone for hours on end' and she 'read[s] over students' assignments, eyeglasses hooked on the nose, feet propped up to pamper legs that threaten an outburst of varicose veins' (123; 125). Not even remotely resembling the 'angry dolls of papier-mâché' (124) of Alicia's first one-woman show that Teresa has just returned from visiting, she has become a docile doll herself, even wishing for Alicia that she will find 'a place [she]'ll want to go back to and call home too' (125) and thus conform to the given pattern. Variant two, 'For the Cynic', offers no better ending, insinuating Alicia's apparently absolute submission to a man named Vicente das Mortes, at the sound of whose whispering she puts on 'a smile that ooze[s] with honey' (132). The cynicism of this ending consists of, first, the fact that it was Teresa who introduced Vicente to Alicia and is thus implicated in her downfall; and second, that Alicia's oozing smile is triggered by Vicente calling her Dulcinea, a common moniker for one's female lover in Spanish-speaking countries, derived from the name of *Don Quixote*'s idealised woman figure.[11] Given the quest structure of the narrative and the explicit references to Cervantes's novel, Alicia's 'smile that oozed with honey' becomes an uncanny image redoubling this idealisation by unrestrictedly accepting it and in turn idealising Vicente das Mortes as the knight in shining armour come to rescue her.[12] Only the third variant, 'For the Quixotic', escapes the conformist's and cynic's 'deathtrap' (118). It is the only variant that does not end in docility and submission. Instead, it holds up the injunction to live up to the insistent imperative by quixotically taking up the difficult journey over and over again. It is no coincidence that the final letter in this variant is letter 1. This arrangement, having the first letter in the novel function as the conclusion to one of its hypertextual story versions and thus not appear in the two other versions at all, emphasises the lack of proper origins and invokes cyclicality and the eternal return to beginning anew. This is also the case in terms of the letter's content, as Teresa outlines her plans to embark on yet another journey to Mexico, to respond tirelessly to the imperative not to cave in, to keep going 'furiously' (22). The home Teresa desires to find turns out not to be Mexico at all but the journey itself. 'For the Quixotic' thus offers a line of flight, an escape route from the dead ends depicted in the other two versions, and this escape consists in the mad nomadicism of quixotic journeying. Apart from 'Mixquiahuala', the topos of the eternal journey is thus the second important figure in Castillo's novel: against settling down and returning home, *The Mixquiahuala Letters* promotes the eternal return of the journey; against mythical origin, virtual repetition; against identity, difference; against Aztlán, Mixquiahuala. Castillo's novel thus echoes Deleuze's warnings against confusing the pure past of virtuality with yet another present, the mythical present. Far from evoking Aztlán, the ground of originary Chicano identity, Mixquiahuala – and this is how politics emerges by means of poetics – in fact constitutes Castillo's Chicana feminist antidote to it. Mixquiahuala as the figure of the virtual grounds and constitutes Teresa's being, is the 'undiscernible' and 'obscure' origin, because it hovers over the groundlessness of the eternal repetition of difference. In contrast to the originary place and time of Aztlán, Mixquiahuala is 'nowhere' and 'never'. It is but the insistence to incessant journeying, with journey being precisely the figure of the repetition of difference. As such, the journey corresponds to Deleuze's third synthesis of the pure and empty form of time, the unfolding of time itself, within which the second synthesis of memory unfolds. The third synthesis is purely formal, devoid of any content (whereas the second constitutes *all* the content), as it offers the *principle* according to which 'time itself unfolds' (DR: 111) and the name of this principle is becoming. Becoming names the originary repetition of difference, the eternal return of the different, the coming of the future, and the production of the new. Letter 1, the beginning of the novel's discourse, thus comes to mark not a starting point but this originary repetition, the principle of becoming, and the future to come. Likewise, in terms of content, Mixquiahuala is not the evocation of a pastoral utopian origin, even though we find occasional bucolic scenes in the novel. These evocations of the pastoral, however, are without exception belied by an underlying sense of threat and danger. Thus, letter 3, in introducing Mixquiahuala, mixes pastoral description with the rhetoric of repression, death, and general danger and unease (25–6). Letter 19, which takes up Teresa's short-lived engagement with a rich Mexican entrepreneur, invokes the pastoral in its description of the man's estate. Of course, the relationship is ill fated and the pastoral reverts into the farcical (66–8). And letter 21, probably the most salient example, in recounting the protagonists' visit to Yucatán, makes clear that there is no pastoral for women (70–4). Such tainted pastoral suggests that *this* kind of utopia is but an illusion. The true utopian moment in the novel does not consist in (male) idealisations of fertility, youth, and perfection but in the incessant movement of becoming. One has to shed all identity and selfhood, the novel suggests, and tap the powers of the virtual, the forces of becoming, to make a difference and engender change. This is vividly expressed in letter 27, which constitutes the culmination of a series of letters at the heart of the novel – letters 18 to 27 – which appear in all versions and always in this order. As such, it is no coincidence that letter 27 recounts one of Teresa's strange dreams. Dreaming in general and this dream in particular play a crucial role in Castillo's novel. Given the prominence of references to and accounts of dreams in the novel, it is surprising that, as far as I can tell, nothing yet has been written about the significance of dreams and correlatively of sleeping in *The Mixquiahuala Letters*. As we will see, falling asleep and dreaming are Teresa's and Alicia's two distinct strategies of 'depersonalization' (Deleuze 1995: 6) or 'becoming-imperceptible' (ATP: 308), of tapping the virtual and immersion in difference.

We have seen how the novel's epistolary and hypertextual form cracks up its representational surface by fracturing both its integrality as narrative and the identity and selfhood of its protagonist. This differentiation of integrality and identity is repeated within the third of the three proposed story variants, which posits originary repetition (rather than the repetition – *Wieder-holung* – of origin) as the narrative's animating principle in terms of both content and form. We will now burrow even further into the narrative by following the trajectory of the dissolution of Teresa's self in order to unearth the dark chthonic caverns of differential narrative.

Metaphysical Dreams

Spirituality and spiritualism, usually in the form of *curanderismo* and *brujería*, are staples of Chicano/a literature. Accordingly, supernatural powers and a *brujo* also make their appearance in *The Mixquiahuala Letters* in an episode which features nocturnal interference by spirits (letters 22 and 24, 74–81; 85–90). It is in letter 22 that we first read about Teresa's spiritistic leanings when she explains to Alicia: 'Nothing you couldn't see and touch existed. i, on the other hand, having been raised by a spiritual healer grandmother who'd believed in the metaphysical way of the universe, couldn't shake off the idea that ghosts existed among us' (76). The term 'metaphysical' here clearly correlates with an esotericism of otherworldly spirits and cosmic energies rather than proper philosophical concerns. What is remarkable, however, is that the novel, in the depiction of the relationship between Alicia and Teresa, advocates the fusion of empiricism (Alicia's reliance on sensory impressions) with metaphysics (Teresa's esotericism). More precisely, the novel takes empirical facts as a given, but propagates their suffusion with metaphysical powers. That spirits suffuse facts becomes apparent when Alicia, due to her no-nonsense empiricism, is not in the least worried by the esoteric séance the two women participate in despite the rather vague but clearly unpleasant premonitions that this occult session engenders. Only the spiritistic Teresa, however, is able to ward off the subsequent nightly visit by a dark spirit (85–90). Since the novel never questions the robustness of empirical access to the world, and never aims at a transcendent other-world in order to sublate thisworldly problems – on the contrary, the novel is concerned with the very material thisworldly problems of the double subjugation of Chicanas as brown women – this episode serves to envision powerfully a supplementary, invisible dimension of spirits and powers. Such a view is very much in line with Castillo's musings on *espiritismo* in her volume of essays, *Massacre of the Dreamers*:

> [E]spiritismo [...] is an acknowledgement of the energy that exists throughout the universe subatomically generating itself and interconnecting, fusing, and changing.
> While subatomic studies may serve as a theoretical basis for social change, on a more pragmatic and immediate level, they offer a personal response to the divided state of the individual who desires wholeness. (Castillo 1995: 159)

Castillo's *espiritismo* clearly belongs to the tradition of modern esotericism.[13] It is but a version of the staple esoteric account of individuality suffused with cosmic energy, where cosmic energy is the guarantor of wholeness, overcoming the state of division and mending the rift. Upon closer scrutiny, Castillo's vision of wholeness seems incongruent with any notion of subatomic powers, however, as it remains utterly unclear how an impersonal cosmic energy can constitute a personal response to anything, unless, of course, one takes these impersonal powers as the ultimate *source* and *ground* of the personal, if one locates one's identity in this cosmic 'elsewhere', if one conceives of wholeness as the work of 'interconnecting, fusing and changing' itself. Such an undertaking finds support in Deleuze's own writings, which are replete with references to the esoteric and occult, from his very first publication on Johann Malfatti (Deleuze 2007b) to his and Guattari's musings on sorcery in *A Thousand Plateaus* (ATP: 264–78), and their evocation of the activity of thought as akin to the 'witch's flight' in *What is Philosophy?* (WIP: 41). Deleuze time and again sifts through the occult and esoteric tradition for the sake of making it fruitful for his philosophical enterprise. Christian Kerslake's *Deleuze and the Unconscious*, the first extended study to focus on this tradition in Deleuze's philosophy, is a veritable treasure chest when it comes to Deleuze's indebtedness to esoteric and occult thought.[14] More recently, Joshua Ramey has placed these references in the larger tradition of hermeticism, one of the roots to which modern esotericism can be traced (Ramey 2012). Following this genealogy, today's esotericism can legitimately be viewed as a kind of folk metaphysics. In what follows, much in the spirit of Deleuze, I will try to translate Castillo's folk metaphysical intuitions into metaphysics proper.

One should also note here that despite its centrality to Chicana literary production, the issue of spiritualism and spirituality is only slowly emerging as focal point of study. Theresa Delgadillo's *Spiritual Mestizaje*, the first sustained account of Chicana spirituality, was published only as recently as 2011. In her book, Delgadillo elaborates on Gloria Anzaldúa's notion of 'spiritual mestizaje', using it as a critical tool for unlocking theological themes in Chicana literature. Given the theological dimension of the work, Delgadillo's insistence on notions of critique and the critical is striking, however. Quoting the single passage in Anzaldúa's *Borderlands* that actually features the term 'spiritual mestizaje', she concludes that it 'underscore[s] its [spiritual mestizaje's] status as a critical process' (Delgadillo 2011: 7). But even a cursory glance at the respective passage seems to suggest something else entirely. To wit, Anzaldúa asserts that, as a *mestiza*, she is 'an act of kneading, of uniting and joining', that the *mestiza* soul is '*el trabajo*, the opus, the great alchemical work; spiritual mestizaje, a "morphogenesis," an inevitable unfolding', and that '[w]e have become the quickening serpent movement' (Anzaldúa 1987: 81). That Anzaldúa invokes processuality is clear, but this process is quite obviously ontological, not critical. This passage is an evocation of ontogenesis: how the *mestiza* is a work, something both formed and incessantly being trans-formed. She is even the quintessence of work (*el trabajo*, great work). The question, of course is, whose work? Who is doing the forming? While the terms 'spiritual', 'kneading', and 'opus' already mark the passage as theological, Anzaldúa is more than explicit about this theological import when she asserts that 'we are the people on the knees of the gods' (80). The *mestiza* is thus the work of gods; she is literally a spiritual *mestizaje*, something kneaded, united, and joined – in short, shaped and formed, by spiritual powers. Spiritual *mestizaje* has nothing to do with the work of critique (unless one believes that gods indulge in ideology critique rather than creation). It is a thoroughly onto-theological term. What Anzaldúa offers here is a sort of esoteric onto-theology – the reference to alchemy and the great work, opus magnum, precisely invoking the esotericism of the Hermetic tradition. Delgadillo is right in regarding spiritual *mestizaje* as an essential term and spirituality as fundamental to the Chicana literary output. She is wrong, however, in aligning this spirituality with the practice of critique. Both Anzaldúa's spiritual *mestizaje* and Castillo's *espiritismo* have genuine metaphysical weight. It is in this vein that I suggest reading the following emphatic assertions by Castillo:

Intensive Narration

> Once the causes for certain obstacles in her [the *espiritista*'s] life are identified and worked through, she does not flounder about as merely a 'survivor,' such as one who has survived a plane wreck and awaits a rescue team (which may never be forthcoming) but uses the new affirmation, that she is and has always been part of the intricate network of life on this planet, to strengthen herself and to share her knowledge with others. Ultimately we seek to propel ourselves into a collective state of being, which is so ancient we will consider it new.
>
> In the long run, spirituality will be a state of being that is not defined, but lived, as a unified self. (Castillo 1995: 160)

Castillo's notion of a unified self seems to render her esoteric spiritualism incongruent with Deleuze's philosophical spiritualism. Upon scrutiny, however, it is exactly this point that makes Castillo's *espiritismo* incoherent in-itself. If spirituality reveals that human selves are part of the much larger 'network of life' understood as a collective state of being, and if this collective state of being is to be equated with the above-quoted 'interconnecting, fusing and changing' of cosmic energy, then it is a mystery how any notion of a unified self could be retained. On the one hand, only the dissolution of unified selves can produce a truly collective state of being. Anything else results in a mere collection of beings. If, however, on the other hand, the notion of the unified self is supposed to refer to a larger, spiritual entity that fuses the many human (or sentient) selves, it remains inexplicable how the differentiation into a multiplicity of selves came about in the first place. If Castillo's collective state of being *is* a unified self, no numerically differentiable selves are possible. In Deleuzian terms, everything here hinges on the crucial difference between implicit and explicit multiplicity, internal and external difference (DR: 298; 23; 29; 97). A crowd of unified selves is a mere explicit multiplicity belonging to the realm of external difference, meaning that there is a certain quantity of selves that can be differentiated from each other numerically: a set of well-defined selves, a collection of beings. In contrast, implicit multiplicity and internal difference cannot be measured by number. They do not extend in space and time but are the pure intensities of multiplicity and difference as such: dissolved selves, a collective state of being that is precisely singular–plural. If Castillo is looking for 'a state of being that is not defined' and that can still account for difference, she will only find it here. Only by becoming multiple and differential can selves achieve a collectivity that is undefined but still distinct. Of course, undefined – obscure – and distinct is precisely Deleuze's definition of the Idea

(DR: 184; 350). This is no surprise, as implicit multiplicity and Idea are basically synonyms (DR: 230–1). Since we already know that the Deleuzian Idea belongs to the realm of the virtual, and that the virtual is Deleuze's name for the transcendental, a collective state of being is a transcendental state. This, indeed, is no surprise either and in fact has to be thus, as it is quite clear that empirically we never fuse with other humans, let alone trees or stones, to form such a collective state of being. But if this collectivity qua implicit multiplicity is virtual, then it is also the productive ground of actual, explicit multiplicity and the generator of the collection of beings. It is the 'differenciator of difference' (DR: 40), producing numerically distinguishable entities. With respect to Castillo's concerns, the collective state of differential being is the ground of unified, identifiable, selves. If this is the case, then reaching for the collective state of being indeed amounts to reaching for one's ground and essence, for that which defines what 'I' am. That which defines me, however, is not a unified notion of 'I' – it cannot be thus since 'I' is that which I am trying to define – but the notion of an absolutely dissolved self pertaining to a state where any 'I' has vanished. Thus, the ground of my self lies outside my self. In order to become truly myself, to reach my essential being, I have to go elsewhere. This elsewhere, due to the topological foldings of the virtual and the actual, is nowhere in particular. It can only be reached by 'leaping in place' (LS: 170), by undertaking a 'curious stationary journey' (D II: 95). This journey consists in shedding one's self, in becoming-imperceptible. In contrast to the inconsistencies of her esoteric non-fiction, Castillo's *The Mixquiahuala Letters* is an impeccable account of precisely such a journey. Apart from the narrative strategies already discussed – the differentiating and fractalising function of epistolarity and hypertextuality – this journey finds its most acute expression in the novel's repeated evocation of the protagonists' state of sleeping and dreaming. Ultimately, it turns out, 'Mixquiahuala' is that 'Never Never Land' which can only be visited via the 'curious stationary journey' and 'leaping in place' of sleeping and dreaming.

The novel presents sleeping and dreaming as the only viable strategies to escape male domination and identification. The two protagonists repeatedly go to sleep in the context of discussions or depictions of male–female interactions, often of a sexual kind and usually clearly marked by male domination, where sleep invariably constitutes a (more or less) deliberate withdrawal from these interactions (as, for example, in letter 11; 45–6). Their dreams, in turn, often have a visionary quality that serves either as prophetic warning (for example, letter 12; 46–7), or as a means to envision a markedly different power structure (for example, letter 27; 101–4). Before turning to a close analysis of these instances of sleeping and dreaming in the novel, I need to establish how far sleeping can be said to amount to becoming-imperceptible, the double movement of both shedding one's self and becoming absolutely oneself.

This not only is an argument that can be made from Deleuze,[15] but also finds strong support in Jean-Luc Nancy's recent non-phenomenology of sleep in his *The Fall of Sleep*. Nancy's text has the virtue of tackling the relation between self and sleep head on. Nancy bluntly states that 'I fall asleep and at the same time I vanish as "I"' (Nancy 2009: 11) while unmistakably making clear that this vanishing of the 'I' amounts to the unearthing of one's essential being: 'It is in the self the sleeper is, as *in self* as the Kantian *thing* can be, that is the being-there, posited, the very position independent of all appearance and all appearing' (13).[16] Falling asleep thus constitutes both the attainment of my innermost self and the dissolution of a distinct 'I':

> I fall to where I am no longer separated from the world by a demarcation that still belongs to me all through my waking state and that I myself am, just as I am my skin and all my sense organs. I pass that line of distinction, I slip entire into the innermost and outermost part of myself, erasing the division between these two putative regions. (5)

A little later Nancy clarifies that sleep's erasure of division between inside and outside with respect to one's essential being constitutes simultaneity per se, as true simultaneity only exists 'in the realm of sleep. It is the great present, the co-presence of all compossibilities, even incompatible ones' (7). Nancy locates the essential self in the fusion of distinctions in an eternal presence. In other words, the in-itself of one's self turns out to be the eternal dissolution in an undifferentiated *apeiron* attainable only through sleep. Nancy's sleep thus epitomises Hegel's dictum of the 'night in which every cow is black' (Hegel 1977: 496). It constitutes a realm that concepts (distinctions) cannot reach. All one can do is cautiously circle the event horizon of this black hole – hence Nancy's poetic non-phenomenology surfing its outer brinks. While Nancy thus articulates the necessary link between dissolution and essence of one's self, he, due to his phenomenological commitments, cannot say much about this dark essence itself. It needs a metaphysician to probe this darkness. This is where we need to return to Deleuze. In contrast to Nancy, and as already indicated, Deleuze self-identifies as a 'pure metaphysician' (Deleuze 2007a: 42), and it is not too difficult to see that Deleuze's conceptualisation of the virtual–actual fold is apt to provide the detailed metaphysical account that Nancy cannot offer. More importantly, Deleuze's topological folding of inside and outside immanentises Nancy's black hole of the in-itself and plants the seeds of conceptual distinction into the obscurity of this darkness. Deleuze's virtual qua realm of the in-itself qua realm of implicit multiplicities or Ideas is precisely not an undifferentiated *apeiron* – it is the incessant differentiation of difference. Accordingly, falling asleep amounts not to a fall beyond the event horizon into oblivious indistinction, but to a plunge into obscurity where obscurity is conceived as the very germ of the distinct: difference itself. Having thus established the relation between sleep and the in-itself, we are now equipped to trace Castillo's esoterico-poetic figuration of sleeping and dreaming in *The Mixquiahuala Letters*.

Sleeping and dreaming pervade Castillo's novel: letters 11 and 28 suggest falling asleep and sleeping as antidotes to male-induced sickness and patriarchy's defining pattern at large. Right after hinting at a possible lesbian relationship between the two protagonists, letter 11 exposes the societal status quo that seems to make such a relationship impossible: 'We weren't free of society's tenets to be convinced we could exist indefinitely without the demands and complications one aggregated with the supreme commitment to a man' (45). Indeed, Teresa castigates and bemoans women's 'need [. . .] to seek approval from man through sexual meetings' (45), as these meetings embody male domination and female subjection. This diagnosis is substantiated and exemplified by the lyrical description of a sex scene between Alicia and an unnamed man that follows these assertions. In this encounter, Alicia is a full subject, in the sense of being aware, being conscious, precisely in the moment of utter exposure, passivity, and subjection when, lying naked on her belly, she gives herself over to the caresses of the man: '*for a moment you were aware of yourself / lay very still and alert and awaiting*' (45). Her '*barriers [. . .] cast away*' (45) are the barriers that kept her from being subjected. Being a subject then, in the triple sense of being aware, of being subjected, and of being thrown under man who acts upon passive woman, the passage suggests, correlates with being defined by '*the circling patterns of his expert fingers*' which '*erase fear*' and '*instill trust*' (45). Against the mainstream philosophical understanding of subjectivity since Descartes, the novel casts being a subject, a well-defined self

– more precisely, a woman subject and self – as a state opposite to autonomy and freedom, as slavery to a pattern – the pattern man's fingers draw – as quoted in the novel's Anaïs Nin epigraph. Man's erasure of fear and instilment of trust are fundamentally a lure into unfreedom. The circling fingers of man – it is no coincidence that the man in this episode remains unnamed, evoking not a particular man but man in general – trace Alicia's body from head to toe, defining her. If being a well-defined self equals dependence and heteronomy, then independence and autonomy can only be gained through acts of desubjectification and depersonalisation. It is here that sleep enters the picture. In the letter's final lines, Teresa, who has witnessed this scene, decides to leave this realm of identity by heteronomy through going back to sleep: '*i closed my eyes / went on / with my nap*' (46). Falling asleep is cast as a method of silent withdrawal. Following Nancy, we can say that this withdrawal is a movement into the dark recesses of one's self, a movement away from heteronomy towards autonomy.[17]

While letter 11 focuses on Alicia, letter 28 exposes the governing patriarchal pattern by means of one of Teresa's sexual relationships. The parallels to letter 11 are striking. Teresa writes,

> High above the trash-ridden streets of Manhattan [. . .] we were snuggled and safe within the tight arms of men who knew how to possess women. [. . .] I was pliable clay to be molded and defined, to envelop him, suit his proportions until a pillow was placed over the mouth to stifle a cry of insatiable hunger. (105)

Men define women, subject them, and women are subjects by conformity to this male patterning only. Again, going to sleep is depicted as the only escape route from this patterning when Teresa, feeling sick due to the odour of a perfumed picture she receives from a former acquaintance, resorts to this tactic: 'Sleep would make the throbbing go away, the clamps at each side of my head stop pressing in, threatening to crush my skull' (107). Sleep is thus depicted as curing male-induced sickness.

Yet another example of this figuration of sleep as withdrawal from a world that is thoroughly man's world occurs when Alicia returns home after an exhaustive journey only to find her lover Rodney cheating on her (precisely as her prophetic dream had suggested). As a reaction, she drops her bags and heads directly for the bedroom: 'The bed hadn't been made and the sheets were musk odored, but you lay down anyway, and closed your eyes' (49). Given the evidence, it is safe to say that *The Mixquiahuala Letters* time and again resorts to the following formula: the empirical world is the world of definition, with definition being solely man's privilege (as acutely exemplified in the novel's depiction of heterosexual relationships); this world is opposed to the transcendental world, which is the world of the obscure and undefined, the no man's land of woman (as manifested in the novel's emphasis on the folding in on oneself that sleep constitutes). In this novel, women never define and men never seem to sleep. That sleep indeed constitutes a bastion against the definitionist and identifying impetus of man and that it is a realm intangible by these operations is driven home forcefully in letter 16 in an episode already alluded to further above when Alvaro attempts to enter the women's only refuge. Since they are staying at Alvaro's place and since they fear his actions after Teresa rejects Alvaro's sexual advances, the two women prepare for the ensuing night by barricading the door to their room before going to sleep. Alvaro returns home after a night out drinking and noisily forces his way in, waking them up. Taking off his clothes and climbing into their bed, leaving Teresa 'sandwiched in the middle' (58), his sole objective is to keep the women from sleeping. In an almost absurd and farcical episode, 'animal-like, vindictive' (58) Alvaro achieves this by means of 'exaggerated snoring interspersed with farting' (58). Devoid of other comfortable sleeping options, the women spend the night 'like a pair of dogs, huddled at the foot of the bed' (58). Together with the aforementioned reference to the 'insomniac nights' (54) that Teresa had spent with Alvaro, this incidence underscores that the novel casts men as wanting their women sleepless, always awake and aware since asleep and unconscious they fundamentally escape their definitions and identifications – to repeat Nancy's words, sleep 'shows of itself only its disappearance, its burrowing and its concealment' (Nancy 2009: 13). Going to sleep is thus tantamount to withdrawing from male-endowed identity and constitutes the novel's most salient act of female resistance. That it really is an act of resistance, in the sense of resisting male intrusion, becomes evident by the fact that Alvaro does not and in fact cannot manage to enter the women's sleep. To enter sleep, one has to fall asleep. But this of course entails giving oneself up and giving one's self over to sleep, partaking in the collective state of being. In this state, however, man can no longer wield the weapons of identification, definition, and subjection. Thus, the only tactic Alvaro can resort to in order to keep the women within the bounds of man's subjectifying pattern is that of sleep deprivation.

Intensive Narration

Now, one might wonder whether, if sleep indeed constitutes the only viable option for women's resistance, this is not a very poor state of affairs. Are not falling asleep and sleeping the epitome of quietism and passivity? Is not sleep, rather than constituting an act of resistance, the ultimate act of capitulation? In curling up and folding in on oneself, in becoming-imperceptible, becoming-zero, does one not simply give up everything, leave everything to man? This counterargument forgets that in Deleuze's differential metaphysics, which has served as our guide thus far, the virtual is the locus of change. There is no change engendered on the level of the actual and every relation between two actual entities has to pass through the virtual. Change on the level of the actual needs to be engineered in the virtual; everything is decided in the virtual. It is in this vein that sleep, qua access to the in-itself, figures as the pathway to change. Sleep has a double function: refusal and retreat in its withdrawal from heteronomy, and affirmation and advance in its access to potential change. In other words, falling asleep is not a mere passive sinking from consciousness into the unconscious but also a way of tapping the transformative powers of the unconscious.[18] Sleep's tapping of the powers of the unconscious is indexed by the dream image. This is fairly well known from Freudian dream interpretation, according to which the dream image precisely manifests the unconscious dreamwork. This invites us to turn to Castillo's evocation of dreams. If woman's becoming-unconscious is to be not just a passive and quietist refusal and retreat but also an active method of empowerment, this needs to become evident in the novel's treatment of dreams. Congruent with the metaphysical reading of sleep as a pathway towards the in-itself, and congruent with the novel's Chicana *espiritismo*, my reading of dreams as they appear in the novel is not situated within the restricted framework of psychoanalysis, which exclusively focuses on the human psyche. Rather, the dream image has to be understood in a larger metaphysical sense. In this vein, the metaphysical dream image, analogous to the psychoanalytic dream image, manifests other, more primordial forces. But these forces are not inherent to the human psyche only – they pertain to a truly metaphysical unconscious pervading all of reality.[19] With this in mind, let us turn to the novel's central dream sequence.

From Alicia's 'mystical' (27) and 'prophetic dreams' (46) to 'the window of dreams' enigma' (47), the 'refuge of dreams' (86), and 'the abyss of the dreamworld' (88), to 'dream inspired town[s]' (55) and the 'dream-like quality of the surroundings' (62), the novel is replete with references to dreams and dreaming. These references invariably evoke an otherworldly quality of the dream, as can be readily inferred from the vocabulary in the examples above (mystical, prophetic, window, enigma, refuge, abyss). In *The Mixquiahuala Letters*, dreaming is not a mere personal experience that might serve as a leverage for the analyst for probing the analysand's psychic depths, but rather indexes an experience of the impersonal as expounded in Castillo's esotericism of subatomic cosmic energies and Deleuze's conceptualisation of the virtual. In short, in Castillo's novel, rather than merely being an effect and providing the image of the (human) unconscious at work, dreaming constitutes a veritable visionary act. With fabulation, a term they hijack from Bergson, Deleuze and Guattari provide the corresponding visionary faculty to these acts (WIP: 171; 230n). Fabulation qua visionary faculty is the proper faculty of speculation, that which makes it possible to go beyond experience in experience. Fabulation is the name for the capacity of embarking on Deleuze's 'curious stationary journey' and making that strange 'leap in place'. In *The Mixquiahuala Letters*, fabulation's work comes in the guise of 'mystical dreams' (27).[20] Teresa's dream in letter 27 constitutes the end point of this fabulatory journey. In this letter, Teresa presents Alicia and the reader with a story of origin which could easily be detected as an invocation of mythical Aztlán were it not for a number of details that do not fit this picture. In fact, the images this micro-narrative evokes produce a counter-Aztlán that sets originary, virtual repetition over against the repetition of mythical origins. The dream is set in a 'provincial town' some time 'between the sixteenth century and the present' (101), its people of mixed blood. That the dream is a narrative of origin becomes evident when the town's existence is traced to the beginnings of time in the dream's invocation of God's creation of the first human. This originary creation is cast as successful only after two failed attempts that produce people too dark and too fair-skinned, respectively. God is finally satisfied with his 'brown, firm and strong' (102) creation, which posits *mestizaje* as originary rather than derivative. That the dream is about origins that exceed filiation and familial ties and thus go beyond the 'familialism' of psychoanalysis (Deleuze and Guattari 1986: 51) is further substantiated in a scene where Teresa enters a house 'with a sense of familiarity' but is 'surprised' when the old woman she meets turns out 'not [to be her] mother' but 'still of [her] people' (102). The dream thus presents a vision of the origin of Teresa's people and simultaneously casts this origin as universal; all people are essentially brown, all people's origin lies in *mestizaje*. While this claim to universality is already at odds with the Aztlán myth's claim as being foundational for a particular ethnic identity, the Chicano appeal to this originary myth is further eroded in the subsequent scene, where Teresa passes 'a group of young people caught up in rhetorical debate' who 'fight and defend theirs with words and ideologies' (102). This is a thinly disguised attack on the Chicano movement's leading figures and strategies, which becomes even more evident a couple of lines further on, when Teresa confronts the group a second time; now they are explicitly referred to as 'intellectuals' and it seems safe to assume that the group consists of men only as Teresa furiously tears open her shirt and yells, '"i am a woman [. . .] but i am first human"' (103). This proclamation again casts feminism as a universalist endeavour in opposition to male particularism.[21] Accordingly, Teresa calls them 'fools', knowing that 'they, too, were scornful of [her] and [her] methods' (102), the narrative thus clearly marking the methodological difference. This difference can be encapsulated thus: empirical and verificationist versus transcendental and speculative. The verificationists are 'word dealers' (103) and thus rely on logic (logos) as their primary method. The dream reveals this to be an utterly ineffective method for facing real and not just formal problems: the word is by no means mightier than the sword when it has to face the 'thundering sound of marching troops' (103), which announce the town's looming downfall. Only fabulatory speculation is adequate to cope with these real problems. Instead of logicians, we need dreamers, witches, sorcerers: this is the quintessence to be drawn from the dream's and the novel's climax, where the method of fabulation (speculation), ontology (becoming of being), and politics (transformative action) meet and merge in one visionary dream image: Teresa pointing her weapon (104). Let me unpack this image. The climax is reached when Teresa, in the face of the marching troops, races to retrieve her gun:

> My weapon. It was my own and i had used it before, fit into my hand like that of a faithful lover.
>
> i made certain that it was fully loaded and loaded another that had been left by someone else. *There was no time!* (103)

In terms of politics, the contrast with the ever-debating 'word dealers' could not be starker. To remain with the image evoked above, swords trump words when it comes to action: not because one cannot do things with words, but because they are utterly ineffective and simply the wrong tool when it comes to dealing with real problems. Reality is not linguistically structured. This is not to say that *Teresa* will defeat a whole army, but it is to say that her *method* harbours the potential to change the course of events, whereas that of the group of young intellectuals does not. The gun thus becomes the vivid figure of her speculative methodology. In terms of ontology, in the framework of the differential metaphysics espoused here, the dream image, akin to the sorcerer's and witch's incantations and visions, is as close as we can get to the non-appearing, the non-phenomenological: in short, the in-itself. It is the image closest to the virtual. We have already established that the principle which grounds, or rather ungrounds, the virtual is the Deleuzian third synthesis of time, the unfolding of time itself, repetitious difference and differential repetition: becoming. As such, becoming does not emerge and happen in time, but is the emergence and happening of time. And this is indeed what Teresa's dream imagines – in the sense of putting into image – in its positing of originary and universal *mestizaje* as synthetic ground, the principle (God) of which is precisely that of difference (two different skin colours inhere) and repetition (two other beginnings persist). That God is a name for becoming, the unfolding of time, is revealed when the dream narrative asserts that this story of synthetic origin marks the 'beginning of time' (102) inaugurated by God 'one eon of a day' (102). The dream draws a difference between eon and time here, with time denoting the time of succession – that is, chronology – which only comes into existence with the human, and eon, the time of God, that grounds and generates chronology. This, of course, is also the distinction that Deleuze makes when he differentiates between Aion and Chronos in his *Logic of Sense* (LS: 186–93). What is crucial to Deleuze's account, however, is that Aion is not split from Chronos. It is not another, prior and transcendent, temporal dimension but folded into Chronos. Teresa's dream narrative embraces this temporal topology in its climactic final moments. The exclamation '*[t]here was no time!*' (103), which is italicised and thus emphasised, not only transports a sense of urgency, but more importantly marks the fact that this dream image fabulates an origin literally out of time. There is no Chronos in this nowhere and 'Never Never Land'. Accordingly, when the sentence following the negation of chronology exclaims that '[t]he moment had come' (103), this is precisely not the coming of yet another moment in the sequence of moments, moment after moment, but the advent of Aion, an eruption *within* Chronos, the moment that harbours 'the history of the world and [. . .] its future, [. . .] all that had lived and died and had been born again'; it is the moment Teresa 'approache[s] an opaque window and point[s] [her] weapon' (104). *This* is the ultimate speculative moment in the novel, this image of Teresa pointing her weapon at an opaque window. This image encapsulates virtual co- and pre-existence, the zero point of chronology ('history and future of the world'), the rebirth of the new ('born again'), originary repetition: becoming. By the same token, it makes clear that the only way to reach becoming is by means of fabulatory speculation. This dream image redoubles on itself – the opaque window – and exclaims: speculation *is* the weapon! This is *The Mixquiahuala Letters'* revolutionary politics, its call to arms: speculate, cast your spells, dream! If one wishes for transformation and regeneration, one has ceaselessly to go beyond the restrictions of empirical life and tap the sources of transcendental becoming.

That fabulation as the faculty of speculation is etymologically related to fabula – story – is no coincidence. In Bergson's coinage, it conceptualises religious myth-making and is indeed translated as myth-making (Bergson 1954: 108). In Deleuze and Guattari's use, fabulation is shorn of its theological import and secularised as a faculty that artists, particularly writers, capitalise on (WIP: 171). It is thus closely allied to the production of art and, specifically, literature. Against Deleuze and Guattari, I wish to suggest that fabulation's true function is the production of stories in the general sense of narrative rather than in the restricted sense of fiction. Fabulation would thus be the faculty to narrate, with narration amounting to the rendition of visionary knowledge. This knowledge has nothing to do with conceptual knowledge. Rather, it is aesthetic in the sense of Baumgarten's original coinage of the term as 'gnoseologia inferior' (Baumgarten 1963: 10). Being less rigorous (and thus inferior) than conceptual knowledge since unable to draw precise distinctions it is adequate to probe obscurity precisely because of this lack – it is still gnoseologia. This characterisation ties in very well not only with aesthetics as being concerned with darkness rather than luminosity, but also with the etymological origin of narration in Latin *gnārus*, having knowledge of, being acquainted with a thing. One of the notorious difficulties in narratology is to reconcile this origin with narration in the sense of fiction, as fiction stems from *fingere* – to form. How can something constitute knowledge and creation at the same time? This question will be further pursued in Chapter 3 under the heading of speculative constructivism. Suffice it to say here that the answer also inheres in Teresa's visionary dream, for when she recounts the myth of the origin of humanity, God's creative act consists in forming clay. To form out of clay in turn is the specific root of *fingere* in the general sense, a root that goes back to the Proto-Indo-European word *dheigh*, which survives in today's English as dough and means to knead. Fiction as *fingere*, then, denotes originary creation in the sense of kneading, shaping into form. 'To fiction', to forge, thus describes the activity of morphogenesis. If narration is an act of knowing and if fiction-making means creating form, then narration, and particularly fictional narration, might well be the adequate means of probing the origins and workings of this making, of acquiring knowledge about morphogenesis. In this sense, narration is, by default, creative *and* speculative. It all boils down to this: in order to narrate, one has to make use of fabulation. In order to speculate, one has to tell a story.

Dream Poetics

Castillo's novel substantiates and exemplifies Colebrook's assertion that

> [t]here is a voice that is other than speech, a sound or intensity that is not the expression of a self or body and that occurs extra-organically as a rhythm or pulsation from which something like a social body or territory would emerge. (Colebrook 2010: 118)

This extra-linguistic, extra-psychosomatic, and extra-organic voice is precisely the voice grounding all voices, what Deleuze, quoting Lawrence Ferlinghetti, calls '"the fourth-person singular"' (LS: 118). Fourth, because it marks an additional dimension to the three grammatical persons, thus going beyond any grammar of person – it is impersonal; person, because it nevertheless inheres in all of the three forms as their immanent condition; singular, because despite this universality it is only one voice, but a voice devoid of a particularity of its own. It is the transcendental ground of all empirical voices, the universal singularity productive of all its particular expressions. This voice is unconscious, impersonal, and non-human, and as such persists in all human, personal, and conscious voices. While these statements concerning voice are obviously metaphysical and not narratological statements, it is my contention that the metaphysics and narratology of voice are profoundly intertwined. This can also be gleaned from the point of view of narratology where, as discussed in the Introduction, Nielsen's concept of the impersonal voice features among the characteristics of unnatural narration. In this vein, the fourth-person singular is the voice that grounds every single enunciation, the impersonal voice that produces any personal account without transcending it. *The Mixquiahuala Letters* takes a first-person account, emphasised in its monologic epistolary form, as its starting point to uncover successively its conditioning fourth-person singular. On the surface level, this is already indicated by the novel's consistent employment of the lower case 'i' whenever Teresa speaks of herself. This can be read as the narrative's acknowledgement of the 'larval subjects' (DR: 100) teeming underneath and constituting the fully developed subject that is 'I'. This foundational fourth-person singular is made tangible in the novel's hypertextual epistles and its valuation of visionary dreams. In fact, if hypertextuality simulates the intensive process of actualisation, the unconscious process of morphogenesis, and if visionary dreams grant access to this unconscious process, then Castillo's novel suggests that, by dint of displaying its hypertextual form and showcasing the powers of visionary dreaming, it has to be viewed as precisely such a visionary dream itself; it is a delirious dream and a veritable act of *brujería* summoning the forces of becoming. It is in this sense that the novel constitutes an instance of intensive narration. *The Mixquiahuala Letters* pursues a dream poetics that is adequate to the fourth-person singular, that voice, that intensity, that rhythm and pulsation that makes things happen, that is creation itself. This dream poetics thus warrants an adequate method of scrutiny. As has been shown, this method cannot rely on a representational framework, as the light of representation cannot enter the 'night' of 'Never Never Land'; it merely makes the shadows recede and announces the relentless reign of luminosity (clarity and distinctness). This reign is built on the excision and exorcism of darkness, a darkness on which it nevertheless depends in order to shine, a darkness without which it would be impotent. In order to dream properly, in order to reach 'Never Never Land', one has to use the sandman's method and sprinkle some dust on one's eyes, distorting and obscuring one's vision; one has to immerse oneself in darkness and dream along. This immersion, this dreaming, is what intensive narration qua fabulatory speculation achieves. It is in this vein that Deleuze pits his anamorphic understanding of the dream against the insistence of psychoanalysis on its essentially tropological nature when he says that 'the dream is not a metaphor but a series of anamorphoses which sketch out a very large circuit' (Deleuze 2008: 54). Why anamorphosis and not metaphor?

Because metaphor emphasises representation. In metaphors, something stands in for something else, whereas anamorphosis is dynamic and transformative. It captures changes in form. While dreams qua metaphors qua signs facilitate hermeneutic decoding – the default methodology of both psychoanalytic praxis and literary interpretation – anamorphic images, in order to be properly seen, need to be viewed through prisms and mirrors. Thus, the method adequate to anamorphosis is not that of hermeneutics but that of speculation[22] – and the method adequate to the analysis of narratives qua anamorphic dreams that of a speculative narratology.

Notes

1. Even where poetics does feature prominently, it is regularly subsumed within a larger political framework. This is as true of earlier criticism like Alfred Arteaga's *Chicano Poetics* and Ramón Saldívar's *Chicano Narrative* as it is of more recent scholarship such as Marcial González's *Chicano Novels and the Politics of Form* (Arteaga 1997; Saldívar 1990; González 2009).
2. Within Castillo scholarship, Ritch Calvin's 'Writing the Xicanista' constitutes a notable exception to the dominant paradigm. Calvin laudably tries to ground the feminist politics of Castillo's literary output in the aesthetics it displays. There is thus considerable overlap in our respective projects. However, in his analyses Calvin never leaves the realm of 'lived experience' (Calvin 2007: 45), the particular Chicana articulation of which he takes to be the focal point of Castillo's œuvre. Thus, while providing a long-needed corrective to it, he still falls squarely *within* the tradition I have outlined above. In contrast, my aim will be to show that Castillo's fiction precisely goes *beyond* the experiential and thus cannot be grasped by any notions of lived experience.
3. For a similar assessment with respect to American Studies' more general transnational paradigm dominating the scholarly discourse over roughly the same period of time, see Philipp Schweighauser's *Beautiful Deceptions* (2016). And just as I was composing this chapter, the *Notre Dame Philosophical Reviews* published a review by Gerald L. Bruns where he notes the still prevalent rift between politics and aesthetics with a clear emphasis on politics at the expense of aesthetics within literary studies as a whole:

    During the last thirty years literary study has become less literary than social and political in its topics and debates. A short list of current critical approaches would include, under the rubric of 'Cultural Studies,' gender studies, ethnic studies, queer theory, postcolonial studies, and, more recently, cybernetics. What holds these pursuits together as a family is a suspicion that careful philological attention to the work of art or literature itself is an aestheticism that holds itself aloof from the real world. (Bruns 2012: n. p.)

My point is precisely that the aestheticism charge is ill advised and devastating to the enterprise of literary studies: by conflating aestheticism with aesthetics and thus casting aesthetics as fundamentally apolitical and otherworldly, cultural studies (in the sense of Bruns's umbrella term) posits an unbridgeable divide between the aesthetic and the sociopolitical. As a result, the aesthetic is exorcised and expunged from literary studies in the interest of 'real world' politics and social change. Such a move entirely misses or, even worse, denies that literary works are part and parcel of the real world *as aesthetic and poetic objects*. Obviously, acknowledging this fact by no means implies that there can be no politics associated with these objects. Rather, it merely means that the political needs to be addressed *on aesthetic grounds*. Seen in this light, cultural studies not only misses out on the most central and essential aspect of literature, but also fails to address the most central and essential aspect of its own enterprise properly as, by expunging the problem of aesthetics, it necessarily produces a skewed account of the politics of literature.

4. The *locus classicus* of such a cultural conception is of course Homi Bhabha's *The Location of Culture* (Bhabha).
5. These are three variations of the consensus view, which holds that the novel expresses the search for, struggle to achieve, and affirmation of some kind of personal and/or collective Chicana integrality. At least one of these variants is explicitly posited in each of the following texts: Bennett 1996: 464; González 1996: 85; Johnson 2004: 56; Madsen 2000: 82; Maszewska 2008: 266; Mujčinović 2004: 33; Walter 1998: 82; Yarbro-Bejarano 1996: 218.
6. Obviously, there are a number of philosophers who can be legitimately viewed as philosophers of difference: most notably, the already mentioned Lyotard, Jacques Derrida, and Martin Heidegger. However, none of these thinkers endorsed a full-blown *metaphysics* of difference, all three in fact being thoroughly anti-metaphysical.
7. The diagram provided by Aarseth illustrates the relation between user functions and text types nicely.
8. N. Katherine Hayles has elaborated on the specifics of electronic literature in both *Writing Machines* and *Electronic Literature* (Hayles 2002b; Hayles 2008). Most recently, Markku Eskelinen provided an extension of Aarseth's cybertext theory that comes with the added value of revisiting and differentiating the existing critical literature on ergodic (not medium-specific) and electronic or digital literature (medium-specific), most notably also comparing and critically evaluating Hayles in relation to Aarseth (Eskelinen 2012: 15–46; 23–5).

9. For a short overview of what she terms first-wave and second-wave hypertext theory and the concomitant role of the reader, see Bell 2011, particularly pages 63–8.
10. Note that this is a mere simulation because it plays out entirely within the realm of the actual. Narratology's events and existents are *always* actual. Whereas real actualisation proceeds from virtual differential elements and their intensive relations to actual states of affairs, and – in the context of narrative – is thus productive of events and existents and their extensive relations, in hypertext fiction this process of production is simulated by means of actual entities only (and indeed could not be done otherwise).
11. This is the respective passage from *Don Quixote* where the knight-errant describes his beloved:

    > [H]er station must at least be that of a princess, since she is queen and lady of my soul; her beauty supernatural, in that it justifies all those impossible and chimerical attributes of excellence, which the poets bestow upon their nymphs; her hair is of gold, her forehead the Elysian fields, her eyebrows heavenly arches, her eyes themselves suns, her cheeks roses, her lips of coral, her teeth of pearl, her neck alabaster, her breast marble, her hands ivory, her skin whiter than snow, and those parts which decency conceals from human view, are such, according to my belief and apprehension, as discretion ought to inhance above all comparison. (Cervantes 2003: 85)

    In truth, Dulcinea is a sturdy peasant woman named Aldonza Lorenço.
12. This idealisation is further emphasised by Teresa's description of Alicia at Alicia and Vicente's first meeting:

    > You danced all night with his cousin, Egberto, who held your *nimble body* taut through merengues and guaguancos. The *tortoise combs* in your *long hair* that was *flaunted* in the faces of the other dancers, gave the illusion of *innocence*. The *ivory, satin dress* with *Cinderella* sleeves *enhanced* it so that Vicente, watching from our table, believed you might love him. (131; my emphasis)

    Of course, Vicente gets up and asks Alicia to dance – knight Vicente has come to take home his Cinderella.
13. There is no doubt about this fact as the statement occurs in the context of a discussion of the New Age movement as it relates to *brujería*, *curanderismo*, and Chicano/a spirituality.
14. Kerslake's book was published in 2007. Given that philosophers usually shun and despise esoteric mysticism, it is no surprise that Deleuze's esoteric intertexts were ignored for such a long time. Kerslake has shown, however, that doing so amounts to ignoring a significant aspect of Deleuze's philosophy. Deleuze, while not being an esoteric himself, had no qualms about appropriating esoteric thought for his own philosophical purposes.

Intensive Narration

15. Deleuze's interest in sleep, sleeplessness, and particularly somnambulism is central among his more obscure esoteric leanings. For an account of this interest, see Kerslake 2007 again.
16. For this reason, Nancy states that there cannot be a 'phenomenology of sleep, for it shows of itself only its disappearance, its burrowing and its concealment' (13). What follows directly from these two statements is that there can only be a *metaphysics* of sleep. Working from within the tradition of phenomenology, Nancy himself never embarks on such a metaphysical project. To him, sleep profoundly remains a state of 'indistinctness', an 'effacement of my own distinction' (7) which cannot be adequately conceptualised. Since Nancy still wants to make positive statements about sleep, however, the only alternative he has left is a kind of phenomenology that allows for speculation but is not metaphysical: hence my term non-phenomenology to capture this endeavour.
17. Conversely, reliance and dependency on man are depicted as going hand in hand with insomnia. See, for example, letter 16's 'insomniac nights' (54) that Teresa spends with Alvaro, 'a man about whom she has serious doubts concerning his legitimate status with the human race' (54); or, more strikingly still, woman's 'inability to sleep' (118) that comes with 'all the humiliation that one is born to and pressed upon to surrender to a man' (117) – Teresa's definition of love – that is painstakingly elaborated in letter 32, a letter that, through its use of the third person, clearly casts Teresa's singular experience as a particular manifestation of a universal pattern.
18. This is precisely the reason why Deleuze was so interested in somnambulism. The phenomenon of sleepwalking makes us aware of sleep as an activity (rather than passivity).
19. Again, for a poignant treatment of the metaphysical unconscious in the context of contemporary philosophy, see Austin 2011. Austin also reminds us that the concept of the unconscious was by no means an invention of psychoanalytic theory but already an important and explicitly metaphysical term in nineteenth-century German philosophy. Psychoanalysis subsequently cut the unconscious down to human size. Austin traces the concept back to F. W. J. Schelling's *System of Transcendental Idealism*.
20. Deleuze himself, rather than discussing dreams, prefers to revert to the more obscure examples of sorcery and witchcraft in his writings. No doubt this is partly due to the claim of psychoanalysis on the dream as its legitimate object of study, and partly due to the fact that dreams are still too close to us. They are very much a part of our experiential world while the same can hardly be said of sorcery or witchcraft. Once more, Kerslake's *Deleuze and the Unconscious* is the book to consult on these issues, particularly on the ambiguous status of the dream

in Deleuze's writings. The most sustained discussion of sorcery and witchcraft in Deleuze's work can be found in the plateau on becoming in Deleuze and Guattari's *A Thousand Plateaus*, where they explicitly propose sorcery as an adequate means for becoming-imperceptible (ATP: 264–78). It is thus important that dreams in *The Mixquiahuala Letters* figure as visionary rather than ordinary dreams, dreams akin to sorcery and witchcraft.

21. This is congruent with recent re-evaluations of feminism. See, for example, Claire Colebrook's 'Feminist Extinction', where she presents feminism as an intrinsically universalist project, both historically and systematically (Colebrook 2012). Castillo's novel certainly confirms Colebrook's assessment.

22. I refer to speculation's 'other' root in *speculum* – mirror, as explained in Michael Inwood's entry on speculation in his Hegel dictionary:

> *Spekulation, spekulativ* and *spekulieren* ('to speculate') come from the Latin *speculatio* ('spying out, reconnoitring; contemplation') and *speculari* ('to spy, observe; to look around'), which in turn descend from *specere* ('to see, look'). (The Latin for a 'mirror' is *speculum*, which gave rise to the German *Spiegel*, 'mirror'). *Spekulieren* developed other senses: 'to count on, rely on; to guess, conjecture', hence, in the eighteenth century, 'to engage in risky commercial ventures'.
>
> *Speculatio* was used by Boethius for the Greek *theōria* ('contemplation'). Augustine, the scholastics (e.g. Aquinas) and the mystics (e.g. Seuse, Nicholas of Cusa) associate it with *speculum*, and, following St Paul (1 Cor. 13: 12), argue that God cannot be seen or known directly, but only in his works or effects, as in a mirror. Thus speculation goes beyond sensory experience to the divine or supernatural. (Inwood 1992: 271)

As has been shown, this reaching for the supernatural and divine is at the heart of Castillo's esoteric *espiritismo* while Deleuze's speculation is not theologically conceived but thisworldly. Sleeping and dreaming as redoubling acts of contemplation, as obscure kinds of seeing, as 'risky [. . .] ventures' into the unknown are perfect examples of such a thisworldly speculative act. This act can be summarised thus: closing one's eyes to see properly. And this is the formula, the magic spell that both constitutes and is perpetuated by *The Mixquiahuala Letters*. In this light (or darkness), the title of Castillo's first manuscript of poems is programmatic for her entire œuvre: 'I Close My Eyes . . . to See' (Castillo 1975).

2
Narrating Sensation: Michael Ondaatje's *The Collected Works of Billy the Kid*

The first page of Michael Ondaatje's *The Collected Works of Billy the Kid* features famous frontier photographer L. A. Huffman's caption to a picture of Billy he allegedly took. Where the picture should be, however, there is nothing but an empty frame. The text thus starts with a forceful problematisation of representation as, contrary to Huffman's statement, Billy is *not* depicted. In addition, the Huffman caption is fictional. *The Collected Works of Billy the Kid* thus immediately signals that the status of the image, that representation will be an issue both formally and in terms of content. This problematic status of representation is in fact already emphasised in the preceding paratext, as the copyright page mentions diverse 'original' sources, the accuracy of which is more than contested (such as Walter Noble Burns's *The Saga of Billy the Kid*), or which simply do not exist (such as Huffman's book *Huffman: Frontier Photographer*, which is purportedly the source of the caption).[1] In addition, the copyright page, referencing the text's intertextual and transmedial nature, also states that the 'comic book legend is real' – a playful comment on the relation between fact and fiction in the vein of the famous quip from John Ford's *The Man Who Shot Liberty Valance*, 'When the legend becomes fact, print the legend' as it applies to the figure of Billy, and as it is taken up on the narrative's first page with the fictional caption to an allegedly factual but non-depicted image of Billy. These observations are reinforced by the fact that the cover (of my Vintage International edition – the original Anansi publication features an Eadweard Muybridge picture of a man on horseback) *does* actually depict Billy by means of a reprint of the so-called Upham tintype – the only authentic image of Billy we have. As a result, Huffman's caption can only accompany an empty frame since the image it purportedly comments on does not exist. As readers, we thus witness a great spectacle: an existing but fictional text accompanies a non-existing but allegedly factual image that is represented as such – an empty frame.

Right from the start, beginning with the paratextual elements,

Ondaatje's narrative thus complicates the relation between fact and fiction. This is, of course, more than fitting in face of the text's protagonist: the legendary Billy the Kid. The very term *legend* itself already denotes such a complex relation. The relation as such, in turn, is precisely that of representation in so far as representation is the name for a particular kind of relation – a relation governed by verisimilitude or analogy – that is said to hold between fact and fiction. The Upham tintype's reception history adds yet another layer to the whole representation problematic as set out on the narrative's copyright and first pages. Throughout much of the twentieth century, scholars believed that Billy was left-handed precisely due to the tintype, not noticing that it was a mirror-image. In this context, it should be noted that in earlier editions, Ondaatje's work carried the subtitle *Left-Handed Poems*, thus, at least by hindsight, reinforcing the shortcomings of representation qua verisimilar mirror-image. Overall, the reliability and coherence of representation are thoroughly shaken from the outset. Of course, this has been duly noted (it is hard *not* to notice) in the scholarship on *The Collected Works of Billy the Kid*.[2] But the treatment of the issue has been limited to either questions of historical accuracy, legend building, and myth in a blend of traditional Western scholarship with scholarship in the flavour of Hutcheonesque historiographic metafiction, or issues of politics broadly understood.[3] A third strain of criticism that runs through the other two focuses on the work's mixed-media aspect.[4] In contrast to these strands of criticism, I wish to suggest that *The Collected Works of Billy the Kid* problematises representation in quite a literal sense: it provides and focuses on the contours of an underlying 'problem' to which representation is the attempted 'solution'. My employment of the problem–solution matrix is, of course, directly taken from Deleuze, where it has basic ontological weight: the realm of representations, phenomenality, the ontic (these terms provide different perspectives on the same issue) constitutes a solution to the problematic make-up of the sub-representational, noumenal, ontological realm.[5] Phenomena answer to questions posed by noumena; representations to the sub-representational; the ontic to the ontological. As the noumenal, sub-representational, ontological realm is the realm of becoming, it follows that becoming is one big problem *explicated* (in the sense of unfolded, developed, brought out) in concrete beings. Since, as we already know, becoming is differentially constituted and made up of sensations and forces, all phenomena, representations, and ontic entities *implicate* or harbour sensations and forces as their ontologically primary constituents. It is precisely this fact and this relation that *The Collected Works of Billy the Kid* makes explicit. Sensations and forces are at the heart of Ondaatje's work, both in the sense of what it takes as its central concern and in the sense of its animating principle. The narrative investigates, makes visible, and elaborates its own constitution and genesis; by exposing its labour of building a bloc, a monument of sensations (WIP: 168–9), it makes tangible the very fact that it is indeed such a monument. Since sensations and forces are sub-representational and invisible, the work is thus a prime example of what Deleuze, quoting Paul Klee, referred to as art's capacity '"[n]ot to render the visible, but to render visible"' (FB: 48).[6] *The Collected Works of Billy the Kid* loses no time in pursuing this task: the empty frame with its accompanying caption at the very beginning sets up precisely the matrix between the *virtual image and its actual double* – a double that, in Deleuzian fashion, *is not built according to the rules of resemblance or analogy*. The representation does not in any sense *look like* what it represents. In short, assuming some sort of verisimilitude as definitional of representation, the alleged representation is *not* a representation at all but a direct *expression*, just in the way solutions are expressions and not representations of their underlying problems. In this context, it is noteworthy to emphasise what the caption actually says. Here it is in full:

> *I send you a picture of Billy made with the Perry shutter as quick as it can be worked – Pyro and soda developer. I am making daily experiments now and find I am able to take passing horses at a lively trot square across the line of fire – bits of snow in the air – spokes well defined – some blur on top of wheel but sharp in the main – men walking are no trick – I will send you proofs sometime. I shall show you what can be done from the saddle without ground glass or tripod – please notice when you get the specimens that they were made with the lens wide open and many of the best exposed when my horse was in motion.* (Ondaatje 1996: 5; italics in the original)

The caption addresses experiments in photography, giving a technical account of how these images were produced, 'with the lens wide open [. . .] exposed [. . .] in motion', and emphasising that Billy's picture was taken with 'the Perry shutter as quick as it can be worked'. There are three important factors to note here: quickly worked shutter, large aperture, and movement. This is not coincidental, as quickly worked shutters and large aperture are needed both for action shooting and for pictures with a clear figure-ground distinction: that is, pictures that present their motif clearly and sharply while they let the background recede in a hazy blur. They thus draw out and distinguish their motif from background noise. This drawing-out is analogous to the process of actualisation where elements are selected, brought together, and drawn out from amongst the virtual frenzy of becoming. The frenzy of becoming in turn is movement in-itself, spatiotemporal process as such. As we know, movement in-itself simply cannot be represented. What can be represented are moving bodies, and from these we can infer movement in-itself. Movement in-itself is precisely the driving interest of the fictional Huffman caption with its emphasis on the 'daily experiments' in taking pictures of 'horses at a lively trot', 'bits of snow in the air', or 'men walking', even taking photos 'from the saddle' with the horse 'in motion' (5). Quite clearly, the impetus behind these experiments has nothing to do with the respective objects that are being photographed – Huffman's experiments are experiments concerning *motion*, as the reference to taking pictures *from* the saddle *while* riding makes abundantly clear; the respective target object is not even mentioned here. Just as we can infer absolute movement from bodies in motion, we can infer Huffman's interest in capturing movement in-itself from his reference to experiments in photography with respect to the movement of bodies. Given that Huffman's aim really is to capture movement in-itself, and given that movement in-itself cannot be captured, it is absolutely *necessary* that the respective result be *nothing* – an empty frame. Representing movement in-itself is simply impossible. It is precisely this impossibility that the first page of Ondaatje's narrative makes forcefully clear. Note that I do not speak of representation here, as there is nothing to be represented, nothing that the representation could resemble in any way. The empty square simply does not look like the failed attempt at representing movement in-itself. Rather, it merely marks the impossibility of this task. But by doing so, it does manage to capture absolute movement in a sense: by bringing about and emphasising the breakdown of representation, it makes tangible the beyond of representation, spatiotemporal process as such, absolute movement, becoming. It is in this sense that the first page of *The Collected Works of Billy the Kid* is an *expression* of becoming. If, on the surface, it gives us an account of how clear and distinct figures can be drawn out from a receding and amorphous background – namely, through quickly worked shutters and large aperture, what could be called techniques of figuration – beneath this surface, it tells us how the obscure and representation-eluding background can nevertheless be made tangible – namely, through techniques of *dis*figuration (on this notion see also the Introduction). The empty frame is thoroughly disfigured – it is utterly cleansed of any figures, there is no figuration left at all.[7] Overall, the caption and empty frame intimate both the production process, the capturing, bringing together, and composition of sensations and forces – that is, actualisation or differen*c*iation – and the motility of these differentials – that is, incessant differen*t*iation. It is in this way that the first page sets the stage for the rest of the narrative.

As an act of disfiguration, the narrative has to present us with some remnants of a concrete figure. This figure is Billy the Kid. Fittingly, and not surprisingly, the narrative redoubles on a thematic level its formal concerns: namely, those with movement and liminality, in so far as these concerns fundamentally make up the classical trope of the American West with its shifting frontier and history of conquest and settlement. It is precisely this theme that is crystallised in the emblematic figure of Billy the Kid. The copyright and first pages thus serve as a dense exposition to and prefiguration of the story to come, in terms of both content and form. As befits this story, it is mostly constituted of sensations of violence and death. These are the affects traded in the American West, the affective currency of westward expansion, the text suggests. Ondaatje thus makes these sensations of violence constitutive not only for his work, but also for America in so far as the American West can be said to be the germinal locus and moment in the history of the modern US. According to *The Collected Works of Billy the Kid*, the story of America is a story of generation through violence, not of *re*generation through violence as Slotkin's classic account of frontier mythology has it.[8] The American West thus unites 'the best and the worst', as Deleuze and Guattari put it (ATP: 7):[9] on the one hand, an acute awareness and susceptibility to the world of becoming, the circulation of sensations and forces as epitomised by Billy's focus on and perfection of his sensory organs as a means to 'become with the world' (WIP: 168); on the other hand, an attunement to the world of affect and percept that only serves one goal – to keep living by putting to death, by killing better than anyone else. Billy's exceptionality when it comes to tapping the forces of creativity and change, his ability for becomings of all sorts, is employed only to bring about one change: that from life to death. Billy is indeed an artist figure,[10] but his only art is that of killing. Creativity = destruction is the formula that best captures Billy. This is the tragedy at the heart of the American story: the frontier as the locus of true potentiality, as the locus that sharpens one's capacity for becoming, is also the locus that most violently aborts this capacity.

Accordingly, what we get in *The Collected Works of Billy the Kid* is both an actualised and completed narrative and one which, in its actuality and completeness, is but a collection of narrative snippets that do not point to an overarching unity at all – the parts simply do not converge. On the formal level, this is achieved in various ways: (1) by means of layout – that is, arrangement of text, blank spaces, typography, and reproduction of photographs; (2) by the employment of voice, as in many instances it is hard to tell whose voice we are listening to – it is impossible to determine whether there is a narrator over and above the whole cacophony of (anonymous) voices; (3) through the treatment of space – even though most of the action is set in New Mexico we are confronted with a disjointed set of settings, from the Chisum ranch to the US–Canadian border and, more importantly, on many pages the whereabouts of what is being narrated remain utterly unclear; (4) by means of the narrative's employment of temporality – there is no discernible chronology to most of the diverse blocks of narrative. Most of the bits and pieces seem to have fallen out of time, utterly absorbed in their very own moment.

In its actualised form, the narrative thus intimates *another* narrative, a narrative-to-come, a virtual story that is not yet actualised into a coherent and consistent entity. It is this liminality of the narrative itself, operating at the limits of the actual, that takes centre-stage in many guises. The thrust of these operations is precisely to go *beyond* these limits, to attain the virtual conditions of narrative. Accordingly, I will next elaborate on the issue of liminality, touching on some of its incarnations in the text, in order then to follow the narrative's trajectory into the realm of becoming that lies beyond this limit. Ultimately, I will show that the collection that makes up *The Collected Works of Billy the Kid* is entirely comprised of sensations. It is in this sense that Ondaatje's work can be said to be narrating sensation, nothing but sensation.

Frontiers and Limits

While *The Collected Works of Billy the Kid* won the prestigious Governor's General Award for poetry, it is praised as a 'visionary novel' on the verso of my Vintage International edition. Similarly, while eminent Ondaatje scholar Sam Solecki explains the omission of *The Collected Works of Billy the Kid* from his book-length study of Ondaatje's poetry *Ragas of Longing* by stating that he simply does not think it is poetry (Solecki 2003: 5), Lee Spinks in his more recent monograph calls it a 'long poem' (Spinks 2009: 48). This uncertainty and oscillation as to the work's genre are indicative of its genre-bending quality. The work seems to be neither a novel nor a collection of poems (or long poem, for that matter). The work's in-between status as regards genre is just one of many instances of liminality it creates and fosters. From the very start, these liminalities have been commented on extensively in the literature on *The Collected Works of Billy the Kid*. This aspect has, in fact, been such a decisive factor in the scholarship that, already by 1993, Barbour can summarise the respective output in an extensive list (mapping the differences he lists on to the characterisations of Pat Garrett and/or Billy, respectively): 'life vs. death, energy vs. stasis, chaos vs. order, creation vs. destruction, affirmation vs. negation, visceral knowledge vs. mental obliviousness, emotional connection vs. its denial' (Barbour 1993: 36). As becomes abundantly clear from this list, however, these liminalities were not understood as such, but as *oppositions* or *contradictions*. In addition, these contradictions are considered as being governed by the 'essential opposition between Billy the Kid and Pat Garrett' (36), which is taken to be structuring the entire text. In contrast, my point is that *The Collected Works of Billy the Kid* occupies and measures the position in-between these terms, and that Billy and Garrett do not make an oppositional pair at all. While there is a host of oppositions in the text, Billy versus Garrett is not one of them, as Billy is the figure that effectively undoes all the oppositions.[11] The narrative does not juxtapose all these terms qua differences but resides in-between in difference itself. One way in which it signals this residence in difference is precisely by means of genre-bending. *The Collected Works of Billy the Kid* is a differential text in the most fundamental sense. As such, the sign 'vs.' in Barbour's enumeration does not primarily mark instances of contra-diction but rather expresses the work of what Deleuze, with recourse to Leibniz, calls vice-diction, the staking out of a problematic field and the selection and gathering of singularities (DR: 56–9; 238–9). All the moments of perceived contradictions in *The Collected Works of Billy the Kid* are thus the actual narrative solutions to their vice-dictive underlying problems, and Barbour's entire list of contradictions needs to be recast in light of this procedure of vice-diction.

It is fitting that Barbour's list begins with the juxtaposition of life and death. Indeed, all ensuing juxtapositions seem to follow from this one, as life versus death arguably comprises all the other contradictory instances Barbour makes out. The centrality of this relation is corroborated by the fact that the narrative stages both the American West and itself as being inaugurated by death, the end of all life. Thus, Billy is dead from the beginning, as on the page following the empty frame-cum-caption he enumerates himself in a list of all casualties that his life directly or indirectly generated. In addition to listing exhaustively the deaths he is responsible for, from 'early friends' to 'Bob Ollinger' to 'birds during practice', the second part of the list is devoted to those killed by Garrett and his men: 'Charlie, Tom O'Folliard / Angela D's split arm, / and Pat Garrett / sliced off my head' (6). Billy is both dead, as the list certifies, and alive, as his narrative voice testifies to. He thus occupies a liminal position between life and death, both dead and alive, encapsulated in the fragment's final statement: 'Blood a necklace on me all my life' (6). That life gives death (the quintessential frontier experience) and that death gives life (to the narrative; to modern America) indicates that the relation is more complex than Barbour's clear-cut opposition allows for. The thematic liminality between life and death as it pertains to the frontier experience is here expressed formally by means of metalepsis, an infringement of narrative levels that directly bears on the limits of representation. Metalepsis is one way to crack up representationality. As such, a metalepsis never *represents* anything; rather, it both expresses the singularities (here, those involved in the *existential* liminality of the American frontier as embodied by the figure of Billy the Kid) that representation fails to capture *and* exposes the shortcomings of representation in general. By eluding it, metalepses go beyond representation. As such, they are at the same time tools for counter-actualisation, instruments for speculative becoming, and expressions of the Deleuzian procedure of vice-diction. In their liminality, metalepses, as all narrative techniques and strategies that defy representation, mark instances of Deleuze's refunctioning of Kairos, the opportune or supreme moment: They operate to 'condense all the singularities [. . .] in a sublime occasion, *Kairos*, which makes the solution explode like something abrupt, brutal and revolutionary' (DR: 239). They operate to turn intensive forces (here, the forces of life, the forces of death) into extensive relations (here, life *versus* death); they are genuine markers of intensity. Since Deleuze characterises '[h]aving an Idea' (DR: 239) precisely by these procedures of vice-diction – the distribution and subsequent explosion of singularities – and since Deleuzian Ideas are by no means merely mental – 'Ideas no more than Problems do not exist only in our heads but occur here and there in the production of an actual historical world' (DR: 239) – Ondaatje's narrative 'has' its Idea precisely in the movement and alignment of its singularities: that is, the sub-representational forces and sensations it harbours. The entryway to these constitutive forces and sensations is then located in the narrative's anti-representational techniques such as metalepsis, or the disjunctive syntheses of the many fusions-in-juxtaposition (all the moments marked by Barbour's 'vs.'). In fact, metalepses are themselves nothing but such a fusion-in-juxtaposition, as they fuse two incompossible narrative levels. *The Collected Works of Billy the Kid* is constituted by a veritable cascade of disjunctive syntheses that, on the level of representation, branch out into contradictions. One such contradiction leads into the next, the entire text unfolding according to the logic of 'vs.', enmeshed in the splendour of the foldings, unfoldings, and refoldings of this operator.[12]

Thus, directly after exposing the existential liminality at stake in his metaleptic list of casualties – and here one should also note that the list itself is constructed according to the logic of 'vs.' as Billy juxtaposes those killed both linguistically ('by me' versus 'by them') and visually (the list is clearly separated into two parts that are set off from each other) – Billy recounts Tom O'Folliard's death. This narrative splinter serves not only to tell how Garrett killed O'Folliard, to establish the themes of violence and death firmly by means of graphic detail, and to characterise Garrett by the affective distance, mental control, and precision of his actions and Tom by the lack of these qualities, but also to introduce yet another recurrent juxtaposition: namely, that of rational thought and madness. O'Folliard's 'mad' behaviour is juxtaposed to Garrett's cold-blooded execution of the task at hand – namely, shooting Tom; while Tom, after being wounded by Garrett, rushes at him cursing, 'too mad to even aim', with 'jaws tilting up and down like mad bladders going', Garrett takes 'clear aim and [blows] him out' (7). O'Folliard's chaotic frenzy is set over against Garrett's clarity and precision. Indeed, the life versus death distinction maps on to the respective characters in different ways: while Garrett *controls* and *commands* the forces of life and death, Tom is *overwhelmed* by them and *fails* to keep them at bay.

This initial presentation of Tom and Garrett is confirmed in the narrative's later characterisations of both. As Billy recounts Tom's story, it emerges as one marked precisely by the struggle for rational command in the service of survival. Billy tells us about Tom's 'big accident' (50) while out in the New Mexico scrub desert to shoot wild horses: his gun blows up on him, leaving him seriously wounded in the face and knocking him unconscious for two days. Tom survives the ensuing 'four days in the desert without food or water' (50) because he expends only the bare minimum of energy needed, sleeps every two hours, all thought reduced to a minimum and focused on survival (before sleeping, he 'plac[es] his boots into an arrow in the direction he was going'; and he only does not cut his hand to have some food because 'he realis[es] he [has] lost too much blood already' (50)). When he finally stumbles into a small village, he is knocked unconscious by the local blacksmith in order to prevent him from drinking too much too quickly – Tom was just about 'to throw himself in water' (51). While Tom's rationality kept him alive *against* the most basic instincts for survival (that is, find something to drink and eat), he would have given in at precisely the moment of his rescue. In order to avoid the suicidal tendencies of his instinctual machinery for survival, his entire system of conscious perception and cognition is shut down and, subsequently, his body placed and tied down in the blacksmith's bed. The loss of *rational* control (which directly results in the loss of control over his own body) is here depicted as Tom's death knell, with death only averted in the last instance by the blacksmith's intervention. As we already know, this will only defer Tom's death until the moment of his confrontation with Garrett, when he will succumb once more to the mad feelings driving him – this time without anyone around to help him counter his impulses.

Tom's struggle for control is epitomised in the repercussions of his accident that leaves his face partially atrophied:

> all the muscles on the left side of his face had collapsed. When he breathed, he couldn't *control* where the air went and it took new channels according to its fancy and formed thin balloons down the side of his cheek and neck. These fresh passages of air ricocheted pain across his face everytime he breathed. (51; my emphasis)

With half his face under his control and the other half eluding it, Tom's life is stranded somewhere in-between. That on the representational level the control versus lack of control dichotomy (which could be recast as Barbour's order versus chaos juxtaposition) maps on to the life versus death dichotomy not only is clear from the preceding story, but also is reinforced by the fact that the most essential ingredient for human life – air – is the most painful for Tom. The forces of life threaten to overwhelm Tom as he lives in a constant state of enstrangement – pure life is constantly made tangible to him – so much so that he needs to soothe it through drugs: 'So he chewed red dirt constantly, his pockets were full of it' (51). The drug functions as a counter-enstrangent so that automatic living, mental control over the forces of life, becomes possible again. Tom's 'mind [is] still sharp' *because* he takes the drug. The 'pain [takes] all the drug' (51), as Billy notes. The breakdown of life, the frontier between life and death, makes life all the more tangible. The pure impersonal sensations that constitute life in-itself register forcefully as Tom's personal sensation of pain. That Tom's pain is not a matter of mere internality is made clear at the very beginning of Tom's story when Billy introduces him in his struggle to keep the pain away, his attempts at not letting it in: 'This is Tom O'Folliard's story, the time I met him, eating red dirt to keep the pain away, *off his body*, *out there* like a melting shape in the sun. [. . .] Out of his skull' (50; my emphasis). This introductory passage not only highlights that Tom takes the drug in order to avoid pain, but more fundamentally posits pain as an autonomous affect 'out there'. Sensation is here posited as an autonomous formless form 'like a melting shape in the sun'. That the shape is melting not only presents us with a certain amorphous quality, but also highlights activity: sensations *are* the becomings of beings. Tom O'Folliard's story and the account of his death at the hands of Pat Garrett present him as being in constant struggle against these forces and sensations of life at the frontier, struggling at the very frontier of life and death itself – a struggle he eventually loses.

I have dwelled on Tom O'Folliard for some time in order to tease out (1) how liminality plays out in several guises on both molar and molecular levels (large aggregates and their constitutive micro-entities) as these pertain to the narrative's thematics (survival at the frontier on the molar level, circulation of affects and percepts on the molecular) and form (from the molar question of genre to the molecular question of the narrative's disjunctive syntheses); (2) how the narrative is attuned to the world of sensation and becoming; and (3) how the text introduces Tom, rather than Billy, as a foil to Garrett. Tom serves as the negative image of Garrett in so far as he *lacks* everything that Garrett has: rationality, control, composure, cold-bloodedness. Garrett is characterised as 'ideal assassin' and 'academic murderer' with the 'mind of a doctor' and 'the ability to kill someone on the street walk back and finish a joke' (28), coupling clinical precision with ruthlessness and a striving for absolute control. That he fears nothing more than disintegration and the loss of control is made forcefully clear in a passage that recounts Garrett's attempt to teach himself to drink *according to a plan*, to become an alcohol addict academically, *forcing* himself '[to disintegrate his mind' (28). According to Garrett's logic, if one fears disintegration, the most rational thing to do is to control disintegration itself. As it turns out, his two-year stint at becoming an alcoholic academically, almost losing out and needing help to overcome his addiction, finally does result in absolute control: '[h]is mind was clear, his body able to drink' (29). While Tom tries to keep disintegration at bay, Garrett takes it fully on board (accordingly, their respective use of drugs also stands in an inverse relation). What they share in common is that both their strategies aim at exercising control: both Tom and Garrett attempt to control the forces of life and death. Ultimately, only Garrett succeeds (as we will see, this only holds true to a certain extent, however). Thus, the opposition here is between Garrett and Tom. Billy, in contrast, does not even try to master these forces. Billy's strategy is not locked within this logic of contrariety, but opens up a *third* option, absolutely *other* to Garrett's and Tom's, as it resides precisely in the very difference between control and lack of control. Billy does not partake in the battle of one-upmanship over the proper control of the forces of life and death, but directly *immerses* himself in these forces. While, in their respective attempts at mastery, Tom externalises and Garrett internalises these forces, Billy simply becomes with them. Billy, the metaleptic figure of the versus-structure, is the personification of becoming itself.

As such, 'Billy' names the two trajectories – ontogenetic and speculative – of becoming: that of figuration, of becoming a figure, the work of actualisation with its composition and distribution (vice-diction) of differential elements (sensations) and their relations (forces), the process of differen*c*iation; and that of disfiguration, of becoming-imperceptible, the work of counter-actualisation with its attendant processes of disintegration and dissipation. It is through the latter movement that the former is excavated, thereby making tangible the groundless movement of becoming in-itself (differen*t*iation) on which everything else rests. These two trajectories can also be encapsulated thus: ontogenetic becoming is the movement from sensation to sensory impression and registration (and, in the case of humans, further on to rational thought) while speculative becoming is the inverse movement revelatory of the first movement and its basis in the continuous movement of sensation in-itself. That this double-movement is indeed the trajectory the narrative follows is made crystal clear when it deliberately and self-reflexively offers the 'slight silver key to unlock it, to dig it out' (20). When Billy proposes, 'Here then is a maze to begin, be in' (20), his statement not only shifts the focus from beginnings to immersion, from *ab ovo* to *in medias res*, but also, in so doing opens up a gap, a fissure as indicated by the removal of the letter 'g', thus highlighting the space in-between, that which bifurcates and differentiates, and ultimately advocates an *immersion in difference*.[13] It is in this vein that the 'maze' that is being offered as the place to be turns out to be a frontier, as the immediately following passage reads: 'Two years ago Charlie Bowdre and I criss-crossed the Canadian border [. . .] the ridge of action rising and falling, getting narrower in radius till it ended and we drifted down to Mexico and old heat' (20). The US–Canadian border thus serves as yet another metanarrative instantiation of liminality as such, of difference in-itself with Billy's and Charlie's trajectory verging towards that limit ('getting narrower in radius'). That this limit determines the radius and thus the 'ridge of action rising and falling' makes liminality constitutive for the unfolding of the story. The passage both clearly alludes to Gustav Freytag's dramatic arc, scrapping Freytag's exposition, climax, and catastrophe/dénouement in favour of a repetitive unfolding of action, and locates the *determinant* of the action in the limit, the frontier, and thus difference itself. It is precisely this limit that Billy and Charlie are continuously approaching until they break off and go somewhere else. In this manner, the passage postulates difference not only as the narrative's ground or condition from which it emerges but also as the goal it is heading towards, thus programmatically declaring its double-movement of ontological determination and speculative excavation. In short, everything here hinges on the 'maze [. . .] to be in' that difference is.

The remaining task has thus been staked out: first to follow the narrative's trajectory of excavation in order then to scrutinise what has been excavated. This means that we now have to see how the narrative simultaneously constitutes and disfigures 'Billy the Kid'; or, more precisely, how the disfiguration of Billy amounts at the same time to his constitution as a character. Billy is a disfigured figure; everything so far points to this fact. The next section is devoted to teasing out that this is indeed the case.

Becoming-Animal, Becoming-Imperceptible

If speculative becoming's work of excavation proceeds from sensory impression and registration to sensation, and if the narrative presents this trajectory through the figure of Billy the Kid, then we need to take Billy's sensory apparatus as our starting point. And focusing on Billy, one immediately notices the wealth of sensory impressions associated with him: from the point of view of Billy everything seems to be colour, shape, noise, smell, texture, and so on. The narrative abounds in passages such as these:

> the house in front of me changed colour – the night, the early morning yellow, the gradual move to dark blue at 11 o clock, the new white 4 o clock sun let in, later the gradual growing dark again. (34)

> We came to the low brooding whirr of noise, night sleep of animals. They were stunning things in the dark. Just shapes that shifted. (36)

> and with a bit the edge of my eye / I sense the thin white body of my friend's wife // Strange that how I feel people / not close to me / as if their dress were against my shoulder / and as they bend down / the strange smell of their breath / moving across my face / or my eyes / magnifying the bones across a room / shifting in a wrist (39)

In addition, there are about half-a-dozen mentions of loose, exposed, or raw nerves (12, 34, 72, 76) in Billy's renderings of his experiences. Since none of the other characters comes anywhere close to being characterised through such attunement to the world of the senses, this gives Billy a peculiar status. It could be said that while Garrett and Tom, like most of the other characters, with their emphasis on rational control where the mind is supposed to reign over and command the body, endorse a clear Cartesian mind–body dualism, Billy is a Spinozist monist, a position that implicates a somaticism of thought. Nowhere is this voiced more explicitly than in the first longer narrative section that serves to introduce Billy and recounts a feverish week-long stay in a deserted barn. Apart from giving an account tinged with a plethora of sensory impressions – among other things, Billy emphasises that 'it was the colour and light of the place that made [him] stay there, not [his] fever' – Billy tells us that once he had settled in he 'began to block [his] mind of all thought', that he '[j]ust sensed the room and learnt what [his] body could do, what it could survive, what colours it liked best, what songs [he] sang best' (17). Billy deliberately suspends rationality – blocking out thought – in order to live by his sensory apparatus, to learn what his body can do, what affects and percepts it is capable of.

What his body can do: this voices almost verbatim Spinoza's fundamentally anti-Cartesian concern with the powers of the body:

> But although these things [that body and mind are one and the same thing conceived under different attributes] are such that no reason for doubt remains, still, I hardly believe that men can be induced to consider them fairly unless I confirm them by experience. They are so firmly persuaded that the Body now moves, now is at rest, solely from the Mind's command, and that it does a great many things which depend only on the Mind's will and its art of thinking.
>
> And of course, no one has yet determined *what the Body can do*, i.e., experience has not yet taught anyone what the Body can do from the laws of nature alone, insofar as nature is only considered to be corporeal, and what the body can do only if it is determined by the Mind. For no one has yet come to know the structure of the Body so accurately that he could explain all its functions – not to mention that many things are observed in the lower Animals that far surpass human ingenuity, and that sleepwalkers do a great many things in their sleep that they would not dare do awake. This shows well enough that the Body itself, simply from the laws of its own nature, can do many things which its Mind wonders at. ('Ethics' IIIp2s; my emphasis)

Spinoza here clearly emphasises that, already on an empirical basis, the mind cannot be said to govern the body, as the body has powers all its own, powers we should be investigating: what a body can do. Now, while this might look as if it merely inverted the Cartesian dualism in favour of the body while maintaining the dualism as such, the thrust of Spinoza's argument is that body and mind (or soul) are two attributes of univocal being (attribute of thought and attribute of extension) and thus not ontologically distinct; the distinction is qualitative not quantitative.[14] Within this framework of ontological univocity and formal diversity, human rational thought is but a particular (though highly developed) expression of the attribute of thought and the human body a particular expression of the attribute of extension. Both harbour respective capacities, powers in line with 'the laws of nature'. Spinoza thus naturalises thought and integrates it into his metaphysics of the modes of existence, the ways or styles of being (there is only one being expressed in many guises – Spinoza's univocity and immanentism). Deleuze puts this naturalisation of thought very succinctly in one of his Spinoza lectures:

Spinoza never defines man as a reasonable animal, he defines man by what he can do, body and soul. If I say that reasonable is not the essence of man, but is rather something that man can do, it changes so that unreasonable is also something that man can do. To be mad is also a part of the power (*pouvoir*) of man. At the level of an animal, we see the problem clearly. If you take what is called natural history, it has its foundation in Aristotle. It defines the animal by what the animal is. In its fundamental ambition, it is a matter of what the animal is. What is a vertebrate, what is a fish, and Aristotle's natural history is full of this search for the essence. In what is called the animal classifications, one will define the animal above all, whenever possible, by its essence, i.e., by what it is. Imagine these sorts who arrive and who proceed completely otherwise: they are interested in what the thing or the animal can do. They are going to make a kind of register of the powers (*pouvoirs*) of the animal. Those there can fly, this here eats grass, that other eats meat. The alimentary regime, you sense that it is about the modes of existence. An inanimate thing too, what can it do, the diamond, what can it do? That is, of what tests is it capable? What does it support? What does it do? A camel can go without drinking for a long time. It is a passion of the camel. We define things by what they can do, it opens up forms of experimentation. It is a whole exploration of things, it doesn't have anything to do with essence. It is necessary to see people as small packets of power (*pouvoir*). (Deleuze 2003a: n. p.; translation slightly modified)

This passage not only describes Spinoza's project in a nutshell, but also renders the thrust of Deleuze's entire philosophy. Instead of asking, in Aristotelian fashion, 'what is this?', Deleuze restlessly poses 'questions such as who? how much? how? where? when?' (Deleuze 2004d: 94), questions designed to determine capacities rather than essences. Or, in other words, the essence of things is determined on the grounds of their capacities; all things, including humans, become 'small packets of power'.

That Billy endorses such a capacity ontology becomes evident in a short passage towards the beginning of the narrative. There, Billy muses, 'If I had a newsman's brain I'd say well some morals are physical must be clear and open like diagram of watch or star' (11). While the subjunctive makes clear that he in fact does not have such a brain and thus does not endorse the respective morals, the statement itself – contrary to its own assertion – marks such morals as *ideal* rather than physical, as an abstraction from the actual physical thing, a diagram *of* the thing (watch or star). For such abstraction, 'one must eliminate much that is one turns when the bullet leaves you walk off see none of the thrashing' – what needs to be eliminated is the actual *physical thrashing*, the mess the bullet makes of the body (a mess that Billy repeatedly describes in painstaking detail throughout the text). In order to be 'clear and open', a requirement that recalls philosophy's obsession with the clear and distinct – the space of rational thought – the moral of the newsman actually *abstracts away* from the muddled mess of the physical, the realm of 'mingled bodies', as Michel Serres's subtitle to his *Five Senses* has it. In contrast, the mingling of bodies is repeatedly emphasised by Billy throughout *The Collected Works of Billy the Kid*. In this very passage, it is the horse's 'neck sweat eating at [Billy's] Jeans' that immediately falsifies the clear-cut distinctions of the newsman evoked by the 'body split at the edge of their [horses'] necks' (11). This is only true at the molar level whereas at the molecular level bodies constantly mingle, form assemblages such as neck–sweat–jeans. There is a distinction, but it is obscure as the distinction (the spilt) bleeds into all directions. The newsman's abstractions result in a moral 'where bodies are mindless as paper flowers you don't feed or give to drink' (11): in other words, a world of Cartesian bodies, lifeless, inert, dead. In contrast, Billy can actually 'watch the stomach of clocks shift their wheels and pins into each other and emerge living, for hours' (11). Billy does not abstract away from the physical thing, he does not determine it on the grounds of transcendent conceptual diagrams, but studies the very thing itself. While the newsman's moral abstracts away from bodies (here, humans) and thus results in a worldview where bodies are intrinsically mindless (here, one should remember that mind is a translation of *psyche*, as is soul, and thus basically names something like an animating principle) – mere inert, dead bodies – Billy advocates the exact opposite: he immerses himself in the very thing (here, a mechanical watch) in order to study, to contemplate, to feel the allegedly inert thing's *animating principle* – for Billy everything is animated, everything is moved and in motion. Billy is a panpsychist, but only in a very restricted sense where psyche denotes neither consciousness, or potential for consciousness, nor any kind of principle of life in the narrow organic sense, but a principle of movement (animation in the sense of movement): that is, the *inherent forces, powers that keep things going* – he precisely sees things as 'packets of power'.[15]

It is in this vein that Billy explores his bodily powers. Rather than submitting his body to the transcendent reign of reason, Billy experiments directly with what he qua body can do, what forces he can sustain and channel. His approach to life is fundamentally *nervous* in the sense that he directly acts on the basis of his nervous system (this is why, as pointed out, the narrative repeatedly emphasises nerves in the context of Billy's experiences). Garrett in contrast is eminently *brainy* in so far as he acts only on the basis of rational thought. These differences in attitude can be described as predominantly perceptive as against cognitive, and thus captured adequately with the terms *aisthesis* and *noesis* respectively. Note, though, that within Deleuze's genetic framework (a framework not present in Spinoza – this is Deleuze's post-Kantian innovation), this is not a dualism of *aisthesis* versus *noesis*, as *noesis* is dependent on, grows out of, and is shot through with *aisthesis*. *Aisthesis* stealthily traverses all instances of 'versus' and brings them down. Rational, conceptual knowledge is thus returned to bodily, nervous, aesthetic knowledge.[16] The upshot of this is that a striving for pure rational thought disregards thought's somaticism, privileges one capacity over a plethora of others, and thus *diminishes* one's powers. What is so difficult for humans about attuning themselves to the powers of the body they are is that these powers operate unconsciously – as soon as something is conscious, it is placed in the space of reason and thought takes over. It is for this reason that one has to block thought deliberately – just like Billy does – in order to unearth one's powers that are *other* than rational thought. In this context, it is no coincidence that both Spinoza and Deleuze refer to animals in their respective discussions. And this is also the source for Deleuze's elaborations on becoming-animal (and of his interest in somnambulism, as mentioned in Chapter 1 and as indexed by Spinoza in the passage quoted above). Indeed, learning what his body can do entails all sorts of becomings-animal for Billy. In the first of these – notably during Billy's stay in the deserted barn – Billy tunes his capacity for '"close-range" vision' by investing in a becoming-animal that turns out to involve one of Deleuze's favourite examples: a pack of rats. As Billy recounts his stay, his account turns into a testimony to the becoming-animal he undergoes:

> There [in the barn] were animals who did not move out and accepted me as a larger breed. I ate the old grain with them, drank from a constant puddle about twenty yards away from the barn. I saw no human and heard no human voice, learned to squat the best way when shitting, used leaves for wiping, never ate flesh or touched another animal's flesh, never entered his boundary. We were all aware and allowed each other. The fly who sat on my arm, after his inquiry, just went away, ate his disease and kept it in him. When I walked I avoided the cobwebs who had places to grow to, who had stories to finish. (17)

Narrating Sensation

As Deleuze (and implicitly Spinoza) indicates, becoming-animal amounts to an attunement to a world prior to cognition, a world marked by the rhythm of sensations and forces, the rhythm of eating (the grain), drinking (the puddle), shitting (posture of the body), the rhythm according to which bodies are distributed in the territory (eat here, drink there, shit over there) and territorial demarcations between bodies are erected (fly, spider, Billy). This rhythm determines the life and death of bodies (for example, in the case of the fly that is caught in the spider's web (17)). This becomes even more evident when the 'hundred or so rats' living in the adjacent granary 'separated by just a thick wood door' enter a deathly state of frenzy after 'a heavy rain storm burst[s] the power' in the already fermenting grain, inducing the rats to go after each other in drunken madness (18). When they start spreading into Billy's barn, Billy joins the frenzy and empties 'the whole bag of bullet supplies [. . .] [t]ill [his] hand was black and the gun was hot and no other animal of any kind remained in that room but for the boy in the blue shirt sitting there coughing at the dust' (18). This account of the powers of fermentation allying themselves with those of the weather spreading like a contagion and taking up hundreds of bodies – including Billy – in their wake almost reads as if it was deliberately crafted to illustrate what Deleuze and Guattari describe as the furor to which becoming-animal opens out. Or, inversely, given the chronology of publication, Deleuze and Guattari's statement – disregarding the elephants – reads as if it was meant to capture this particular passage from Ondaatje's text: 'There is a complex aggregate: the becoming-animal of men, packs of animals, elephants and rats, winds and tempests, bacteria sowing contagion. A single *Furor*' (ATP: 268). This furor is precisely the furor of the spreading and circulation of forces and sensations: the capacities inherent in grain (fermentation) are coupled with those of the storm and rain (speeding up the fermentation process) to unleash the forces of destruction and death inherent in the pack of rats (the capacities to claw and bite multiplied by sheer number and relative speed) and to induce Billy to use his deadly powers in turn. Even though he sits on the window sill where the rats cannot reach him, Billy's killing is anything but distanced and rationally driven. This is indicated by the fact that he uses up his entire bullet supplies and also that he refers to himself as an animal – 'no other animal [. . .] but [. . .] the boy' remains. '[T]he power in those seeds' traverses and criss-crosses the barn, determining the distribution of bodies (the spreading of the rats, Billy's retreat to the window sill, bullets flying 'between the wooden posts') and '[bringing] drunkenness into the minds' not only 'of those rats' but ultimately also that of Billy as he is swept up by the furor, the economy of affects and percepts (a barn, some grain, to ferment, to rage, to run, to bite, to shoot, some wood, some dust, a pack, and so on) determining everything in that place at that moment (18). Rather than exerting rational control, Billy attunes himself to this world of affects and percepts, becoming with the world rather than being in the world (WIP: 168).

The crucial mediating role of the senses between sensation and rational thought is brought out sharply and reinforced when viewed from the other side – that of thought – in a passage narrated by Pat Garrett. Pat tells us about being trapped in the Mescalero, dusty plains where 'your eyes would be speckled and frosted with sand. Dust and sand stick to anything wet as your eyeball, or a small dribble from your nostril [. . .] Your ears are so blocked that you cannot hear for a good while afterwards' (42). After two days in the Mescalero it is in such a state that Pat arrives at the Chisum ranch, in 'total silence', his 'mind blasted', and 'passe[s] out on the bed' (42). While Billy lives in a world replete with *sensa* or *qualia*, Garrett, in Heideggerian fashion, notices the importance of his sensory apparatus only at the moment of its utter breakdown. Not coincidentally, this is also the moment when his consciousness blacks out, thus intimating a relation of causality that goes from sense impression to thought. After recovering, his 'mind awake[s]' the very moment he hears that Billy is also a guest at the ranch. This is the first time Billy and Garrett meet and their encounter provides the reader with two diverging approaches to the use of the senses. As soon as they are restored, Garrett employs his senses *in the service of* rationality, observing and cataloguing Billy's behaviour (noting his custom of eating only 'with his right hand', his 'ridiculous' postures, the left hand's constant 'fingers exercises', his clothing style, the witty smile and humour (43)), but he cannot make head nor tail of it (44). Garrett unwittingly gives us the reason why this is the case when he – correctly – states that Billy's 'imagination [. . .] was usually pointless and never in control' (43), a use of the imagination that is utterly alien to Garrett as Garrett strives to control his imagination to the highest possible degree. Garrett figures as the man of the active Kantian syntheses that go from intuition to imagination to the concept. Controlling one's imagination thus means properly employing it as the faculty of image-making in the service of conceptual knowledge. Imagination is but a step in the movement towards proper rational thought. As we have seen, Billy's imagination is but the first step in the opposite direction: that is, he is a man of the Deleuzian passive syntheses that dissolve rational thought in the spatiotemporal processes of morphogenesis, a movement that goes from intuition–imagination to the pure past to the pure and empty form of time itself (DR: 90–114; see also my Chapter 1). While Billy's imagination serves his immersion in the world of sensation and thus entails dissolution and the loss of the applicability of a category such as control, Garrett's serves the extraction and organisation of information in rational thought and thus entails integration and the exertion of control; while Billy constantly becomes with the world, Garrett tries to master it; while Garrett pursues reason, Billy opts for sensation. Billy is engaged in the athleticism[17] of many a becomings-animal (the intuition of life and death); Garrett pursues the judgement of a calculating thought (the geometry and algebra of life and death).[18] In short, Billy is the artist; Pat is the scientist–philosopher. This is why Garrett initially does not understand Billy. And then, the cat incident happens: Sally Chisum's cat, poisoned by a snake bite, hides under the house, dying, and there is no possibility of retrieving it. Since, judging from the occasional noises it makes, the cat is suffering terribly, Billy offers to kill it, which Sally happily accepts without asking how. The ensuing spectacle is remarkable. Through a veritable becoming-cat, almost on all fours, sniffing and listening acutely, Billy is able to detect the silent cat's whereabouts under the house and to kill it with two gunshots fired through the floorboards.[19] This is what a body can do: *aisthesis* at work. While Garrett is the epitome of the *rational* killer, Billy is an *aesthetic* killer. Pat calculates death; Billy feels it.

Crucially, their different approaches towards life and death can also be read off their different relations to animals. While, as we have seen, Billy is incessantly taken up in all sorts of becomings-animal, Garrett collects stuffed birds (88). Garret's approach to animals is that of a scientist, a diagnosis that is confirmed by the description of how he goes about unpacking and preparing a seagull he receives by mail including a reference to the 'rubber glove' (88) he wears that casts him as a surgeon, a precise dissector, epitome of the rational man, the one who observes and analyses animals from a transcendent vantage point. In all this, it is important to remember that Billy does not work as Garrett's foil (or vice versa, for that matter). Rather than functioning antithetically, Billy opens up the space underlying all contradictions. Aesthetics and thought are not presented as working according to the logic of contradiction. Rather, as corroborated by the account of Garrett's Mescalero incident, aesthetics serves as the instigator and ground of thought. The narrative makes sure that we do not misread it on this point. Similar to staging an opposition between Tom O'Folliard and Pat Garrett, the narrative introduces another foil to Garrett in the person of a certain Livingstone, who presents us with the perversion of Garrettian rationality – indeed, the narrative speaks of the 'perverse logic' (61) of Livingstone's actions – by 'clinically and scientifically' (61) inbreeding dogs into madness, eventually being killed and eaten by them:

> In three years he had over 40 dogs. The earlier ones he just let loose, they were too sane. The rest, when the vet found them, were grotesque things – who hardly moved except to eat and fornicate. They lay, the dogs, when they found his body, listless as sandbags propped against the 14 foot fence Livingstone had built. Their eyes bulged like marbles; some were blind, their eyes had split. Livingstone had found that the less he fed them the more they fornicated, if only to keep their mind off the hunger. These originally beautiful dogs were gawky and terrifying to that New Orleans vet when he found them. He couldn't even recognize that they had been spaniels or were intended to be. They didn't snarl, just hissed through the teeth – gaps left in them for they were falling out. (61)

Both the account of Livingstone's practice and its explicit characterisation as following a 'perverse logic' present Livingstone as Garrett's antithesis in so far as Livingstone's actions manifest the *corruption* (perversion) of rationality (logic). Garrett's rationality is once more juxtaposed to madness. Like Tom, Livingstone thus amounts to an *inverted* (etymologically synonymous with perverted) Garrett, his negative double. This juxtaposition of Garrett and Livingstone reminds us again that, even though one might be tempted to construct such an opposition, opposing Billy to Garrett will not do. Garrett versus Livingstone is yet another dichotomy that serves to highlight the fact that Billy explores the difference inherent in all dichotomies: that is, the differential ground that determines the distinctions between terms. Just as he endorses an *other* way of killing to that of Pat and Tom (where Tom figures as madness qua *lack of* rationality), he embodies an *other* relation to animals than Garrett and Livingstone (where Livingstone figures as madness qua *excess of* rationality). Billy, as the instantiation of the versus-structure, is a figure of the disjunctive synthesis as the *determinant in intensio* of differences *in extensio* (he could thus be said to figure as the madness of becoming, a madness that is not defined as the negative of rationality). If we return to Deleuze's discussion of Spinoza quoted above,

Narrating Sensation

we can say that while Garrett figures as the human being's power to be reasonable – that is, to wield rational thought, and Tom and Livingstone manifest the power to be unreasonable – that is, being mad, Billy is the figure of power as such. Since this power is precisely the power of affects and percepts – what a body is capable of – Billy is the figure of Deleuzian sensation. And he is this by dint of incessantly undergoing all sorts of becomings that open out on to the realm of sensation.

Before turning to this realm of sensation in more detail, let me briefly dwell on another passage, as this passage allows me to bring together both the importance of sensory experience as the starting point for explorations in the realm of sensation *and* its importance in the process of the determination of thought. It underscores that sensory experience assumes the mediating position between these two realms, the space of sensation and the space of reason. In addition, the passage metanarratively emphasises the role of writing, the role that the telling of the story plays within this conundrum. Thus, when Billy – while there is no grammatical indication that the narrative voice is indeed Billy's, the content of the passage seems to suggest as much – writes that 'The acute nerves spark / on the periphery of our bodies / while the block trunk of us / blunders as if we were / those sun drugged horses' (72), he once more emphasises the liminality of the senses as they are located on the periphery between a body's inside and outside. The senses are presented as bleeding into both directions; they are the locus of hybridity and the liminal capturers of intensity; they constitute the body's proper zone of intensity. This status and role of the senses is further emphasised when Billy asserts that he is 'here with the range for everything / corpuscle [range for the molecular], muscle [range for the molar], hair [the thin line connecting exteriority with interiority]', and that 'those senses [. . .] want to crash things with an axe' – making clear that it is the senses that open things up for us – that they are 'the mind's invisible blackout', its 'intricate never / the body's waiting rut' (72). The senses operate in darkness, where the light of thought has not yet emerged; they are our guide and compass *before* thought has even entered the scene.[20] The senses map the outside, and it is on the basis of their cartographic work that thought then operates on the inside.

Billy conveys this relation in a series of verses that go from the movement of blood to the movement of his fingers to the movement of thought:

> the blood from my wrist / has travelled to my heart / and my fingers touch this soft blue paper notebook / control a pencil that shifts up and sideways / mapping my thinking going on its own way / like light wet glasses drifting on polished wood. (72)

Since these verses immediately precede the ones quoted above, the passage in its entirety repeats *both* the narrative's explorative movement that goes from thought (that is, representation) to the senses (i.e., the apparatus of perception/registration) to sensation (that is, the imperceptible) as set up and staged on the very first page with the empty frame and caption, *and* the movement of becoming-imperceptible that representational thought has to undergo in order to excavate its constituting affects and percepts. In this context, the role of writing and storytelling is revealing: in this passage it seems that writing – inscription – is the paradigmatic activity of an extended mind that brings into play its various elements – notebook, fingers, circulation of blood, pencil – in order to map thought's drifting movement, to organise it and to make it intelligible, to lay it out in the representational space of reason. But the image of the cobwebs that have 'stories to finish' (17) quoted further above in the context of Billy's becoming-animal during the barn episode situates this organisational work in a much larger ontological framework that precisely concerns the composition of sensations. This is not so much a question of the *extension* of rational human mind as of its *emergence*. The cartographic work of the blood–finger–paper–pencil assemblage is *constructive* and *constitutes* the movement of thought that, in its drifting, is then recursively able to retrace this mapping. This double-movement of thought maps exactly on to the double-movement of narrative from its virtual nascent state ('stories to finish') to its actualised completion (*The Collected Works of Billy the Kid*) and the ensuing doubling back in a trajectory that makes its very own construction tangible.

In accordance with Deleuze's statement that 'becoming-animal is only one stage in a more profound becoming-imperceptible in which the Figure disappears' (FB: 25) we now have to follow Billy further down this path of dissipation in order finally to attain the realm of sensation. Only then will we have unearthed the Idea inherent in *The Collected Works of Billy the Kid*; only then will we be able to say what the constitutive elements of its process of emplotment and narrativisation are.

The Realm of Sensation

Billy's becoming-imperceptible is showcased with exceptional clarity in two scenes, once when Billy and his posse are captured by Garrett and his men, and then at the very moment of his death, emblematically confirming the creation = destruction equation. After Garrett and his men capture Billy and his gang, they take them to jail, zigzagging through the desert in order to evade lynchers, 'legs handcuffed with long 24" chains under the horse, hands bound to the bridle. Five days like that', almost going 'mad from saddle pain [...] all going grey in the eyes' (76). The subsequent two pages evoke the violence, cruelty, pain, and madness of this experience as its hallucinative, feverous quality is unfolded. In this unfolding, sensations *become sensible* by means of the narrative's techniques of thematic and formal disfiguration. This making tangible of sensation via disfiguration is most acutely on display as Billy undergoes a veritable becoming-sensation, as he is reduced to a 'soft shell-less egg wrapped in thin white silk' (78), a 'block of sensations' (WIP: 163; 167), a sculpture made of affects and percepts, a 'monument' (WIP: 164; 168) built from sensations. On the content level, Billy is cut open, flayed, and then literally turned inside out. On the formal level, the passage abounds in lyricisms, sentence fragments, lack of punctuation, and figures of repetition effecting a broken syntax, the disfiguration of language, what Deleuze and Guattari refer to as making 'the standard language stammer, tremble, cry, or even sing' (WIP: 176). Disfiguration thus makes tangible both the conditions of any figuration whatsoever – that figures are constituted by sensations – and the implication of these constitutive sensations in generated figures. Figures express sensations by giving them a body, by embodying them (WIP: 177). In a fundamental sense, figures *are* sensations. Here, then, is how Billy's disfiguration proceeds:

> On the fifth day the sun turned into a pair of hands and began to pull out the hairs in my head. Twist pluck twist pluck. In two hours I was bald, my head like a lemon. It used a fingernail and scratched a knife line from front to back on the skin. A hairline of blood bubbled up and dried. Eleven in the morning then. The sun took a towel and wiped the dried dribble off, like red powder on the towel now. Then with very thin careful fingers it began to unfold my head drawing back each layer of skin and letting it flap over my ears.
>
> The brain juice began to swell up. You could see the bones and grey now. The sun sat back and watched while the juice evaporated. By now

the bone was dull white, all dry. When he touched the bone with his fingers it was like brushing raw nerves. (76)

If there is a much better example for Shklovsky's insistence on the capacity of art to 'return sensation to our limbs' (Shklovsky 1998: 6) then I have as yet to find it. Already upon reading these first few lines one *feels* the sensations attendant on travelling under such extremely adverse conditions: namely, tied, on horseback with almost no rest, under extreme heat and lack of food and water. How is this feeling conveyed? First, it is conveyed through effecting the simultaneous acuteness and discombobulation of the senses, particularly of the tactile. But note that the personified sun also evokes the sense of sight, as do the references to the colours grey, white, and red, and the various descriptions of objects (such as Billy's head) and actions (such as the sun cutting Billy's head). In addition, there are several references to sounds such as the bubbling up of blood, the flapping of the skin against the ears, and the swelling up of the brain juice. While the senses of smell and taste can only be inferred indirectly from this passage (via objects like the lemon, for instance), they do feature explicitly in the latter sections of the passage to which I will turn shortly. Second, it is conveyed through the slow but continuous intensification of pain, culminating in the 'brushing [of] raw nerves'. This is achieved through presenting pain as something *that forces itself in from the outside*, slowly, meticulously, and with cruel precision, increasing in intensity as it makes headway. This presentation in turn is effected through the personification of the sun, casting it as a deliberate actor that breaks in by means of surgical precision, all the while keeping a disinterested distance ('the sun sat back and watched'). Pain methodically works itself in and up to its highest point of intensity. This is only the beginning, though, as the narrative continues:

> He took a thin cold hand and sank it into my head down past the roof of my mouth and washed his fingers in my tongue. Down the long cool hand went scratching the freckles and warts in my throat breaking through veins like pieces of long glass tubing, touched my heart with its wrist, down he went the liquid yellow from my busted brain finally vanishing as it passed through soft warm stomach like a luscious blood wet oasis, weaving in and out of the red yellow blue green nerves moving uncertain through wrong fissures ending pausing at cul de sacs of bone then retreating slow leaving the pain of suction then down the proper path through pyramids of bone that were there when I was born, through grooves the fingers spanning the merging paths of medians of blue matter, the long

> cool hand going down brushing cobwebs of nerves the horizontal pain pits, lobules gyres notches arcs tracts fissures roots' white insulation of dead seven year cells clinging things rubbing them off on the tracts of spine down the cool precise fingers went into the cistern of bladder down the last hundred miles in a jerk breaking through my sacs of sperm got my cock in the cool fingers pulled it back up and carried it pulling pulling flabby as smoke up the path his arm had rested in and widened. He brought it up fast half tearing the roots off up the coloured bridges of fibres again, charting the slimy arm back through the pyramids up locked in his fingers up the now bleeding throat up squeezed it through the skull bones, so there I was, my cock standing out of my head. (76–7)

Having opened Billy's skull and brain, the sun now proceeds to turn him inside out literally, working its way from the brain down to the guts, causing his entire sensorium to explode. This is effected through a plethora of directly sense-related verbs and adjectives (I have counted almost 30), enhanced by presenting them in congeries (for example, 'red yellow blue green'), by means of synaesthesia ('liquid yellow'), and by inscribing them in a wealth of figures of repetition – from anaphora ('Down [. . .] down [. . .] down [. . .]' and so on) to geminatio ('pulling pulling') to conduplicatio ('long cool hand'). Via the sun's downward movement *The Collected Works of Billy the Kid* replicates in a nutshell the entire narrative's downward trajectory from brain to gut, from rational thought to pre-cognitive feeling, from cognition to aesthetics, while the ensuing upward motion unearths the aesthetic and brings it up to light, establishing it as the prime mode of relation; the brain is replaced by the cock, sensuality itself, standing out of Billy's head – a veritable antenna of sensitivity.[21] In a final step, Billy's highest point of becoming-sensation is arrived at when the sun, now using two hands, finishes its work:

> They [the hands] picked up the fold of foreskin one hand on each side and began the slow pull back back back back *down* like a cap with ear winter muffs like a pair of trousers down boots and then he let go. The wind picked up, I was drowned, locked inside my skin sensitive as an hour old animal, could feel everything, I could hear everything on my skin, as I sat, like a great opaque ostrich egg on the barebacked horse. In my skin hearing Garrett's voice near me on the skin whats wrong billy whats wrong, couldnt see him but I turned to where I knew he was. I yelled so he could hear me through the skin. Ive been fucked. Ive been fucked by Christ almighty god Ive been good and fucked by Christ. And I rolled off the horse's back like a soft shell-less egg wrapped in thin white silk [. . .] (77–8)

His antenna of sensitivity now covering him wholesale, Billy has finally metamorphosed into pure sensation, the 'soft shell-less egg' of intensity. He dissolves in the intensities of the virtual realm, has become a body without organs, that 'intense egg defined by axes and vectors, gradients and thresholds, by dynamic tendencies involving energy transformation', that designator of 'intensive reality, which is not undifferentiated, but is where things and organs are distinguished solely by gradients, migrations, zones of proximity' (ATP: 182). Indeed, Deleuze and Guattari equate the egg and the body without organs – 'The BwO is the egg. [...] The egg is the BwO' (ATP: 181–2) – as the body without organs is the 'intense germen' (ATP: 182) of the organised, fully developed body. Thus, when Billy the Kid becomes Billy without Organs (BwO) he attains his generative matrix, the egg of differential elements and relations, the 'axes and vectors' of sensations and forces determining him (in the passage above these are clearly sensations of duration, exhaustion, pain, dryness, heat and so on, and forces like friction, tension, gravitation). Aesthetic knowledge, the direct apprehension of becoming, means to enter becoming itself. In order to apprehend becoming *one has to become*. *Aisthesis* entails becoming-imperceptible, entails being dispersed in becoming, immersion in difference itself.

That this happens whenever representation breaks down or is made to break down, at acute moments of representational crisis, is emphasised through repeated images of brain damage, as in the passage above where the sun makes Billy's brain evaporate in order to replace it with his cock.[22] The apotheosis of such crisis is attained when Billy recounts his final moments: 'AND I KNOW I KNOW / it is my brain coming out like red grass / this breaking where red things wade' (95). This is a forceful image that short-circuits knowledge with *aisthesis*. Formally ruptured by means of metalepsis (Billy recounting his own death), on the content level, representation is killed off, its breaking apart marked by the advent of death. Billy's proclaimed knowledge is neither the conceptual knowledge of death, nor the simple perceptual registration of things that Billy might be perceiving just before he dies. Rather, it is knowledge *as* aesthetic experience where the *aisthesis* of dying is determined through the affects and percepts assembled in this death, the movement of: a break, a brain, some red, to wade. The verses make clear that this knowledge takes place outside the brain, outside of cognition, at the point where cognition, the brain, literally breaks. In fact, there is no thought adequate to dying since dying implies the death of thought. Knowledge of death thus is equal to an absolute becoming-imperceptible, becoming-sensation, becoming-non-human, that is, equal to dying itself: a breaking wading redly. This is the moment where epistemology meets up and coincides with ontology, where the movement of knowledge topples over into the movement of becoming, where thought disseminates in being. Accordingly, this happens at the farthest limit of experience, the experience of death, the experience of the end of experience, its ultimate crisis and rupture. It is here, at this moment of rupture and breakage, the climactic moment of speculation, that the *beyond* of experience becomes manifest. By the same token, the beyond of actual narratives is attained: the sensations and forces that make up the death of Billy are those that make up the narrative at hand *in so far as it is the narrative that assembles and composes the figure of Billy*. In doing so, the narrative engages in the construction and composition of a plethora of sensations and forces, as made tangible in Billy's (and the narrative's) trajectory of becoming-imperceptible.

Having thus 'captured' movement in-itself, becoming, or the unfolding of time itself, the narrative immediately makes clear that such capturing necessarily amounts to the impediment of movement (this is why Deleuze and Guattari speak of *monuments* of sensation) by way of a thought experiment: if one were to dig up Billy's body, what would one see? Bones, leg irons, a bullet in the skull, silver boot caps (97). What is it that we see here, in this odd assortment? The answer is quite simple: we see the violent impediment of movement, a movement to which the silver boot caps bear witness. Both movement of thought (bullet in the skull) and movement of the body (leg irons) have been violently brought to a halt. This short passage vividly renders the unmaking of becoming as it makes clear that Billy, the quintessential nomadic figure, has been forced to settle in permanently, literally reterritorialised – six feet under – in a wooden box. There could be no more forceful and more haunting image of settlement than this one. The whole image is aptly captured in the fragment's final line: 'His legend a jungle sleep' (97). In a sense, if one thinks of the etymology of the word, we are presented with nothing but Billy's legend here, as legend means nothing other than 'things to be read'. The things to be read here are those enumerated above. And when we read them they tell us a story of violent capture and stoppage. And what has been captured and stopped has been put to sleep. If *The Collected Works of Billy the Kid* is historiographic metafiction in any sense, then it is so only in the sense of this paradigmatic passage, in the sense of its meta-legending: its display of the truth of fiction at work, a truth that reveals legending as constructing. This construction and composition is precisely that of becoming as exposed by Billy's many a becomings-other. And this, Billy's sensitiveness to and capacity for all sorts of becomings, and the jungle-like texture, darkness, noisiness, splendour, and teeming impenetrability of becoming, have been put to sleep with Billy's death. Note that this, again, is not a mere thematic concern but a forceful metanarrative comment on the very fact that the narrative at hand is but *another* act of legending, another assembly of signs, another version of Billy's story to be read, and thus necessarily buries the movement it seeks to unearth. Thus, the only option that remains is to expose *its own complicity in this burying*, showcasing that creation (of the actual) always means destruction (of the virtual). The only way to do this is to linger in the space in-between, to dwell at the frontier between the actual and the virtual, to make camp in the zones of intensity. In this sense, frontiers are always zones of intensity. And in this vein, *The Collected Works of Billy the Kid* attempts to reopen and reawaken the powers of becoming buried in Billy's legend, to rekindle the intensive forces of nomadicity at play at the American frontier, powers that were submerged and violently erased in its progressive settlement. *The Collected Works of Billy the Kid* unearths and seeks to redeploy these forces at work, the constant strife between de- and reterritorialisation as it pertains to the frontier, emblematically rendered through the final moments of Billy and his last encounter with Garrett.

When Garrett finally gets Billy and kills him, he does this in a very atypical manner. In contrast to his characteristic distanced, cold, and precise academic killing, Garrett gets Billy only by entering a veritable becoming-Billy while Billy simultaneously undergoes a becoming-Garrett. Garrett exclusively relies on Billy's method of aesthetic killing as he, in utter darkness, follows the lead of his senses *feeling* Billy in order to bring him down (92–3).[23] It also becomes clear that Garrett, rather than controlling the action as is his usual custom, is swept up by the event when he is about to burst out into laughter (and thus quickly shoots his gun before he gives himself away) (93). In other words, abandoning the light of rational thought, Garrett enters the dark caverns of pre-cognitive *aisthesis*. On the content level, this is expressed through the darkness of Pete Maxwell's room, a darkness inimical to Garrett's rational calculations. At the same time, at this decisive moment, Billy forgets his aesthetic expertise as he seeks to *determine* who this man is that is lying in Pete's bed: 'He leans forward again and moves his hands down the bed and then feels a man's boots. O my god Pete quien es?' (93). This one time Billy disregards the affects and percepts he otherwise is so adept at intuiting – his nemesis is not Pat Garrett, but his forgetfulness as to the world of becoming. Ultimately, what brings about Billy's death is the simultaneous deterritorialisation of Garrett and reterritorialisation of Billy. *The Collected Works of Billy the Kid* occupies the outpost on the frontier between these two movements, a grand counter-actualisation of the Turner thesis reopening and inhabiting the frontier.[24] In this, the narrative is not so much interested in a *particular historical* moment, however, but in the moment of intensity as it opens out to the grand circulation of affects and percepts, the economy of sensations. As such, it sets itself apart from narratives that give in to and foster their reterritorialising lures, as exemplified in the dime novel excerpt it incorporates. 'Billy the Kid and the Princess' (99–102) is a prime example of burying the affective and perceptive economy of a life at the frontier as it reduces Billy to a stock-figure of pseudo-romantic romance, a conventionalised story of ready-made perceptions and affections where Billy's only role is to rescue the princess repeatedly and finally to be rewarded with her affection and kisses with the prospect (and clear indication) of final settlement and a calm territorialised life.

Again, we have to be careful. The antidote to such territorialisation is *not* to strive to escape territorialisation for good – this would merely turn bodies into utterly bodiless ethereal spirits. Indeed, the narrative presents its own territorialisation when it repeats the initial empty frame at the very end, but this time with a small picture of Ondaatje as a kid dressed in cowboy gear in the lower right corner; a concrete image has been drawn out of the initial state of pure virtuality. The narrative thus assumes a territory, stakes its claim, occupies a little ground, inhabits a small plot of its own. This territory, in turn, is immediately deterritorialised, precisely because it is not absolutised so as to bury and occlude the virtual from which it was won and which exceeds it (the picture occupies only a small section of the frame). The narrative does not claim to represent, to stand in verisimilarly for, the story of Billy the Kid but singularly expresses the forces, the lures, the affects as they are crystallised in Billy the Kid by dint of constructing this very figure (kids – just like Billy and Micky – know the world of affects). The picture does not represent little Michael representing Billy the Kid. This is not a game of representations – the similarities are superficial and rather ridiculous (neither Billy nor any cowboy actually looked like that). Rather, the narrative captures precisely this fact: namely, that as a representation of the story of Billy the Kid the narrative at hand is but ridiculous and a failure. Instead, it unfolds from virtuality to actuality, from the empty frame to the frame with the small picture. This is why the bulk of the narrative is *literally couched between* these two frames, occupying the liminal space in-between and thereby rendering the crystallisation process visible.

Rendering the crystallisation process visible is precisely what Deleuze means when he says that art is diagrammatic: that it diagrams the distribution of formless forces throughout the work (FB: 127). If, with reference to Derrida's grammatology, I said in the Introduction that all grammar rests on metaphysical production, then art as diagrammatic indeed produces diagrams of this production: by making explicit its own generation via the distribution of forces, which always come accompanied by sensations as their 'carriers', art makes tangible the general matrix of generation as such. Deleuze thus underpins any grammatology with a diagrammatology, to borrow John Mullarkey's term (Mullarkey 2006: 174; 190–1). In this sense, diagrammatology is an adequate term to capture art's very own speculative activity. When Billy, in a passage already discussed further above, calls the newsman out for producing mere *conceptual* diagrams of things, he does so because this comes at the expense of the *sensational* diagrammaticity of things themselves. These two senses of the diagram are repeatedly evoked throughout *The Collected Works of Billy the Kid*, most prominently so in an account of Billy trapped inside a shadowy building, waiting.[25] Billy's voice first presents a veritable geometry of the place and situation, precisely determining the location of his body within these coordinates:

> This nightmare by this 7 foot high doorway / waiting for friends to come / mine or theirs / I am 4 feet inside the room / in the brown cold dark / the doorway's slide of sun / three inches from my shoes / I am on the edge of the cold dark / watching the white landscape in its frame / a world that's so precise / every nail and cobweb / has magnified itself to my presence. (74)

This diagram of extensive relations, where everything is clear and distinct with its position determined in relation to other positions, then gives way to this:

> I am here on the edge of sun / that would ignite me / looking out into pitch white / sky and grass overdeveloped into meaninglessness / waiting for enemies' friends or mine. (74)

The diagram of extensive relations has become a diagram of intensive relations where nothing is clear and distinct any more as the blue of the sky and the green of the grass are dissolved in whiteness. This seeming dissolution and collapse of distinctions are aptly captured by the photographic trope of overdevelopment. Overdevelopment is a means to amplify contrast. And indeed, the passage initially presents us with a situation of extreme contrasts, a chiaroscuro narrative: inside darkness versus outside lightness. However, at a certain threshold of overdevelopment, the extreme contrast, the highest differentiation, results in indistinction; the clear distinctions, the magnified nails and cobwebs, collapse into white light. To wit, this is but how things *appear to us* (in this case to Billy) while *in themselves* they teem with difference. The object thus indeed becomes meaningless for us, as it seems to lack distinction. Nothing can be distinguished – sky not from grass – and everything bleeds into one another. To reappropriate Hegel's famous saying, this is the daylight in which all cows are white.

There could not be a better image for the virtual: what appears to be amorphous, featureless, indistinct is, in fact, *differentiated to the highest degree*. The virtual is unrepresentable precisely because of this: one cannot represent pure difference. If one tries, all one achieves is the uniformity of whiteness – just like the empty frame on the first page. As Deleuze puts it in *The Logic of Sensation*, this is 'the separation of bodies in universal light and universal color [. . .] the union that separates [. . .] a monochromatic eternity. An immense space–time unites all things, *but only by introducing between them the distances of a Sahara, the centuries of an Aion*' (FB: 70). This is but a reformulation of *The Logic of Sense*'s disjunctive synthesis and of *A Thousand Plateaus*' magic formula 'PLURALISM = MONISM' (ATP: 23), the formula that captures the topological folds of the virtual–actual relation. As we have seen, the failure of representation is not without merit, as it makes the inadequacy of representation explicit. The breakdown of representation allows for flickers of the virtual; it presents the dance of differentials in its monochromatic splendour – the white of the day, the black of the night, the yellow of the desert, the green of grass, and the blue of the sky. This is representation pushed to its limit, at which point the dualism it set up is finally torn to a shambles, where it gives way to its underlying genetics and truly morphs into expression. By now, it should come as no surprise that Billy here again occupies the space in-between, standing 'on the edge of cold dark' that is at the same time the 'edge of sun' (74). It is only by occupying liminal zones of intensity that one can draw the diagram of forces and sensations. *The Collected Works of Billy the Kid* is diagrammatic in precisely this sense.

Ultimately, the contours of the diagram Ondaatje's narrative draws are determined by the chiastic interweaving of two figures of *kyklos*. While on the content level, the death of Billy is first taken up as a mere empirical fact (in the list of casualties at the beginning) and then unfolded in order to make palpable its singular transcendental circulation of sensations and forces (in Billy's account of dying), on the formal level, the first page's empty frame indexes the transcendental realm of constitution (how to produce a picture that captures movement) and its repetition at the very end focuses on the empirical fact that is drawn out from it (the picture of Michael Ondaatje as cowboy). In so doing, the narrative adequately expresses the double-movement of ontogenetic and speculative becoming: on the formal level, it necessarily proceeds from its virtual constitutive elements to its actual form – from the pure and empty form of time (movement in-itself; becoming) to the fully developed individual entity (*The Collected Works of Billy the Kid*) – what, hijacking Ricœur, I term configuration or emplotment; on the content level, it takes the reverse path of decomposing the fully individuated entity (the figure of Billy the Kid) to attain its constitutive elements (the sensations and forces at play in Billy's various becomings-other) – what I call the movement of disfiguration. Note that this clear distinction between form and content does not hold, though. The emplotment of form – morphogenesis – clearly involves the constitution of content. What is being constituted is a singular individual with a singular form and a singular content. The disfiguration of content – speculation – likewise clearly involves the deformation of form. What is being unearthed is the universal Idea in its variability. The narrative thus unfolds what could be called a grand Spinozist parallelism and identity of form and content, body and soul, enhanced by Deleuzian geneticism.[26] Chiasmus, *kyklos*, parallelism: what drives this narrative (and, by proxy, narrativity at large) is incessant repetition, the repetition of repetition, the repetition of the differenciator of difference. Nietzsche's eternal return in the guise of Deleuze's difference and repetition (the repetition of difference and the difference of repetition) thus becomes the recipe for the abolishment of all dualisms in favour of a monism that is a pluralism: 'All dualism does is reveal a ghost facing a skeleton. All real bodies shimmer like watered silk' (Serres 2008: 25). *The Collected Works of Billy the Kid* violently crashes through all these empty dualisms precisely in order to capture the *shimmering* of bodies, the body without organs, the virtual discoteer ecstatically dancing away, immersed and dispersed in the stroboscope of sensations.

Notes

1. For details on the origin and composition of the caption and the book it is allegedly taken from, see the respective footnote in Douglas Barbour's monograph on Ondaatje (Barbour 1993: 222n16).
2. Since virtually every comment on the text deals with this central feature in one way or another, I content myself with referring to the two major studies by Douglas Barbour and Lee Spinks (Barbour 1993; Spinks 2009).
3. For the former, see, for example, Hochbruck 1994 and Bethell 2003; for the latter, Hillger 2006 and Marinkova 2011. I should also say here that both Marinkova and Spinks present their readings of Ondaatje in light of a certain Deleuzianism. However, this Deleuzianism – one that is rampant in literary and cultural studies – to a large extent neglects Deleuze's metaphysics and directly short-circuits the texts under scrutiny with a Deleuze-inflected politics. This is rather unfortunate, however, as Deleuze's politics rest on his metaphysics. The result of such short-circuiting is that becoming is read as political rather than metaphysical (this is the case in Marinkova's recourse to Deleuzian micropolitics), or that talk of intensities and sub-representational forces remains on the level of historicity as it maps on to a past–present relation (this is the case in Spinks). No doubt, this kind of Deleuzianism was at least partially triggered by the sequence of translations of Deleuze's opus, with the *Capitalism and Schizophrenia* project, one explicitly political that, however, *presupposes* the earlier metaphysical work, coming early on. This led to a first wave of *political* Deleuze scholarship *at the expense* of his metaphysics. It is only within the last ten to fifteen years that Deleuze's metaphysics has garnered more attention. The point here is not to say that one should do Deleuzian metaphysics instead of politics, merely replacing the focus of attention, but that Deleuze's politics cannot be unmoored from his metaphysics.

   It is no coincidence that the rise of scholarship (at least within the Anglophone world) on Deleuzian metaphysics coincides roughly with the detailed and arduous explanatory work of Daniel W. Smith.

Smith's work, much of which has just recently been collected in his *Essays on Deleuze* (Smith 2012), has without doubt paved the way for a more scrupulous discussion of Deleuze, and still remains unmatched in its scope and – crucially – accessibility.
4. Again, some examples will do: for earlier treatments, see MacLulich 1981 (photography) and Grace 1992 (comics); for a more recent one, see again Marinkova 2011 (cinema).
5. Deleuze's elaborations on the problem–solution matrix pervade the entirety of *Difference and Repetition*, but passages on pages 77, 203, 225–6, and 230, and the whole of Chapter 5 are particularly relevant.
6. It should be noted that visibility here stands in for all perception. While, to a certain extent, the phrase can thus be said to foster ocular-centrism, one should not forget that Klee's coinage is in the context of painting (as is Deleuze's use in *The Logic of Sensation*). Deleuze picks up on it and widens it such that it applies to perception per se, quite similar to his use of the terms 'vision' and 'visionary'. In 'Literature and Life' Deleuze makes this clear by referring to 'visions and auditions' (Deleuze 1997: 5) instead. Compare also the notions of 'haptic space' and 'haptic vision' in Deleuze and Guattari's discussion of nomad art in *A Thousand Plateaus* (ATP: 543–51) and in Deleuze's *The Logic of Sensation* (FB: 99–129). Haptic vision is the intuitive immersion or '"close-range" vision' needed to attain haptic space, a space that is 'as much visual or auditory as tactile' (ATP: 543–4). 'Haptic' thus refers to the virtual's tangibility in principle, its potential of being felt independently of the use of any particular sense; or, more precisely, it refers to the fact that virtuality can *only* be felt, passively, as it is 'not the given but that by which the given is given' (DR: 176). This is indeed what Deleuze terms 'the primary characteristic' of an encounter: that its object 'can only be sensed (and is at the same time imperceptible)' (DR: 176). It is imperceptible, because the Kantian *active* syntheses cannot reach this domain *outside* of the given; only perceptible, because the Deleuzian realm of passive syntheses is the realm of a fundamental *passivity* and *passion*, the realm of that which affects (and thus constitutes) a given body: that is, the realm of sensation. It is via this notion of haptic vision that Deleuze develops the important concept of the diagram in his book on Bacon: it is precisely through its diagrammaticity that art makes the virtual tangible, that it renders perceptible the imperceptible object of encounter, that it pries open an entryway to the realm of sensation. I will return to this concept in the last section of the present chapter.
7. Note that the caption plays a very important role in this, as it is only due to the caption that we expect the frame to have figures, to present a figuration of some sort. The caption is the last trace of figuration, the final moment before utter dissolution. If the narrative only featured

an empty frame without caption, we would not be able to discern the process of disfiguration; we would have an instance of abstract storytelling akin to abstract painting, a situation where disfiguration has already happened, whereas, as it is, the first page now is more akin to the concrete disfigurations of a painter like Francis Bacon. The traceability of the process of disfiguration is the major reason why Deleuze was drawn to Bacon's paintings and did not particularly like abstract art. This becomes evidently clear in his book on Bacon, where he states this explicitly (FB: 84–6). In this vein, the four otherwise quite diverse narratives I am scrutinising in this study are all akin to Bacon's paintings in so far as they are narratives of disfiguration. I am not sure what the narrative analogue to abstract painting would look like and whether such a work even possibly exists – it would have to be some form of ultra-experimental writing in which any trace of any kind of figuration has been erased. Maybe visual poetry like Fritz Lichtenauer's, such as his 'Textteppiche' and *Buchstäblich*, and some of the pieces in *Visual Poetry in the Avant Writing Collection* fit the bill (Lichtenauer 1994; Lichtenauer 1991; Bennett 2008). I fail to detect figuration there. Note that such artworks are thoroughly anti-representational, but fail to problematise (in the Deleuzian sense) representation. They are negative art akin to negative theology in so far as they operate according to a logic of incessantly saying what they *are not* without ever being able to say what they *are*. 'This is not a representation' is the slogan of abstract art. In this, abstract art still adheres to representation; it is simply its negative form. In any case, the process of disfiguration – of disfiguring representation – is essential to both Deleuze's elaboration of speculative becoming (or counter-actualisation) and my elaboration of a differential narratology based on Deleuze's speculative account. In this context, *The Logic of Sensation* is a crucial work, as it is here that this process is most clearly elaborated. It is also here that Deleuze's statement from *Difference and Repetition*, that in a transcendental empiricist framework aesthetics becomes the 'apodictic discipline' (DR: 68), gains consistency. Given this, and given the relative scarcity of critical work on the book, *The Logic of Sensation* is certainly one of Deleuze's most underrated works.

8. See Slotkin's magisterial trilogy, *Regeneration through Violence*, *The Fatal Environment*, and *Gunfighter Nation* (Slotkin 1973; Slotkin 1994; Slotkin 1998). *The Collected Works of Billy the Kid* posits the generation through violence thesis explicitly and directly when it raises the question as to the motive and reason for all the violence: 'A motive? [. . .] Was there a source for all this?' (54). The answer turns out to be just more violence, as the reason given, by way of a graphic account, is the atrocious murder of Tunstall (which triggered the Lincoln County War). The source of all the violence is violence.

9. This phrase from the introductory plateau of *A Thousand Plateaus* is not employed gratuitously here, as Deleuze and Guattari's paradigmatic example is indeed America, and particularly the American West. They even go so far as to speak of 'the rhizomatic West' (ATP: 21). Given this, and given the explosion of Deleuze scholarship in the past decade, it is not surprising that Deleuze and Guattari have been explicitly taken up in recent scholarship on the West. See particularly Campbell 2008, which avails itself of the above-mentioned Deleuzo-Guattarian expression for its title. See also Buchanan 2001a, which discusses the American West in terms of a 'pure expression that has affect, but not content' and 'more a structure of perception and feeling [. . .] than an actual place' (77).
10. This has been claimed by several commentators; see, for example, Nodelman 1980 and Wart 1985.
11. Indeed, I have already recast Barbour's creation versus destruction opposition as the creation = destruction equation that defines Billy.
12. On the Deleuzian concept of disjunctive synthesis, see the 'Twenty-Fourth Series of the Communication of Events' in *The Logic of Sense*, particularly pages 199–201.
13. Here one could also note that the maze, the labyrinth, is the figure of difference *par excellence*, as expounded both in Deleuze's first Nietzsche book (NP) and in *The Fold*. This conundrum is taken up and elaborated on in Chapter 4.
14. In short, Spinoza's parallelism of body and soul is a monism (and not a dualism) precisely because body and soul *are one and the same thing* considered under *different aspects*: namely, those of extension and thought respectively. On Deleuze's reading of Spinoza's real distinction of the attributes as formal distinction, see Duffy 2006: 95–102.
15. Panpsychism has had quite a surge recently on both sides of philosophy's analytical-continental divide. For a great overview ranging across the divide and presenting the state of the art in all its diversity, see Skrbina 2009.
16. Again, Deleuze says this explicitly in *Difference and Repetition*: 'Something in the world forces us to think. This something is an object not of recognition but of a fundamental *encounter*. [. . .] [I]ts primary characteristic is that it can only be sensed' (DR: 176). Thought is thus triggered by a sensual encounter – this is Deleuze's empiricism; what can only be sensed, however, is precisely the imperceptible and as such needs another method, that of '"close-range" vision' – this is his transcendentalism. Together, these two aspects constitute the method of transcendental empiricism.
17. On the Deleuzian notion of athleticism in the context of disfiguration, see FB: 13–18. But also note Garrett's reference to Billy's tendency to assume 'ridiculous positions, feet locked in the chair's arms, or lying

on the floor with his feet up' (43–4) already mentioned above, which display a striking similarity to the distorted postures of Bacon's figures as discussed by Deleuze.

18. Apart from Garrett's characterisation as an academic murderer and his drinking experiment, this becomes particularly evident in the accounts of Garrett's killings, as, for example, the murder of Tom O'Folliard as discussed above or the incident that leads to the capturing of Billy, Wilson, and Dave Rudabaugh that is presented (by Billy) almost like a basic arithmetic operation (an impression enhanced by the actual use of numbers):

> Snow outside. Wilson, Dave Rudabaugh and me. No windows, the door open so we could see. Four horses outside. Garrett aimed and shot to sever the horse reigns [sic]. He did that for 3 of them so they got away and 3 of us couldnt [sic] escape. He tried for 5 minutes to get the reigns [sic] on the last horse but kept missing. So he shot the horse. We came out. No guns. (48)

19. This is the respective passage, which is worth reproducing in full here:

> He stood up and took off his boots and socks, went to his room, returned, he had washed his hands. He asked us to go into the living room and sit still. Then he changed his mind and asked us to go out of the house and onto the verandah and keep still and quiet, not to talk. He began to walk over the kitchen floor, the living room area, almost bent in two, his face about a foot from the pine floorboards. He had the gun out now. And for about half an hour he walked around like this, sniffing away it seemed to me. Twice he stopped in the same place but continued on. He went all over the house. Finally he came back to a spot near the sofa in the living room. We could see him through the window, all of us. Billy bent quietly onto his knees and sniffed carefully at the two square feet of floor. He listened for a while, then sniffed again. Then he fired twice into the floorboards. Jumped up and walked out to us. He's dead now Sallie, don't worry. (44–5)

20. This becomes clear when the senses are described as the 'body's waiting rut', thus highlighting that the senses, not rationality, direct the body. The additional sexual innuendo of this passage, indicated by the use of the word 'rut' and the allusive 'palms [. . .] that move in dreams over your women night', not only reinforces sensual experience, but also, considering Claire Colebrook's recent theorisations of sex as the paradigmatic expression of the 'truth of the relative' (2014: 151), further underscores the quintessential role of sensual experience in opening the body up to this realm of the relative: that is, the realm of the versus-structure, that of circulating affects and percepts, difference in-itself.

21. Again, Colebrook's theorisation of sex as the truth of the relative further accentuates the force of this image; since *aisthesis* is here established as isomorphic with relationality as such, the sexual organ qua organ of *aisthesis* invokes *the truth of the aesthetic*.

22. Just to mention one more such passage that involves brain damage: 'bang it went was hot / under my eye / was hot small bang did it / almost a pop / I didn't hear till I was red / had a rat fyt in my head / [. . .] / floating barracuda in the brain' (38). It is no coincidence that this passage, that, as I read it, presents us with another scene of death (or at least of being wounded), very possibly Billy's, uses animal imagery (rat, barracuda) in order to convey the sensations and forces of dying: redness, heat, noise of shot, acceleration, disorientation, and so on.

23. This is not only shown in the account of the killing but also reinforced in the ensuing dialogue between Garrett and Deputy John Poe: '"*Pat,*" replied Poe, "*I believe you have killed the wrong man.*" "*I'm sure it was the Kid,*" responded Garrett, "*for I knew* **his voice** *and could not have been mistaken*"' (103; italics in the original, my bold).

24. In 1893, in a talk delivered to the American Historical Association, Frederick Jackson Turner famously elaborated on the consequences of the closed frontier, the fact that what he took to have been America's driving force – westward expansion – was no longer possible. This talk and several more of his essays on the topic are collected in his *The Frontier in American History* (Turner 1986).

25. Apart from the ensuing account and the passage discussed further above, the two senses of the diagram also unfold in the rendition of Billy's death when the narrative, as shown, not only gives us a diagram of forces and sensations, thus mapping the intensive relations attendant on his death, but also a 'diagram of [. . .] Pete Maxwell's room' that maps its extensive relations including the bed, the wall, the window, the porch – in short, the distribution of bodies in space (92).

26. For how Deleuze's geneticism renders Spinoza's univocity even more univocal – ridding Spinoza of his remnants of equivocity – see Peter Wolfendale:

> The principle of univocity is at minimum the idea that every entity is said 'to be' in the same sense. This idea originated with Duns Scotus, was taken up by Spinoza, and pushed even further by Deleuze. The crucial point to understand here is that there are at least two ways of interpreting the principle: as the **univocity of predication** (e.g., that the property of *intelligence* is ascribed to God in the same way it is ascribed to humans) and the **univocity of existence** (e.g., that God is said to *exist* in the same sense as humans are said to exist). Each of these is opposed to an **analogical** conception of Being, in which we take some things 'to be' in a sense which is merely analogous to the sense in which a privileged category (e.g., the *divine*) is said to be. As we should be able to see, Spinoza follows Duns Scotus in restricting univocity to predication. He takes Substance to share the same **attributes** as its modes in a non-analogical way. However, this is founded upon viewing Substance and modes as distinct **types of existent** to which other logical categories apply analogically: as supranumenary [sic] and enumerable (**quantity**), self-grounded and other-grounded (**causation**), atemporal and temporal (**time**),

etc. Deleuze's atheism demands that this deeper equivocity must be eliminated, along with the residual privileging of Substance it represents. [...] [The plane of immanence] is his attempt to make Substance turn around the modes, by conceiving it not as **analogous** to individual modes, but as the **condition** under which modes can be individuated. (Wolfendale 2012: n. p.; italics and bold in the original)

3

Sensational Realism:
Colson Whitehead's *The Intuitionist*

In its emphasis on verisimilitude and its depiction of social relations, Colson Whitehead's *The Intuitionist* is a realist novel and thus deviates substantially from the more experimental set-ups of Castillo's and Ondaatje's narratives discussed in Chapters 1 and 2. While *The Mixquiahuala Letters*' and *The Collected Works of Billy the Kid*'s respective forms emphasise and enact incompleteness, processuality, and divergence (a series of disconnected narrative and poetic vignettes in Ondaatje's case; a set of letters that present the reader with three divergent story variants in Castillo's), nothing like that holds for Whitehead's novel. *The Intuitionist* can be described as a realist African American alternate history detective novel, clearly structured into two parts, which are subdivided into another two parts respectively. Several commentators have labelled it a postmodern novel (Bérubé 2004: 163; Liggins 2006: 365; Russell 2007: 46), but this characterisation at best holds in terms of literary history, not form. While it might thus be a postmodern novel, it is certainly not a postmodern*ist* novel. Michele Elam even describes it as employing a 'naturalistic' tone (Elam 2011: 120). Ramón Saldívar proposes his own term, speculative realism, to account for the 'revisions of realism and fantasy into speculative forms' he sees at play in novels such as Whitehead's (Saldívar 2013: 3).[1] I suggest that the term altermodern, as theorised by Armen Avanessian and Anke Hennig, who provide a *literary historical* contextualisation and a *formal* qualification, best captures the novel's form. Thus, while it may be too early to herald it as a (literary) historical term, the altermodern comes to designate a specific poetics. Following Nicolas Bourriaud's original emphasis on time and temporality, Avanessian and Hennig meticulously tease out the time-related ramifications of altermodernist narrative fiction. In doing so, they stress the importance of grammatical tense. In their account, a specific use of the present tense becomes the most significant marker of the altermodern and its negotiation of temporality, narrativity, fictionality, and reality – all issues that are at the heart of *The Intuitionist*, which indeed is a present-tense novel.[2] Since this altermodernist poetics is perfectly compatible with a realist style,[3] *The Intuitionist*'s realism can be further qualified as altermodern realism.

The novel tells the story of Lila Mae Watson, the first female African American elevator inspector and an Intuitionist. Set in an alternate twentieth-century US metropolis where elevator inspection is a prestigious municipal government job, the book describes the inspection business as divided into two warring factions, the Empiricists and the Intuitionists.[4] As befits their respective names, Empiricists rely on careful observation and technical details while Intuitionists directly 'feel' the elevator's condition. Even though, inexplicably, the Intuitionists have a 10 per cent higher accuracy rate, they are viewed with suspicion by everyone else. This is due not only to their unverifiable method, but also to the fact that Empiricism is the traditional method of the craft while Intuitionism was only introduced much later through the writings of James Fulton, a former Empiricist, whose two-volume work, *Theoretical Elevators*, shook up the business. *Theoretical Elevators* is the Intuitionist bible, so to speak, with James Fulton – already dead when the novel sets in – the enigmatic guru of the movement, notorious across the divide for his eccentricities. In a society clearly patterned by latent and not-so-latent racism and sexism, being an Intuitionist thus leaves Lila Mae triply stigmatised despite her 100 per cent accuracy rate. It is within this context that Number Eleven, one of the newly built elevators in the city's Fanny Briggs Memorial Building, which Lila Mae had been assigned to inspect, crashes. That the accident, which luckily harms no one, happens while the city's mayor visits the building together with Bill Chancre, the chair of the Department of Elevator Inspectors and an Empiricist, sets off all kinds of speculations concerning the accident. The speculations are further fuelled by the fact that it is election time, with a new department chair to be elected and the respective Empiricist and Intuitionist campaigns at their height. In short, everything looks as if Lila Mae has been set up and Number Eleven sabotaged. This is the novel's initial set-up, gradually revealed on its first twenty-seven pages.

As befits a realist detective novel, the ensuing story unfolds linearly, if punctuated by analepses that, in a traditional fashion, serve to flesh out characters and to provide contextual information. The story is driven by the protagonist's search for the culprit responsible for the alleged act of sabotage that brings about the elevator accident at the beginning of the novel and propels the entire action. The narrative situation is also fairly traditional, heterodiegetic with focalisation moving between zero and variable. None of this is very demanding for the reader, and narrative voice and perspective are always easily discernible and attributable. Everything in *The Intuitionist* is crafted so that it strives towards and converges on its final moment of revelation, the solving of yet another whodunit riddle, a solution that would convey a satisfying Kermodian sense of an ending – except it turns out that there has never been such a riddle to be solved in the first place. What Lila Mae discovers in the end is the very fact that there was nothing to be discovered; the accident turns out to have just been that, an accident. Something she *does* discover on the way, accidentally as it were, are the remnants of Fulton's notebook that contain a draft of the third volume of *Theoretical Elevators*. The parallel evolution of Fulton's story, which initially constitutes a subterranean counterpoint to the main theme only to move increasingly into the foreground in the second part of the novel, complicates the picture considerably. The more Lila Mae tries to find out about the Fanny Briggs accident, the more she detects about Fulton's life as an elevator inspector. Parts of Fulton's notebook that were sent anonymously to the press, the elevator industry, and the two warring factions of elevator inspection reveal that Fulton, in the final days of his life, apparently managed to construct the black box – the perfect elevator. Underneath the surface of Lila Mae's hunt for the saboteur and the moves and tricks of departmental politics (including mobster involvement replete with bullying, kidnapping, and torture) the novel gradually reveals the hunt for Fulton's black box, instigated and propelled by two of the elevator industry's big players (Arbo and United), as the all-determining factor behind the scenes. This doubling of storylines, however, is only one intricate moment within the novel's several patterns of duplicity that range from the Empiricist–Intuitionist feud to that between Arbo and United, to the two-part structure and substructure of the novel.[5] That the two main parts of the novel are entitled 'Down' and 'Up' not only emphasises the novel's thematic concerns with elevators and their respective down- or upwards trajectory, but also names the governing pattern of all the novel's doublings: namely, the division between surface appearance and hidden depth. This is evident not only in the two schools of elevator inspection where Empiricists are solely concerned with the material surface body of elevators and Intuitionists exclusively focus on their immaterial hidden 'soul', but also in the relation between the two contrapuntal storylines. The true figure and apotheosis of the surface-depth dichotomy, however, is the enigmatic Fulton himself. He both embodies the Empiricism–Intuitionism divide, as he wrote the standard Empiricist textbook and became the department chair before founding and turning to Intuitionism, and, as Lila Mae eventually discovers, was also of mixed race, half-white, half-black, passing as white his entire adult and professional life.

As might have become clear by now, the novel's realist appearance does not keep it from developing an extremely intricate and complex 'experimental' depth. Indeed, paraphrasing Elam, one could say that *The Intuitionist passes* as a realist novel, but that underneath its surface of clear structure and distinct story rumbles a dark depth of mixtures and experiments.[6]

When the novel on its very last pages has Lila Mae discover that the accident was just an accident and subsequently opt out of the business of elevator inspection to continue Fulton's project and work on the incomplete third volume of his *Theoretical Elevators*, the two storylines, surface and depth, converge. This convergence, however, conveys anything but Kermode's sense of an ending as it converges on *the divergent itself*, the very moment of bifurcation, the virtual before its actualisation. This is evident in Lila Mae's rejection of *inspection* in favour of *creation* as she not only sits down to finish Fulton's third volume, but also truly to bring about the 'second elevation' (61, 64, 100, 182, 198) inherent in Fulton's black box: that is, she sits down to prepare for 'the city to come' (255), to *construct* the future itself. The novel thus ends with the very activity of creation, the production of the new. Very far from conveying a sense of closure, then, the novel's ending is in fact an opening up: as we witness Lila Mae engaged in channelling, concerting, composing singularities – manifested in her activity of writing – we witness the novel's opening up to the future.

This image of writing qua creation qua facilitation of the future has its correlative image of reading. It is no coincidence that Fanny Briggs, the woman whose name the eponymous memorial building carries, was a 'slave who taught herself how to read' (12). In reading the novel, we actually trace Lila Mae's Briggsian endeavour of teaching herself how to read – how to read the accident, how to read Fulton's works, how to read the Empiricist–Intuitionist feud – how to get to 'the bottom of things' (56), as the novel puts it. As it turns out, getting to the bottom of things requires a different speed of reading, a slowing down. The German word for slow-motion, *Zeitlupe* – literally 'time magnifier' – more aptly expresses what is at stake here: viewing *time itself*, the unfolding of time. This is the lesson Lila Mae learns, that she teaches herself. As we will see, only once she has become an adept reader in this sense can she embark on the enterprise of writing; only once she has mastered the art of reading time, can she venture to configure time. However, neither Empiricism nor Intuitionism provides the means for such mastery. While the immanentism of Empiricism cannot penetrate below the surface of appearances, Intuitionism provides depth only at the cost of rendering it transcendent. While Empiricism is down to earth but depthless, Intuitionism gains a different world of heavenly spheres only by forsaking earth. In other words, while Empiricism does not allow for speculation, Intuitionism rescues it at the cost of abstraction, making speculation an empty gesture. In the first case, speculation cannot get off the ground; in the second case, it cannot regain the ground. In *The Intuitionist*'s language, neither method gets at the 'elevatorness' (62) of elevators, as both miss the elevator's essential motility: up and down, up and down. The only option that remains, the option that Lila Mae eagerly seizes, is the option prefigured in all the novel's dualisms, the option embodied by Fulton himself: the method of reading – speculation – has to be an *intuitive empiricism*, or, in Deleuze's terms, a 'superior empiricism' (DR: 69). Only a superior empiricism can reconcile immanence with depth. This indeed is the story of *The Intuitionist* as it renders Lila Mae's metamorphosis from Intuitionist to Superior Empiricist. In the course of this trajectory, what Lila Mae detects, what she ultimately reads in time, are the very dynamics of the *passing* of time. These dynamics are encapsulated in what Deleuze terms the *event*, the 'distribution of singular points' in the idea (DR: 237). It is thus no coincidence that Lila Mae's discovery concerns precisely the nature of the initial accident. Finding out that there were no actants behind the accident of Number Eleven, she detects the accident qua event, as its very own occurrence, the actualisation of singularities – in a word: *becoming*. Once she is equipped with the knowledge of the passing of time, with the knowledge of the event qua becoming, Lila Mae sits down to create a future.

It is by the means of presenting reading as the speculative endeavour par excellence and writing as its correlative act of creation that the novel promotes what Isabelle Stengers has called a speculative constructivism, the affirmative facilitation of events.[7] There is no construction, there is no creation without speculation; and speculation is empty and useless if it is not inherently creative. Only a

Sensational Realism

speculative constructivism, with superior empiricism as its adequate method, results in the production of the new and the effectuation of change. Accordingly, as readers of the novel we should heed its advice and co-embark on its 'stationary journey' (D II: 95) of reading in slow-motion – the viewing of time, the discovery of the event. Only then will we be able to uncover its dark depth underneath the glistening surface, its distribution of singularities, the subterranean forces and sensations grounding its plot with its events and existents. Only then will we uncover the *reality* of the narrative beneath its *realist* surface.

Intuitionism and the Black Box

Both Empiricism and Intuitionism are concerned with epistemology, the knowledge of things. However, they differ in both the methods of acquiring this knowledge and their respective conceptualisations of knowledge itself. The crucial role knowledge plays in *The Intuitionist* also becomes evident in the fact that knowledge and the lack of knowledge are explicitly thematised throughout the novel. Thus, early on, the narrator says this about Lila Mae's inspection of a defective elevator: 'She is right about the overspeed governor. She is never wrong. She doesn't know yet' (9). The assertion that she does not know yet is repeated shortly after in the context of her self-perceived role in departmental politics (15). In general, her state of ignorance concerning the events unfolding is repeatedly emphasised (41, 60, 93). At the same time, it is asserted as often that she is never wrong (197, 227, 255). In fact, at the end of the novel, her initial state of ignorance (in both senses of the term as marking deliberate disregard and simple lack of knowledge) – 'She is never wrong. She doesn't know yet' – has been transformed into the certainty that only lack of knowledge propels expeditions into the unknown – 'She is never wrong. It's her intuition' (255). Being the novel's very last words, they convey how Lila Mae rejects the clarity and distinctness of recognition or detection (conceptual knowledge or knowledge proper), the staple ends of detective fiction, in order to affirm the obscure adventures of speculation (intuitive knowledge or intuition proper). Only now has she become a true intuitionist, a prospector instead of an inspector, on the look-out, mining the future.

The affirmation of speculation maps perfectly on to her activity of writing qua production of the new, as an operation of creation, as nothing new can come from the already known (that is, the recognised and detected). With such an understanding and practice of writing she is, of course, in very good company, as writers have repeatedly understood the mining of the unknown to be *the* mark of creativity. Thus, one of the greatest twentieth-century fiction writers, Thomas Pynchon, remarks in the introduction to his collection of early stories, tellingly titled *Slow Learner*:

> Everybody gets told to write about what they know. The trouble with many of us is that at the early stages of life we think we know everything – or to put it more usefully, we are often unaware of the scope and structure of our ignorance. Ignorance is not just a blank space on a person's mental map. It has contours and coherence, and for all I know rules of operation as well. So as a corollary to writing about what we know, maybe we should add getting familiar with our ignorance, and the possibilities therein for ruining a good story. (Pynchon 1985: 15–16)

In short, Pynchon suggests that we become acquainted with our ignorance and that we probe this ignorance in order to produce a good story. More strongly still, Deleuze asks,

> How else can one write but of those things which one doesn't know, or knows badly? It is precisely there that we imagine having something to say. We write only at the frontiers of our knowledge, at the border which separates our knowledge from our ignorance and transforms the one into the other. Only in this manner are we resolved to write. To satisfy ignorance is to put off writing until tomorrow – or rather, to make it impossible. (DR: xx)

That knowledge acquisition is a slow process is not only underlined by the title of Pynchon's book, but also explicitly mentioned in Whitehead's novel in the passage already partly quoted above: 'Things are happening too fast for [Lila Mae] to convince herself that she does not need time to think, to get to the bottom of things' (56). Getting to the bottom of things takes time. Since, when she gets to the bottom of things, she discovers that this bottom is the event (the accident), the distribution of singularities, becoming, or the unfolding of time itself, this also means that Lila Mae literally needs time to think, as without the conditioning work of time there would be nothing: that is, no thing at all, not even thinking. It is thus that reading and writing qua thought qua the superior empiricist activity of speculative constructivism are invariably bound up with time. Thought probes (reading) and configures (writing) time, but this probing and configuring are itself contingent on time. Thought – reading and writing – is thus but one (human) *expression* of the

Sensational Realism

unfolding of time itself. 'Timing' indeed 'is everything', as Sjoerd van Tuinen puts it in his speculative constructivist discussion of mannerism (Van Tuinen 2014b: 468). It takes time for Lila Mae and, concomitantly, us readers as we accompany her, to reach this point, the revelation of both the event as such and the eventness of reading and writing qua thought: in other words, the revelation of 'timing' as 'the bottom of things'.

Throughout the book, it is made explicitly clear that Empiricism, as its name already indicates, only deals with phenomena (that is, the appearance of things)[8] and Intuitionism with their immaterial conditions. Intuitionism is thus essentially a form of idealism. This becomes evident in the novel's first description of Intuitionism at work:

> This elevator's vibrations are resolving themselves in her mind as an aqua-blue cone. [. . .] The ascension is a red spike, circling around the blue cone, which doubles in size and wobbles as the elevator starts climbing. You don't pick the shapes and their behavior. Everyone has their own set of genies. Depends on how your brain works. Lila Mae has always had a thing for geometric forms. As the elevator reaches the fifth floor landing, an orange octagon cartwheels into her mind's frame. It hops up and down, incongruous with the annular aggression of the red spike. Cubes and parallelograms emerge around the eighth floor, but they're satisfied with half-hearted little jigs and don't disrupt the proceeding like the mischievous orange octagon. The octagon ricochets into the foreground, famished for attention. She knows what it is. (6)

The intuitionist method evokes the abstract ideal conditions of Kantian transcendental idealism evident in its use of abstract forms (the geometrical 'genies') and the fact that these forms are mental (they are 'in her mind'). While the account of Lila Mae's intuitionist practice thus *exemplifies* its transcendental idealism, the first excerpt from Fulton's *Theoretical Elevators* presented in the novel *asserts it explicitly*. In a passage from the first volume, Fulton basically dishes out Kant's Copernican Revolution: 'We conform to objects, we capitulate to them. We need to reverse this order' (37–8).[9] This Kantian transcendentalism, or, in Quentin Meillassoux's words, correlationism,[10] is further accentuated in one of Lila Mae's reminiscences of her days at the Institute for Vertical Transport, when she remembers discussing in class the Fultonian Dilemma of the Phantom Passenger, the question of what happens to the elevator when it is called but the prospective passenger decides to leave before the elevator arrives. How would Fulton answer the problem of the phantom passenger he raises but does not himself resolve? The set of answers the novel provides to this question by means of the contributions of several students to the discussion in class parades four paradigmatic philosophical positions vis-à-vis the dilemma. Thus, Gorse, a fierce advocate of Empiricism and common sense, replies that the elevator arrives, the doors open, they close again and that is it. Johnson, advocating a panpsychist hylozoism, suggests that the elevator arrives but the doors do not open, as there is no incentive for them to do so – 'the vertical imperative does not apply' (101), as he says. Bernard in turn proposes what very much looks like an orthodox Heideggerian pragmatist ontology:

> If, as the index of being tells us, the elevator does not exist when there is no freight, human or otherwise, then I think in this case the doors open and the elevator exists, but only for the loading time. Once the doors close, the elevator returns to nonbeing – 'the eternal quiescence' – until called into service again. (101)

Lila Mae, finally, gives us an explicitly correlationist interpretation:

> 'Fulton is trying to trick the reader. An elevator doesn't exist without its freight. If there's no one to get on, the elevator remains in quiescence. The elevator and the passenger need each other.' [...] 'And if we set up a film camera in the hallway to see what would happen, what would we see when we developed the film, Watson?' [...] 'By leaving the camera there, you've created what Fulton calls "the expectation of freight". The camera is a passenger who declines to get on the elevator, not a phantom passenger. The film would record that the doors open, the elevator waits, and then the doors close.' (101–2)

Existence is here (as in Bernard's case) clearly rendered in terms of the for-us: that is, givenness. The elevator can only be said to be, to exist, when it is given to us; otherwise it remains in 'quiescence' – waiting to be called up and given again.[11] Taking the Intuitionist notion of being to denote existence per se rather than givenness, Gorse replies, 'Just because you can't see it doesn't mean it's not there!' (102). Ironically, this is, of course, precisely the line of argumentation for which Empiricists usually castigate Intuitionists.[12] Accordingly, Professor McKean, who lost one arm in the war, reverses the argument on Gorse by asking whether there is an arm in his jacket sleeve or not. Naturally, Gorse says that there is nothing in McKean's sleeve, to which McKean replies, 'That's the funny thing [...] My arm is gone, but sometimes it's there' (102).

Let us unpack this dispute: Gorse claims that there are things one

Sensational Realism

cannot see, which nevertheless are there. The thing is there existentially, but sometimes it is gone perceptually. McKean in turn claims that there is no-thing which one can plainly see, that sometimes nevertheless is something: that is, the thing is gone existentially, but sometimes it is there perceptually. These are two entirely different claims. While the first claim is about the existence of the unperceived, the second is about the perception of the non-existent; the first claim is about the empirically unverifiable (ironically brought forward by an Empiricist), the second claim about the empirically verifiable but hallucinative. It is no coincidence that McKean juxtaposes Fulton's *phantom passenger dilemma* to *phantom limb sensation*.[13] He thus seems to suggest that the empirically unverifiable has to be probed by the means of intuition (the human means of non-conceptual registration). What sounds counterintuitive – namely, sensing what cannot be sensed – is precisely how Deleuze defines intuition. According to Deleuze, only intuition – direct apprehension – gets at what he calls the *aistheteon*, 'the being of the sensible', in contradistinction to the *aistheton*, 'a sensible being' (DR: 176). As such, the *aistheteon* is *both* what can only be sensed *and* imperceptible (see also Chapter 2 and the Introduction):

> It is not the given but that by which the given is given. It is therefore in a certain sense the imperceptible [*insensible*]. It is imperceptible precisely from the point of view of recognition – in other words, from the point of view of an empirical exercise of the senses in which sensibility grasps only that which also could be grasped by other faculties, and is related within the context of a common sense to an object which also must be apprehended by other faculties. Sensibility, in the presence of that which can only be sensed (and is at the same time imperceptible) finds itself before its own limit, the sign, and raises itself to the level of a transcendental exercise: to the 'nth' power. (DR: 176)

What Deleuze asserts here contra Kant is not only that the empirically imperceptible can be sensed by means of the transcendental use of the faculty of sensibility, but also, more importantly, that this use has the *being of the sensible* as its object, that by which the given is given: in short, the thing in-itself. This is why Deleuze can say that

> Empiricism truly becomes transcendental, and aesthetics an apodictic discipline, only when we directly apprehend in the sensible that which can only be sensed, the very being *of* the sensible: difference, potential difference and difference in intensity as the reason behind qualitative diversity. It is in difference that movement is produced as an 'effect', that

phenomena flash their meanings like signs. The intense world of differences, in which we find the reason behind qualities and the being of the sensible, is precisely the object of a superior empiricism. This empiricism teaches us a strange 'reason', that of the multiple, chaos and difference (nomadic distributions, crowned anarchies). (DR: 68–9)

Superior empiricism thus directly apprehends the *aistheteon*, the thing in-itself, and it discloses it as chaotic and differential. Along these lines, *The Intuitionist*'s juxtaposition of the phantom passenger dilemma with phantom limb sensation advocates that the imperceptible and the hallucinative, that the unknowable and the speculative need to be fused. This is exactly the slogan of Deleuze's superior empiricism: speculate into the unknowable, make yourself a body without organs, embark on a becoming-imperceptible. Or, in the image of *The Intuitionist*, make yourself a phantom limb – pure sensation.

While such speculation is merely indexed via the positing of the Dilemma of the Phantom Passenger (without further discussing it) in the first volume of Fulton's *Theoretical Elevators*, the second volume actively envisions it. In contrast to Volume 1, Volume 2 now reverses the Kantian Copernican Revolution and advocates finding concepts adequate to objects. In a similar manner, it now also drops the earlier dismissal of perfection – 'perfection provides no incentive for improvement, and nothing is perfect' (38) – in order to pursue the perfect elevator actively:[14]

> Ants have it easy for speaking in chemicals. Food. Flight. Follow. Nouns and verbs only, and never in concert. There are no mistakes for there is no sentence except the one nature imposes (mortality). [. . .] The perfect elevator waits while its human freight tries to grab through the muck and find the words. In the black box, this messy business of human communication is reduced to excreted chemicals, understood by the soul's receptors and translated into true speech. (86–7)

Fulton makes clear that words, concepts, need to become adequate to the black box. That this adequation can only happen via the soul's receptors registering excreted *chemicals* and thus being able to converse in the true idiom of chemistry (just like ants) marks the turn from transcendental idealism to a naturalised transcendental. In this vein, intuition aims at reality's direct apprehension by the soul. This direct apprehension of intuition is *anterior to* and *productive of* conceptual knowledge – concepts only come afterwards. In this context, it is worth remembering that *theoria* is the Greek synonym of Latin *speculatio*, and that both *theorein* and *speculari* mean to observe, to look at from an elevated point of view. Etymologically, elevation and speculation go hand in hand. Fulton's book title – *Theoretical Elevators* – is thus a quasi-pleonasm (elevated elevators), doubling and subsuming two inverse movements: up and down. These movements equally apply to both the activity of elevators as they shuttle from floor to floor *and* the activity of speculation as it ascends only in order to turn its attention to what it has left behind, to survey the field below. Given this doubling, one can say that Fulton's programme is *meta-theoretical* as it theorises the nature of speculation itself. It is a speculation on speculation. While Fulton's first volume still dismisses speculation as an impossible task (noumena are unknowable), the second volume takes it fully on board and envisions it as the only viable task (instigating expeditions into and experiments with the unknowable). This trajectory from anti-speculation to speculation finally comes into its own in a passage from Fulton's lost notebook that begins the novel's final section, part two of 'Up'. Since this passage is so central I reproduce it here in full:

> By the ninetieth floor, everything is air, but that's jumping ahead a bit. It starts with the first floor, with dirt, with idiocy. As if we were meant for this. As if this is what fire meant, or language. To crawl about, prey to the dull obviousness of biology, as if we were not meant to fly. To lift. It starts on the first floor, with the grub's-eye view of the world: dirt. What will happen: it will move from the first floor, from safety, from all you've ever known and that takes a bit of recalibrating your imagination. To recognize that come-hither look of possibility. Trust in the cab, made by people like you, trust is the worst of it: it was made by people like you and you are weak and you make mistakes. They have incorrectly imagined this journey, misfigured the equipment necessary. By the fifth floor, the unavoidable consideration of physical laws, the slender fragility of the cables holding the car. Your own fragility. The elevator does not complain, climbs in a bubble of safety, fifteen and sixteen and twenty-six floors and no mishap: well that's no comfort, the accident could come at any time, and the higher up the worse it will be. Could anything survive a fall from this height? They say they have safety devices but things can go wrong and things often go wrong. Giddy at forty – made it this far. And yet still so much to say goodbye to if this is the end. This floor, fifty, where they all wait, those who will not receive apologies, the dead, those who have been wronged and are too low now for reconciliation. Those broken by your passage, the odd ricochets of your passage to this ride: there's nothing to be done. There is only the ride. At seventy-five no turning back. No need for safety devices because there's only up, this ascension.

It is not so bad, this thing, that world falling away below and there are sturdy cables and a fine cab, dependable allies. Even the thought, *if there were only more time*, possesses no weight here, for nothing has weight, it has all been taken care of, the motor can handle any mass differential between the cab and the counterweight, that's its job, and what wish could possibly weigh so much that the machine could not accommodate it? Half enjoying it now. The walls are falling away, and the floor and the ceiling. They lose solidity in the verticality. At ninety, everything is air and the difference between you and the medium of your passage is disintegrating with every increment of the ascension. It's all bright and all the weight and cares you have been shedding are no longer weight and cares but brightness. Even the darkness of the shaft is gone because there is no disagreement between you and the shaft. How can you breathe when you no longer have lungs? The question does not perturb, that last plea of rationality has fallen away floors ago, with the earth. No time, no time for one last thought, *what was the last thing I thought last night before I fell asleep, the very last thought, what was it,* because before you can think that thought everything is bright and you have fallen away in the perfect elevator. (221–3)

This entry from Fulton's notebook is an extended meditation on the risks and anxieties of speculation. It traces the movement of ascension as the movement of theory/speculation, a movement away from the earth, away from dirt, a literal deterritorialisation. Riding the perfect elevator thus amounts to a becoming-elevator, a becoming-imperceptible, to making oneself a body without organs. Correlatively, the highest movement of thought, the most adventurous speculation, leaves the distinctions of rationality and thought behind: becoming-imperceptible ('there is no disagreement between you and the shaft') one has made oneself a body without organs ('you no longer have lungs'). Having thus abandoned the 'last plea of rationality', one has 'fallen away in the perfect elevator' (222–3). The upward movement of speculation brings one down into the very things themselves, beyond experience *of* there is pure becoming with, becoming-elevator. In this, the two movements of upward and downward coincide – as Deleuze puts it, they are 'one and the same movement' (Deleuze 2004a: 24) – and elevation becomes a falling away. This is the moment where epistemology and ontology meet. Importantly – coinciding with the passage's thematic concern with the beyond of rationality – this meeting of epistemology and ontology is rendered in a highly *literary* rather than *logical* style. This is necessarily so given intuition's fundamentally aesthetic (according to Deleuze) and outright phantasmatic (according to McKean) nature. In short, speculation is *artistic* and *art* the pre-eminent site of speculation. Note that saying this is but a paraphrase of 'speculative constructivism'. Essentially, to be a theorist means to be an artist and vice versa. 'Theory' and 'art' merely denote two aspects of one and the same thing: speculation and construction, reading and writing, knowing and creating, having an idea and executing it.[15]

Two temporalities are correlated with these two aspects: the anteriority of the past and the posteriority of the future. Past, in so far as what is being known has already happened, is already catalogued and shelved and what is being read needs to pre-exist the reading. Future, in so far as what is being created is not yet actualised, is yet to come and what is being written does not yet exist. In speculative constructivism, these disjunctive temporalities are merged and form the *temporal* corollary to the *spatial* coincidence of upward and downward movement, of the falling away of elevation. The proper time of speculative constructivism is thus the future past: *what will have been*. Note that this is not the time of prophecy, which revels in the *what will be* of the simple future. Rather, the futurity of the future past is that of *fictional narrative*, which combines fiction-making, the future-oriented act of creation (what will be), with narrative retrospection (what was). In the reading experience, the *what will be* is manifest in the forward-looking suspense of the story's fictional here and now, while the *what was* is incarnated in the backward-looking discourse of the narrative instance. As Avanessian and Hennig have shown, this antinomic double-temporality comes to the fore most explicitly in altermodern *present-tense* narrative fiction. The present tense and its disjunctive synthesis of past and future thus become the hallmark of the altermodern. Avanessian and Hennig have to be lauded for their extremely rich and sophisticated discussion of the altermodern present-tense novel and for bringing to light its fundamental asynchronicity. However, as their analysis is *linguistic–phenomenological* in nature, they align fiction with the actuality of the present (as incarnated in the reading process) rather than with the virtuality of past and future inherent and insistent in every actual present moment. While, from the point of view of the *phenomenon* – that is, the fictional narrative as it is being read, fictionality marks the here and now *within* the story told and narrativity the retrospection of its telling, from the point of view of *metaphysics* – that is, from the perspective of the unfolding of time itself, fiction marks the act of creation unfolding, the virtuality of a future to come, and narrative – in this narrow traditional sense – its recursive capturing.

In this vein, futurity is not and cannot be found *in* the given fictional narrative, as Avanessian and Hennig rightly point out (108). Rather, it is the dimension that the fictional narrative opens up to and facilitates. As such, the altermodern present-tense novel marks not merely *asynchrony*, as Avanessian and Hennig maintain, but also a more fundamental *achronicity*, the 'pure and empty form of time' (DR: 108, 109, 111).[16] My point is precisely that fictional narratives, with altermodernist narratives as particularly salient examples, not only *endorse* the metaphysical point of view but also actually *embody* it. They are frozen time. Hence, a phenomenological treatment is insufficient and needs to be grounded by a metaphysics of time. It is this entire spatiotemporal conundrum that is encapsulated in *The Intuitionist*'s black box.

The black box is first mentioned as

> the infamous design problem from [Lila Mae's] school days: What does the perfect elevator look like, the one that will deliver us from the cities we suffer now, these stunted shacks? We don't know because we can't see inside it, it's something we cannot imagine, like the shape of angels' teeth. It's a black box. [. . .] [T]he next elevator, it is believed, will grant us the sky, unreckoned towers: the second elevation. Of course they're working on the black box; *it's the future*. (61; my emphasis)

The black box is thus introduced as the figure of both the imperceptible and the not yet actualised, in short, virtual futurity. In fact, we need to take the novel at its word here: the black box is the future itself. Constructing the black box thus amounts to bringing about the future. And this is precisely the task that Fulton had embarked on, as a dialogue between Lila Mae and Mr Reed, an Intuitionist official, reveals:

> 'The diary shows that [Fulton] was working on an elevator, and that he was constructing it on Intuitionist principles. From what we can tell from his notes, he finished it. There's a blueprint out there somewhere.' [. . .]
> 'I don't see how that's possible, [. . .] I mean from an engineering standpoint. At its core, Intuitionism is about communicating with the elevator on a nonmaterial basis. "Separate the elevator from elevatorness," right? Seems hard to build something of air out of steel.' [. . .]
> 'They're not as incompatible as you might think' [. . .] 'That's what Volume One hinted at and Volume Two tried to express in its ellipses – a renegotiation of our relationship to objects. To start at the beginning.' [. . .] 'If we have decided that elevator studies – nuts and bolts Empiricism – imagined elevators from a human, and therefore inherently alien point of view, wouldn't the next logical step, after we've adopted the

Sensational Realism

Intuitionist perspective, be to build an elevator the right way? With what we've learned?'

'Construct an elevator from the elevator's point of view.'

'Wouldn't that be the perfect elevator? Wouldn't that be the black box?' [. . .]

Which part of Fulton's writing affected her most? The first line that comes to her head is an incandescent flare: *There is another world beyond this one*. (62–3)

This conversation traces Fulton's engagement in the 'renegotiation of our relationship to objects' and the transformation that this renegotiation took from Volume 1 to Volume 2 to the unfinished Volume 3: while initially Fulton's writings at best hint at the Kantian intelligibility but unknowability of the black box in Volume 1 and in the fashion of negative theology do not directly discourse about it though the black box is at its heart in Volume 2, Volume 3 tackles the task of constructing it head on. The first two volumes can thus indeed be said to be pointing to 'a world beyond this one' with Volume 2's elliptical invocation of this beyond accounting for its 'mystic voice', as Lila Mae characterises it (254). But Lila Mae's thoughts towards the end of the conversation – referring to a trivial remark about the weather by Mr Reed – already index the immanentisation of this beyond *and* the possibility of accessing it: 'This slow debate about the rain: it's not about rain at all, but the fragility of what we know. We're all just guessing. The second elevation, she thinks. The new cities are coming' (64).[17] As it will turn out, Volume 3 affirms precisely this fragility of knowledge and the concomitant necessity of speculation, the essentiality of guesswork, of placing one's bets, of groping one's way through darkness. In other words, since the black box is imperceptible, the only adequate means to 'know' it is to make oneself imperceptible in turn, to embark on a becoming-imperceptible, as indeed the above quoted excerpt from Fulton's notebook demands. It is the trajectory of becoming-imperceptible that Fulton has chosen for himself and that Lila Mae takes up in turn. Such becoming-imperceptible warrants the fusion of the Intuitionist and Empiricist methods, the methods adequate to transcendence and immanence respectively, in order to attain an immanence endowed with depth. This fusion of methods is indeed what Lila Mae discovers in Fulton's work once she has embarked on the Briggsian apprenticeship of reading, once she reads his work differently:[18]

> Lila Mae should have seen the black box and the new cities of the second elevation because Fulton's first writings were technical, arcane investigations of the mechanism. *Toward a System of Vertical Transport* is still a basic text for Empiricist thought. No one knows enough about his history to place his design genius in relief [. . .] The black box explains all. It was Fulton's odd perceptions that made him a technical wiz, his way of finding the unobvious solution that is also the perfect solution. It also allowed him, Lila Mae sees, to pierce the veil of this world and discover the elevator world, and a world needs inhabitants to make it real. The black box is the elevator-citizen for the elevator world. (100)

What characterised Fulton, then, as Lila Mae now recognises, was the extraordinary combination of genius in design and a particular perceptive sensibility and the relation and combination of these assets: his extraordinary perceptiveness made him such a great designer. In short, Fulton was the epitome of a speculative constructivist. And it is the Fultonian lesson of speculative constructivism – how to perceive and how to design; that is, how to read and how to write – that Lila Mae takes to heart.

Speculative Constructivism

Passing and its inherent relation to imperceptibility, difference, and temporality have been singled out as constituting *the* formal and thematic axes around which the novel develops. On the content level, passing emerges as the imperceptible and differential conditioning work of time as it applies to Fulton's life and career and as it applies to Lila Mae's endeavour to get 'to the bottom of things' (56). On the formal level, passing emerges as the novel's imperceptible experimental conditioning of its realist surface. In analogy to Fulton's and Lila Mae's superior empiricism we could thus say that formally the novel proceeds according to an experimental realism. In contradistinction to the overt experimentalism of postmodernist poetics, the covert experimentalism of the novel's realism is captured by Avanessian and Hennig's conceptualisation of altermodernism. Having brought together these diverse strands with their respective emphases on imperceptibility, difference, and temporality, we are now in a position to qualify this stealth experimentalism better.

Sitting in her room at the Intuitionist House and waiting for Natchez, the Intuitionist House's temporary African American servant who claims to be Fulton's nephew and offers to help (but will

Sensational Realism

eventually turn out to be an Arbo corporate spy), Lila Mae contemplates elevators and Intuitionist theory:

> She disassembles elevators in her mind and imagines that there is a discrepancy between the mass of the elevator before disassembly and after. That this mass returns when the elevator is reassembled. Fulton did not write that, she extrapolated it from the second volume of *Theoretical Elevators*. [...] She thinks her creations adhere to the spiritual side of Fulton's words, while the rest of the movement gets dizzy in the more recondite apocrypha. An unforeseen loss in mass. A mystery. (132–3)

Lila Mae's mereotopological reflections about elevators also hold for the novel she appears in. Mereotopology fuses mereology, the study of part–whole relations, with topology, the description of spatial connections (Casati and Varzi 1999: 2, 4–5, 11, 30) and thus infuses mereology with an account of connectivity which it otherwise lacks. In this vein, the entire narrative is apparently mereotopological: one narrative (whole) – two parts ('Down' and 'Up') – each of these parts has another two parts (part 1 and part 2) – these parts in turn have many sub-parts with their boundaries clearly marked by three asterisks. This is an exact enumeration of the novel's parts and sub-parts:

Down, part 1: 18 sub-parts
Down, part 2: 19 sub-parts
Up, part 1: 12 sub-parts
Up, part 2: 11 sub-parts

One might continue to determine further sub-parts such as the recounting of particular events and existents, but this is where things start to get fuzzy, since no clear distinctions can be drawn any longer. On this molecular level, mereotopology no longer suffices to describe the narrative's structure. On this level, we can no longer discern parts (the mereology aspect) that connect (the topology aspect) in order to forge a whole. Rather, elements incessantly fold into one another in such a way that the same existents (for example, characters) and events (for example, the Fanny Briggs accident) pop up throughout the diverse parts and sub-parts, are reshuffled and rearranged. Just like Fulton's elevator, *The Intuitionist* amounts to more than the sum of its individual parts. This is so because the spatial aspect of the novel's structure (clear demarcations of space with clear boundaries) is complicated by its temporality. Time is something that neither mereology nor topology nor mereotopology can satisfactorily account for – mereotopology can only describe it in terms of parts and their connections but not in its essential unfolding. Mereotopology only sets in after the fact, once an occurrence or event has taken place, has unfolded. It is thus but an instrument of representation.[19] Analogously, the apparent mereotopological set-up of the novel can only be diagnosed as such after the narrative has unfolded. It is not the parts and their connectivity that constitute the narrative, but the narrative's unfolding that constitutes its parts. In other words, mereotopological identity is grounded on relational difference, the differential elements and relations of becoming: that is, relations engender parts and wholes. Or, put differently, in the relation between parts and wholes what comes first is precisely their relationality; the relation precedes and produces its terms.

While the novel's surface identitarian mereotopology only reluctantly reveals its ground in differential time, the narrative's appurtenance to the alternate history genre explicitly emphasises temporality. That counterfactual novels such as alternate history novels are intimately bound up with time lies in their very nature. Avanessian and Hennig make clear that, in contradistinction to mere historical novels, the temporality involved in altermodern alternate history novels does not just concern the past, however.

> Altermodern *what-if-novels* [they say] do not just modify (on the level of *story*) our image of the past *or* (on the level of *plot*) the past itself, they do not just pose the question of access to the past, but the much more fundamental question of the formation of time, including that of the past. (Avanessian and Hennig 2012: 87–8; my translation)

In Deleuzian terms, they precisely enquire into the fracturing 'pure and empty form of time' (DR: 108, 109, 111). Thus, in altermodern counterfactual narratives such as alternate history novels, time is essentially out of joint (a fracture; a caesura) and a pervasive achronicity holds sway. In *The Intuitionist*, this fundamental achronicity of the counterfactual set-up becomes evident in an analepsis to Intuitionist House and to Lila Mae engaged in rereading Fulton's books:

> She understood that the library *would* be empty *if* these scholars *knew* Fulton was colored. No one *would have* worshipped him, his books probably *would* never *have been* published at all, or *would* exist under a different name, the name of the plagiarizing white man Fulton *had been* fool enough to share his theories with. She read the words in her lap, horizontal thinking in a vertical world is the race's curse, and hated him. She

had been misled. What she had taken for pure truth had been revealed as merely filial agreement. And thus no longer pure. Blood agrees, it cannot help but agree, and how can you get any perspective on that? Blood is destiny in this land, and she did not choose Intuitionism, as she formerly believed. It chose her. (151; my emphases)

Lila Mae's counterfactual musings, as grammatically marked by the conditional mood, denote but a virtuality. The counterfactual essentially falls out of (chronological) time. But this falling out of time, its fundamental achronicity, precisely sheds light on the unfolding of time, on how things came to be what they are. Counterfactual achronicity thus serves to determine temporal facts. In analogy and with recourse to this deployment of counterfactuals in determining factual states of affairs, Jon Cogburn and Mark Allan Ohm recently suggested the following relation between truth and fiction:

> [N]ote that counterfactuals are already in a sense fictional since they concern states of affairs that are not actual. Many true stories about what the actually existing hammer would do involve states of affairs that will never actually come to be and new future objects that will never exist. It is true that one could use this hammer to build a birdhouse that one never does actually build.
>
> Thus [. . .] fictions are necessary in a more originary sense than what we have claimed [. . .] The good writer's ability to discern what would really happen were some set-up incarnate is just a development of an ability that is fundamental to all cognition. Non-fictional, true propositions only get their content because the concepts involved can occur in true fictions. But then fictions themselves are genetically necessary in the very strongest sense. One could not have non-fiction without also having fiction. (Cogburn and Ohm 2014: 224)

Let me stress that Cogburn and Ohm rely on a representational account of fiction. Their conclusion that 'one could not have non-fiction without also having fiction' is a statement about epistemology and only applies to 'cognition', as they themselves make clear. According to Cogburn and Ohm, non-actual fiction sheds light on actual facts. In this context, it is important to note that Lila Mae's counterfactual thinking is employed precisely to discuss the status of truth, and that this discussion is doubled up and raised to a metalevel by dint of being an instance of counterfactual reasoning in a counterfactual novel. In this vein, Lila Mae's counterfactual musings can be read as metafictional commentary on the counterfactual set-up of the novel. Thus, the task is to determine what truth is established by (1) Lila Mae's counterfactual reasoning and (2) the counterfactual discussion of truth within a counterfactual set-up. Obviously, the answer to (1) is race as *the* factor of social predetermination in this society at this time and its (seeming) inescapability ('blood is destiny in this land'). As to (2), the answer looks somewhat like this: if such a world were incarnate, blood would mean destiny. Since this world, even though it is counterfactual, looks strikingly like the twentieth-century United States, the novel basically suggests that blood *is* destiny in the United States *today*.[20] This is only one part of its truth, however, since the novel precisely tells the story of Lila Mae's endeavour *to escape the seeming inescapability* by means of constructing the black box, by bringing about the second elevation and thus *creating the future*. While changing the temporal status quo and thus the present is impossible since the present simply is what it is, creating the future is not. In fact, creating the future *is* inducing change. This, then, is the truth the novel at hand produces. And it is on this point – creating the future by inducing change – that the novel's thematic and formal concerns converge so as to be indistinguishable.

Bringing about change, however, presupposes the affirmation of the irreversibility of the present moment. This diagnosis is confirmed in the opening scenes of 'Up', the second part of the novel, when Lila Mae attends the Funicular Follies, the elevator inspectors' annual party. The narrative recounts how Lila Mae manages to enter the building unnoticed and how she remains unseen throughout the party: due to her skin colour, she is mistaken for a servant. The point is reinforced when the narrative states, 'This is her first Funicular Follies. She understood that this night was for all the Department but her' (153). Lila Mae takes advantage of this invisibility. Accordingly, when, in her newly acquired role as servant, she is ordered to bring one of her white colleagues a new fork, the man does not recognise her. This image of imperceptibility is amplified by the fact that Lila Mae picks up a *used* fork, which she cleans only superficially: 'She has wiped off any visible remains of this new fork's recent trip through the grease and rinds of the garbage pail and envisions the extravagant bacteria metropolis that will thrive in his stomach. Invisible and insidious. Like her' (153). This explicit analogy between Lila Mae and the invisible bacteria on the apparently clean fork not only casts African Americans and people of colour as invisible, thus paying homage to *the* great twentieth-century African American novel, Ralph Ellison's *Invisible Man*, but also twists Ellison's image of passivity so that Lila Mae becomes a genuine danger that contagiously spreads through the city.[21] This twist is also very much gendered: Invisible Woman is not just that, but her invisibility is dangerous to the status quo. The status quo has been infested, and the disease spreads stealthily. In this vein, *The Intuitionist* inverts one of the *Invisible Man*'s narrator's most famous statements and affirms that the truth is the darkness and darkness is the truth. In Whitehead's narrative, Ellison's eternal return of the same as incarnated in the novel's circular structure has become the eternal return of the different, an open spiral instead of a closed circle. One could thus say that the novel's formal structure is analogous to the used fork. Apparently shiny and clean (that is, realist), it is infested by invisible impurity (that is, experimentalism). This point is taken up and reinforced again in the novel's very last pages, which depict Lila Mae's rejection of elevator *inspection* in favour of *creation* as she embarks on the construction of the black box. The fact that this construction is manifested in *writing* is yet another inversion of Ellison's novel, which ends with the protagonist abandoning writing. While in *Invisible Man* writing in its passivity has no impact on the actual course of events and needs to be abandoned, in *The Intuitionist* Lila Mae's writing of Volume 3 of *Theoretical Elevators* not only emphasises the production of the new and the facilitation of the future but also the very means of this production: namely, *composition* in the sense of *emplotment*: the very activity of the writer and storyteller, the arranging of matter such that it results in a story. The ending of *The Intuitionist* thus fuses the construction of the future with the composition that writing constitutes envisioning the *emplotment of the future*. Whitehead *repeats* Ellison, but with a difference. Indeed, difference and repetition govern the entire novel. In Whitehead's differential repetition of Ellison, Lila Mae emerges as the figure of repetition itself as she repeats thrice: Fanny Briggs in her apprenticeship of reading, Fulton in his constructivist writing, Invisible Man in his imperceptibility. This mania of repetition is the exact opposite of the incapacitating neurotic repetition compulsion of Freudian psychoanalysis:[22] 'The past (as condition) and the present (as agent) are here transformed into dimensions of the future (the creation of the new): repetition as metamorphosis' (Smith 2013: n. p.). Lila Mae qua figure of repetition is the embodiment of this futural metamorphosis. By extension, and by dint of Whitehead repeating Ellison and Invisible Woman repeating Invisible Man, Whitehead's novel can thus also be understood as the futural transformation of African American literature.[23]

Let us return to Lila Mae and the Funicular Follies and observe how the narrative depicts Lila Mae's recognition and affirmation of the irreversibility of the status quo. Having just witnessed a blackface minstrel performance by two of her colleagues and the ensuing standing ovations, Lila Mae returns to the kitchen:

> In the kitchen, the other colored workers do not speak on what they have just seen. [...] Lila Mae does not mention it either, telling herself that it is because she does not know the silent women she has been working with, whom she has not talked to all evening for her concentration on the Follies. She tricks herself that that is why she does not mention what she has seen, tells herself it is because she is undercover and speaking to them might trip her up, a dozen other reasons. She thinks the other women are so beaten that they cannot speak of the incident, when all of them, Lila Mae included, are silent for the same reason: because this is the world they have been born into, and there is no changing that. (157)

Indeed, there is no changing this fact; there is no changing that she has been born into *this* world. This recognition amounts to an expression of Lila Mae's *amor fati*, the affirmation of the necessary contingency of life into which she has been thrown. In analogy to the relation between Deleuzian and Freudian repetition, Deleuzian *amor fati* – 'to will the event' (LS: 170) – is the exact opposite of fatalism, as it is this very affirmation of *amor fati* that makes it possible to induce change. Only once Lila Mae embraces *amor fati*, only once she affirms the current state of affairs in their contingency, will she have overcome the fatal deadlock of the status quo and be able to *produce* change. It is through recasting the role of writing that *The Intuitionist*'s Invisible Woman becomes the affirmative inversion of Ellison's essentially sceptical Invisible Man.

Another seemingly minor reminiscence illustrates what is at stake in this production of change. In an analepsis to Lila Mae's first days in the metropolis, the novel tells us how, having lost her way and looking for the subway entrance, she meets a black man called Freeport Jackson and lets herself be convinced to join him for a drink in a nearby hotel bar. During their ensuing conversation, it occurs to her that while '[s]he had long reckoned on the promise of verticality, its present manifestation and the one heralded by Fulton's holy verses', she 'had never given a thought to the citizens. Who the people are who live here' (176). Lila Mae's encounter with Freeport Jackson serves to portray these people, notably *her* people, as Freeport Jackson embodies them. In this context, it is telling that Freeport Jackson is a salesman selling skin lightener and hair straightener, and thus means to alter the appearance of things, not the things themselves. In addition, these means serve to disguise a particular appearance so that the thing disguised – the appearance of blackness – fits in better with the respective inimical milieu. This, indeed, is only *apparent* change changing nothing. Quite on the contrary, it caters towards the status quo. In order to induce *real* change, something else is needed, something that changes the milieu and thus inaugurates the city and the people to come. This seemingly insignificant episode with Freeport Jackson serves to highlight that such change is not possible with the people who are already here, people like Freeport.[24] What is needed is a new people, a people to come, and this new people and its new city are contained in Fulton's black box. They are the people of the future. This is confirmed in a passage from Fulton's second volume of *Theoretical Elevators*:

> *The race sleeps in this hectic and disordered century. Grim lids that will not open. Anxious retinas flit to and fro beneath them. They are stirred by dreaming the contract of the hallowed verticality, and hope to remember the terms on waking. The race never does, and that is our curse.* The human race she thought formerly. Fulton has a fetish for the royal 'we' throughout *Theoretical Elevators*. But now – who's 'we'? (186)

'We' is the people who sleep, the people who are here. But while Fulton thus acknowledges that the grounds on which to act are presently lacking, the very fact that he put this acknowledgement into writing and offered it up to be read displays 'a speculative trust in a future ground, a vision of "a new earth and people that do not yet exist"' (Van Tuinen 2014b: 467).

Just as with Freeport Jackson and the people to come, the existing metropolis will not do and must give way to the city to come:

> She hadn't considered all the implications of the second elevation. They will have to destroy this city once we deliver the black box. The current bones will not accommodate the marrow of the device. They will have to raze the city and cart off the rubble to less popular boroughs and start anew. What will it look like. The shining city will possess untold arms and a thousand eyes, *mutability itself*, constructed of yet-unconjured plastics. It will float, fly, fall, have no need of steel armature, have a liquid spine, no spine at all. Astronomer–architects will lay out the heliopolis so that it charts the progress of the stars through heaven. (199; my emphasis)

The city to come not only is imagined here as mutability itself – that is, virtual becoming – but also is referred to as 'heliopolis', thus alluding both to the original Egyptian name of ancient Egypt's Heliopolis, 'Place of Pillars', a name more than suitable for the vertical future

Lila Mae envisions, and, more importantly, to the Enneads (the nine Gods) and the respective Heliopolian cosmogony as captured by its Greek name, 'City of the Sun' – that is, to the solar mattering of matter itself, the becoming of matter. What Lila Mae envisions here is thus indeed the creativity of time itself, the different/*c*iation of virtual elements and relations, the distribution of singularities contained in Fulton's black box. If the black box, the imperceptible, is the future, then the novel's Afrofuturist astronomer–architects are the builders of an entirely new world, a new cosmos. The metropolis gives way to the heliopolis, the principle and centre of the 'mother city', gives way to unprincipled and decentred stellar becoming, the earthly ground to 'universal ungrounding' (DR: 114).

The most pressing question is, of course, that of how to bring about the future, how to induce change, how to construct this new city and how to invent the people to come. The answer is contained in Fulton's notebook: '*It works, and all that is left is to deliver to the cities. [. . .] [I]t required principles – a way of thinking – I thought I had abandoned*' (206). The way of thinking Fulton thought he had abandoned is, of course, Empiricism (after all, he used to be an Empiricist himself). It is in these two lines that Fulton makes unmistakably clear that, in order to design and produce the perfect elevator, Intuitionism and Empiricism need to be fused. Thus, when Ben Urich, a journalist working for the most important elevator business journal, *Lift*, calls Lila Mae out for her alleged naivety, Lila Mae knows better:

> Did you think this was all about philosophy? Who's the better man – Intuitionism or Empiricism? No one really gives a crap about that. Arbo and United are the guys who make the things. That's what really matters. The whole world wants to get vertical, and they're the guys that get them there. If you pay the fare. (208)

Indeed, *The Intuitionist*, by advocating a superior empiricism, shows that neither pure idealist thought, nor experience-led empiricism, nor the pragmatics of political intrigue suffices to bring about the perfect elevator. Lila Mae will contest and counter the economy-driven creation of the future precisely by fusing the two philosophical schools, by forging a method out of the disjunctive synthesis of empiricism and intuitionism. In the end, when she sends off the remnants of Fulton's notebooks to both parties, she does this in awareness of the fact that the industry might be the one who literally makes the things, but only in so far as they rely on a *plan* to build. The execution of actually building things is contingent on the *design* according to which these things are to be built. Lila Mae is that designer. That she also becomes the builder, that she in the end assumes her role as speculative constructivist, is instigated by her discovery of the catastrophic accident.

The Catastrophic Accident

When Lila Mae finally returns to the Fanny Briggs Memorial Building to inspect once more the site of the accident (another return and another repetition) she finds '[n]othing', and this nothing 'tell[s] the truth': namely, that the Fanny Briggs incident 'was a catastrophic accident' (227). Number Eleven's free fall was nothing but a chance happening, a sudden overturning and reversal of fortune (the etymological sense of catastrophe): that is, the eruption of the new. It is this contingency, this accident, this event, or, rather, contingency and eventness *in general* with this particular accident just being one manifestation of the general contingency of the event as such, that propelled and pulled the entire narrative. Actual narratives are (un)grounded by chance happenings (within a particular milieu). It is accidents that make up the essence of things, events that determine their actants, a gathering of singularities and their subsequent eruption that bring about states of affairs. Milieu in this case means: racism, segregation, sexism, paternalism, chauvinism, institutional politics. Within this milieu the singular event, the catastrophic accident erupts:

> Something gave in the elevator for no reason and its brother components gave in, too. A catastrophic accident. The things that emerge from the black, nether reaches of space and collide here, comets that connect with this frail world after countless unavailing ellipses. Emissaries from the unknowable. (227)

The catastrophic accident denotes the unknowable, the in-itself and is thus of cosmological scope. Note that while the reason for the accident is not determinable, this does not entail that the catastrophic accident is a manifestation of Meillassoux's principle of unreason – that nothing happens for a reason, that anything can happen without a reason – since the principle of unreason is precisely the correlative to Meillassoux's claim to absolute knowledge.[25] Here, however, having no reason merely means that the reason is unknowable, not inexistent. The catastrophic accident, the event, *is* the unknowable.

And it is precisely the unknowable that triggers speculation in the first place. As van Tuinen puts it, 'Only what has no essence or reason becomes a matter of speculation' (Van Tuinen 2014b: 467).

Lila Mae registers the ineptitude of both Intuitionism and Empiricism in living up to the event and the imperatives of speculation: 'What her discipline and Empiricism have in common: they cannot account for the catastrophic accident' (227). The reason for this is that, in fact, both schools miss the elevatorness of elevators. While Empiricism negates a distinct elevatorness apart from its empirical constitution and set-up (the elevator simply is its extensive elements and relations), Intuitionists locate the elevatorness in its correlation to the passenger, a correlation that transcends both passenger and elevator (the elevator becomes its co-relation; on this point, see my discussion on the phantom passenger dilemma above), thereby missing the thing in-itself. In order to capture the elevatorness of the elevator one has to try and penetrate the darkness of the unknowable and unearth the occurrence of the elevator, the event that constitutes the elevator. Things in themselves are *intensive events*, are their very own occurrences. In order to reach the unknowable realm of elevators (and things) one has to join the Empiricists' immanent extensity with the Intuitionists' transcendent intensity in order to forge an intuitive empiricism, an elevated empiricism, a superior empiricism: an empiricism of immanent intensity. In short, one has to make Intuitionism's otherworldliness thisworldly, to make it inhere in the things themselves rather than constituting some sort of transcendent ether. Or, from the point of view of empiricism, one has to implant the realm of the intensive at the heart of the extensive, equipping every actual thing with its virtual germ and germination. This is precisely what Lila Mae gets at when she recapitulates her inspection of Number Eleven:

> Did the genies [the elevator's spirits] try to warn her, were they aware, twitching at times, forbidden to make plain their knowledge but subtly attempting to alert her through the odd wiggle and shimmy. She wouldn't know what to look for. Whatever signal the genies may or may not have dispatched through her darkness went unread. She imagines the proximity of the catastrophe sending ripples through the darkness from the future, agitating the genies with impending violence. It's irrelevant. She didn't see it. (227–8)

What Lila Mae could not penetrate is precisely the *virtual event*, the pending catastrophe, the future. The ever-approaching ripples in the darkness, the future to come: that is precisely the Deleuzian process of different/ciation, the gathering and agglomeration of singularities, futurity as such. In order to reach this realm, what is needed is *amor fati*, the willing of the event.

Unsurprisingly, the investigators at the last incident of total free fall in the US thirty-five years prior to the Fanny Briggs incident 'never found any reason for it. Total freefall. What happens when too many impossible events occur, when multiple redundancy is not enough. Scratching heads over this mystery of the new cities' (228). No reason can be given for total free fall because it is not predictable, it is a contingent eruption within the given occurring 'against probability [...] because it is beyond calculation. It's fate. They won't find any reason for this crash, trace the serial number back to the manufacturer, interrogate an arthritic mechanic's trembling fingers. This was a catastrophic accident' (228). Total free fall, in Heideggerian fashion, makes palpable the fact that every thing is its very own reason in so far as the reason cannot be deduced from any thing outside the thing in question (manufacturer, mechanic's fingers); every real thing has a real reason inherent in it. This reason cannot be calculated probabilistically by the means of pure reason for the very fact that it is *singular* – it has nothing to do with probability. This insight constitutes Lila Mae's epiphany as she 'reroute[s] the incident to her own purposes: it was a catastrophic accident, and a message to her. It was her accident' (228–9). Making this her accident precisely implies going beyond both the Empiricists and the Intuitionists, trying to penetrate the unknowable: 'Even Fulton stayed away from the horror of the catastrophic accident: even in explicating the unbelievable he never dared broach the unknowable. Lila Mae thinks: out of fear' (229). Lila Mae is fearless; she affirms all the risk inherent in experimenting with the unknowable, the risk of speculation. She affirms the catastrophic accident, embraces *amor fati*.

When, towards the end, the narrative announces the successful completion of Lila Mae's Briggsian apprenticeship – 'In the last few days she has learned how to read, like a slave does, one forbidden word at a time' (230) – this announcement implies that, now, she possibly would be able to read the genies that went unread (see the quotation above). Lila Mae's becoming-Fanny Briggs captures at once the novel's thematics of racial uplift and its formal enactment of its speculative 'falling away'. Fanny Briggs is the figure that is being disfigured in this narrative – a disfiguration that has already taken place before the novel gets off the ground both in the collapse of Number Eleven and the excision, apart from this little trace concerning reading, of Fanny Briggs from the narrative. Fanny Briggs is thus the disfigured figure that has to be read and that prompts writing, the name of the event. Lila Mae's Briggsian apprenticeship thus amounts to an exercise in *amor fati* entailing the hard labour of reading things and the experimentation of writing, the two divergent exercises of speculative constructivism, in order to immerse herself in the 'mutability itself' that the heliopolis, the city to come – that is, virtuality and the future itself – constitutes. Only then will the production of the new, will change be possibly effectuated.

As the narrative asserts, '[c]atastrophic accidents are a-million-in-a-million occurrences, not so much what happens very seldom but what happens when you subtract what happens all the time' (230). They are the remarkable happenings among the unremarkable ones, singular events amongst regular occurrences.

> They are, historically, good or bad omens, depending on the time and place, urging reform, a quest for universal standards of elevator maintenance, or instructing the dull and plodding citizens of modernity that there is a power beyond rationality. That the devil still walks the earth and architecture is no substitute for prayer, for cracked knees and desperate barter with the gods. (231)

Catastrophic accidents are those encounters that force us to think, that put us on to the path of speculation that leads beyond the (Kantian) representational architectonic, beyond the light of rationality and into the darkness of the earth (or elevator shaft), the ground infested with demonic spirits, the things' 'fundus animae' (Baumgarten 1963: §511, 176), their 'dark ground' (Schelling 2006: SW I/7 358; 27), sensations and forces (Deleuze).

Against Urich's allegations and against Arbo's self-conception that 'Arbo creates the future' while 'inspectors' merely 'serve the future' (246), the novel shows that neither inspectors nor companies create the future – only theorist–artists do, theorist–artists in the sense of those who take the risk and embark on expeditions into unknown darkness in order to return with something new. In this sense *theorein*, or *speculari*, is tantamount to the praxis of creation and theorist–artist becomes the name of *the forger of the future*. To be a theorist–artist is to be a believer

> in a dispositional basis for future existence, thought and action and to be transformed by this belief. In other words, it is to speculate on the virtual

becoming of what is actual, i.e., the real ideas inherent in the interstices of any actual situation. Whether in philosophy, science or art, speculative thinking is an art of pure expression or efficacy, an art of precipitating events: an art that detects and affirms the possibility of other reasons insisting in a concrete situation as so many virtual forces that have not yet had the chance to emerge but whose presence can be trusted upon to make a difference. (Van Tuinen 2014b: 438–9)

Accordingly, Lila Mae enjoys the fact that the new room into which she has moved at the end of the novel in order to complete Fulton's book looks out on to a factory, as she herself has become a factory of ideas, the facilitator of the composition and emplotment of singularities to bring about the second elevation:

> Much of what happened would have happened anyway, but it warns her to know that the perfect elevator reached out to her and told her she was of its world. That she was a citizen of the city to come [. . .] She returns to the work. She will make the necessary adjustments. It will come. She is never wrong. It's her intuition. (255)

Lila Mae indeed makes all the difference, as she is literally a difference maker. Embracing *amor fati* and becoming-imperceptible, she has attained the event, the passing of time. Lila Mae has become yet another name and yet another manifestation of the catastrophic accident.

Notes

1. Let me note that I have strong reservations about this term due to Saldívar's ill-informed and misconceived appropriation of the eponymous philosophical movement. Let me just mention four points, the first two symptomatic, the last two substantial, that confirm my diagnosis: (1) Saldívar enlists Alain Badiou instead of Iain Hamilton Grant, whom he forgets (while mentioning all other founding members) as a speculative realist, which is simply wrong (Saldívar 2013: 5); tellingly, the two times Grant's name appears, it is misprinted: once in a footnote, which refers to him as 'Iaian', and once more in the bibliography, where he is merely listed as Iain Hamilton; (2) he attributes the term 'weird realism' to all of the original four thinkers, even though it applies only to Harman's philosophy; (3) he conflates speculative realism and object-oriented philosophy (13–14); and (4) he suggests that 'weird [. . .] realism [. . .] posits the speculative possibility that we may be able to imagine the conditions under which the thing in itself and its phenomenal form might coincide' (14), which is the description of a Hegelian *idealist*

programme and precisely what speculative realism ardently argues *against*.
2. Curiously enough, this crucial feature of the novel has not garnered any attention.
3. Note that this characterisation goes against Allison Gibbons's definition of altermodernist fiction in her entry for *The Routledge Companion to Experimental Literature* (Gibbons 2012).
4. Critics diverge in their assessment of the novel's timeframe and setting. While Lauren Berlant speaks of a 1964 New York and Elam more cautiously situates the events in a 'post-civil rights era metropolis with distinctly pre-civil rights era racist sensibilities', Michael Bérubé points out several inconsistencies which support the view that setting and time suggest an even more generic twentieth-century US metropolis (Berlant 2008: 850; Elam 2011: 118; Bérubé 2004: 169). I follow Bérubé here. His observation is also very much in line with Avanessian and Hennig's emphasis on altermodern asynchronicity. Both these insights play into my reading of the novel's counterfactuality further below.
5. This essential feature has, of course, already been noted. See, for example, Alison Russell, who explicitly states that '[d]uplicity is at the core of the novel' (Russell 2007: 48).
6. Against Saldívar, who believes that 'this is not a narrative of passing' and that 'passing is the least interesting aspect of this story' (Saldívar 2013: 10), I side with Elam, who stresses the thematic *and* formal significance of passing in the novel. However, when conceptualising passing as the passing from one world to another, she fails to elucidate the temporality at the heart of these passages (Elam 2011: 119–24). As I will show, the passing at stake is not that between worlds (social, political, theological) but that of time itself.
7. The concept is developed in several of Stengers's articles, some of which are conveniently brought together in a German publication that carries the concept in its title – *Spekulativer Konstruktivismus* (Stengers 2008).
8. Perhaps the most striking passage in this respect appears at the beginning of part two, 'Up', during the account of singer Great Luigi's performance at the Funicular Follies, the elevator inspectors' annual party, when the narrator says about the arch-Empiricist department chair: 'Chancre makes a great show of mouthing the words with the tenor [the Great Luigi] even though it's obvious from a cursory inspection that he's never heard note one of this song before. *Appearance is everything*' (149; my emphasis).
9. This is the respective famous passage from Kant's preface to his *Critique of Pure Reason*:

> Up to now it has been assumed that all our cognition must conform to the objects; but all attempts to find out something about them *a priori* through concepts that would extend our cognition have, on this pre-supposition,

come to nothing. Hence let us once try whether we do not get further with the problem of metaphysics by assuming that the objects must conform to our cognition, which would agree better with the requested possibility of an *a priori* cognition of them, which is to establish something about objects before they are given to us. This would be just like the first thought of Copernicus, who, when he did not make good progress in the explanation of the celestial motions if he assumed that the entire celestial host revolves around the observer, tried to see if it might not have greater success if he made the observer revolve and left the stars at rest. (Kant 1998: B/XVI)

10. In his *Continental Realism* Paul Ennis has convincingly shown that correlationism primarily targets transcendentalism (Ennis 2011).
11. Note that 'quiescence' marks the fact that Intuitionism does not amount to a full-blown Berkeleyan *esse est percipi*. Quiescence is not non-existence, but non-givenness. It is thus a synonym of the Kantian noumenon, the thing in-itself that is thinkable but not knowable.
12. Both the irony and the misreading it is based on also seem to escape the Intuitionists themselves as Lila Mae takes Gorse's comment to exemplify the 'fundamental battle' (102) between the two schools.
13. Vilanayur Ramachandran and Sandra Blakeslee's *Phantoms in the Brain* is the classic account of phantom limb sensation (Ramachandran and Blakeslee 1988).
14. Even though Fulton's almost Heideggerian 'Kehre' is explicitly pointed out in the novel, most commentators tend to treat the *Theoretical Elevators* as a continuous project. This conflation covers up the internal conflicting tendencies of Intuitionism and thus loses sight of the school's dynamism, which to a large extent also accounts for Lila Mae's own transformation. This conflation is particularly regrettable since one thus also loses sight of the novel's most acute concern, that of *transformation as such*: metamorphosis, becoming, the passing of time.
15. Van Tuinen's forthcoming book, *Matter, Manner, Idea: Deleuze and Mannerism*, discusses precisely this relation with respect to mannerism and its emphasis on both *ingegno* and *disegno*, *idea* and *maniera*; that is, the brain and the hand, the ideal and the manual. In this context, it should not be surprising that it is with mannerism that *theoretical* training is introduced to art practice, as manifested in the establishment of art schools:

> [Art] begins to develop its own, strictly artistic knowledge that is to be taught in special academies, e.g., the Florentine Academy of the *arti del disegno* which transformed art from studio craft into philosophical study, accompanied by critical literature on aesthetic problems. For the first time, concepts of art, criticism and art history are articulated as such and form a kind of closed circuit – a discourse – in which artists inspire critics and historians who write for well-trained practitioners. (Van Tuinen 2014b: 441)

It is also in this context that Lila Mae's obsession with and the text's several references to Fulton's handwriting, as well as the simple fact that Fulton's lost notebook is written by hand, assume additional significance (205, 253, 254). The first of these passages even explicitly links ideas to their execution by the hand: 'She [...] practiced Fulton's handwriting for hours. [...] For an entire semester Lila Mae wrote her class notes in that hand [...] As if the mechanics of delivering the idea to the physical world were half the process' (205).

16. It is telling that in their appropriation of Deleuze, Avanessian and Hennig stop short of discussing the passive syntheses of time, particularly the third, the synthesis of the future, as they do not believe the passive syntheses to impinge on their analysis (Avanessian and Hennig 2012: 253). Their focus on the active syntheses indeed ties in with their phenomenological project. However, their project thus misses out on the deeper metaphysical ramifications. This difference in outlook can also be cashed out in the following manner: where Avanessian and Hennig emphasise language's *poietic* capacity to structure time, I hold that time ultimately structures language. In my reading, language assumes *aisthetic* and *noetic* functions, but ontological *poiesis* is a matter of time alone.

17. This insight is ultimately responsible for Lila Mae's change of mind. At the end of this conversation she is no longer content with finding out what happened at the Fanny Briggs Memorial Building and boldly announces: '"I want to find the black box"' (65).

18. This difference in reading is, of course, triggered by the very discovery of Fulton's own imperceptible secret: that he was half-black. It is this imperceptible difference manifested in Fulton's passing that makes all the difference. The lesson Lila Mae learns pertains not so much to the fact that Fulton was of mixed race but to the fact of *passing*: the imperceptibility of difference and the difference that imperceptibility itself makes. The same insight accounts for Fulton's very own transformation. While he initially penned Volume 1 as 'a joke' (232, 236), out of resentment fuelled by the imposed necessity and consequent ramifications of his passing, the very fact that his blackness had to remain imperceptible in order for him to progress in his life and career as an elevator inspector, he finally comes to *affirm* imperceptibility. This affirmation results in Volumes 2 (Intuitionism proper) and 3 (Superior Empiricism) respectively.

19. Note that Casati and Varzi do not claim otherwise. On the contrary, and as the subtitle of their book makes clear, they are explicitly concerned with the representation of space, our 'spatial competence' (Casati and Varzi 1999: 2). On the relation of mereotopology to time, see particularly their Chapter 10.

20. On the novel's setting and temporal framework, see my comments in note 4 above.
21. *The Intuitionist*'s reference (and reverence) to Ellison's novel has, of course, long been noted. It is even mentioned on the book's cover blurb. However, no one has ventured to propose the specific relation I suggest here. In addition to *Invisible Man*, Russell identifies several other precursors she takes Whitehead's novel to be 'Signifyin(g) on' (Russell 2007: 59), most notably Pynchon's *The Crying of Lot 49* and Ishmael Reed's *Mumbo Jumbo*. For a veritable vade mecum of literary and paraliterary cross-references and intertexts (including several of Edgar Allen Poe's stories and Marvel Comics' *Daredevil*), see Tucker 2010.
22. The compulsion to repeat was first theorised by Freud in his 'Remembering, Repeating, and Working-Through', originally published in 1914 (Freud 2001).
23. One could say that *The Intuitionist* participates in and expands on the discourse of 1990s Afrofuturism as it not only fuses the themes of technology, science, and race – the staple hallmarks of Afrofuturist writing – but also takes the title of Mark Dery's inaugural 1993 article literally: 'Black to the Future' (Dery 1993). Isiah Lavender III explicitly reads *The Intuitionist* as Afrofuturist (Lavender 2007). It is worth noting in this context that Lisa Yaszek recently penned Ellison's *Invisible Man* as a 'proto-Afrofuturist' novel (Yaszek 2005: 299). Given Whitehead's differential repetition of Ellison and the novel's explicit speculative foray into the *genesis of the future*, *The Intuitionist* could arguably be called a meta-Afrofuturist novel. In this sense, *The Intuitionist* is itself a black box.

    One should also mention here that Saldívar, in addition to his notable blunders regarding speculative realism mentioned above, in the very same piece also proceeds as if he did not know about Afrofuturism: '*The Intuitionist* is a novel that falls into a mixed set of genres, inventing a category we might call, broadly speaking *Afrofuturism*, or simply *black speculative fiction*' (Saldívar 2013: 7). Given that the term was coined in 1993, one can hardly uphold that Whitehead's 1999 novel invents the category.
24. It is notable that Freeport Jackson, like Natchez, is a telling name. These names invoke the cities of Natchez and Jackson, Mississippi, and the associated Klan activities and killings (Natchez) as well as general turmoil during the Civil Rights era. Also, both cities allude to yet another great twentieth-century African American writer, Richard Wright, who was born near Natchez (which has a historic marker commemorating Wright) and spent part of his youth in Jackson. In addition, 'Freeport' aptly triggers ambivalent associations ranging from freedom and liberty to Liberia and the Middle Passage.

25. For an incisive discussion and critique of Meillassoux's principle of unreason, see Sistiaga 2012: 47–72. Van Tuinen 2014a compares Meillassoux's inversion of the principle of sufficient reason to Deleuze's affirmative revision.

4

Real Folds:
Mark Z. Danielewski's *House of Leaves*

To date, *House of Leaves* has overwhelmingly been read in light of its mediality, the question of technology, and digital culture at large. Apart from the oft-quoted pioneering articles by Brian W. Chanen, Mark B. N. Hansen, N. Katherine Hayles, and Jessica Pressman (Chanen 2007; Hansen 2004; Hayles 2002a; Pressman 2006), three out of five essays dealing with *House of Leaves* in the first book project exclusively devoted to the works of Danielewski read the novel through this lens (McCormick 2011; Evans 2011; Thomas 2011). Add to that another two essays from *Revolutionary Leaves* (Aghoro 2012; Bilsky 2012), the second such project, and the excellent chapter from Alexander Starre's *Metamedia* (Starre 2015) and it becomes clear that mediality and the digital make up the predominant paradigm in Danielewski scholarship. Another recent foray into this very territory comes from Mark C. Taylor, who gives the topic a theological bent, going so far as to conclude that *House of Leaves* is the manifestation of 'the Web' as 'the "embodiment" of God today' (Taylor 2013: 155). While these critics are right in emphasising the novel's engagement with mediality, technology, and digitality, this engagement makes up just one aspect of a much larger metaphysical concern – a concern that registers in Taylor's onto-theological reading – weaving together issues ranging from narrativity to the act of reading, from discussions of representation to more general questions of matter and spirit. In doing so, *House of Leaves* explicitly and directly – arguably more so than any of the other narratives considered in this book – explores the workings of difference, culminating in nothing less than the projection of a veritable differential cosmology.[1] This cosmology is as much a matter of what is presented as it is one of presentation itself. Both the narrated and the narration suggest an inherently fractured, fractalised, differential world. In other words, difference becomes the guiding principle of both the created world *and* its creation. Since the means of creation are those of narrative, *House of Leaves* comes to embody the correlation between a differential cosmology and a differential narratology. The sufficient reason of what could be called *House of Leave*'s narrato-cosmogony is precisely the abyss of difference, becoming's 'universal ungrounding' (DR: 114).

This ungrounding manifests itself most tangibly in the ever-shifting labyrinthine void permeating the novel's titular house, revealing that there is literally nothing at its foundation. The labyrinth *is* the house's unground. That the house and its labyrinth assume cosmological significance becomes clear in the many references to cosmology throughout the novel, most notably so when the protagonist Will Navidson, in one of his letters to his wife Karen, states that 'our house is God' (Danielewski 2000a: 390). This God, however, is but a philosophical God, a formal moniker denoting the house's overall surface finite stability and underlying infinite variability. Coincidentally, Deleuze and Guattari have ventured to propose the terms *ecumenon* and *planomenon* to capture precisely this relation between stability and variability (ATP: 56–81). Ecumenon, of course, derives from *oikoumene*, Greek for 'the inhabited world', and *oikos*, house. In Deleuze and Guattari, the inhabited world, the world as house, the cosmos as dwelling place, is built on and cut through by the planomenon. In short, the stability and steadfastness of the house is unsettled, ungrounded, by the destabilising activity of its ever-moving fundament. That in *House of Leaves* this fundament is a labyrinth is no coincidence. Etymologically, labyrinth derives from the Greek word for double hatchet as it originally denotes the 'palace of the double hatchet'. Its provenance is the Minotaur myth, which assumes a central role in *House of Leaves*, as does myth in general. The double hatchet becomes the symbol for the labyrinth's doublings and bifurcations, *and* their cutting through and differentiation of the unity and stability of the surface house. Since the novel, by means of its ¼ inch anomaly – the fact that the house is a ¼ of an inch larger on its inside than on its outside, topologically connects these two floors, the lower floor of the labyrinth and the upper floor of the house, the resulting construct is a folded surface plane endowed with depth to be traversed infinitely: Deleuze and Guattari's infinitely folded mechanosphere or cosmos (ATP: 77–82, 566).[2] Ultimately, the house and labyrinth on Ash Tree Lane function as an allegory of cosmological scope akin to the allegory of the baroque house in Deleuze's *The Fold*. In addition, and reminiscent of Deleuze's overturning of Platonism (DR: 71; LS: 291–316), *House of Leaves* inverts the traditional onto-theological grounding function of myth, as it employs myth – in both of its senses of fable or

Real Folds

legend and plot or emplotment, in a word: narrative – precisely to unground, destabilise, and differentiate any higher unity or principle. It is by undertaking a differentiation of the world (cosmos) and its unfolding (narrative) that *House of Leaves* establishes difference itself as a non-principle instead: *an-archē* or unground.

Folding

One of the names Deleuze gives to the workings of difference is that of folding. In addition to the resonances sketched above, there are two concrete reasons why the fold promises to be a rewarding conceptual tool for a reading of Danielewski's novel. First, Deleuze uses it when discussing the characteristics of the labyrinth both in his *Nietzsche and Philosophy* and in his book on Leibniz, *The Fold*. Second, he explicitly discusses the concept of the labyrinth in conjunction with that of the house when he introduces the allegory of the baroque house in the opening pages of *The Fold*. Here we learn that the baroque house is made of two floors: below we find the 'pleats of matter' and above the 'folds in the soul' (TF: 3), each level constituting a labyrinth of its own. Deleuze writes,

> A labyrinth is said, etymologically, to be multiple because it contains many folds. The multiple is not only what has many parts but also what is folded in many ways. A labyrinth corresponds exactly to each level: the continuous labyrinth in matter and its parts, the labyrinth of freedom in the soul and its predicates. (TF: 3)

The labyrinth with its folds is thus the adequate figure for the multiplicity of both matter and soul. Note that the root of the word *multiplicity* is the Latin word *plica*, meaning fold, as becomes obvious when we consider the English synonym *mani-fold*. A multiplicity literally contains many folds and is folded in many ways. The baroque house thus names the many folds of matter and soul.

Let us add to this what Deleuze has to say about the labyrinth in his book on Nietzsche:

> It designates firstly the unconscious, the self; only the Anima is capable of reconciling us with the unconscious, of giving us a guiding *thread* for its exploration. In the second place, the labyrinth designates the eternal return itself: circular, it is not the lost way but the way which leads us back to the same point, to the same instant which is, which was and which will be. But, more profoundly, from the perspective of the constitution of the eternal return, the labyrinth is becoming, the affirmation of becoming.

> Being comes from becoming, it is affirmed of becoming itself. [...] The labyrinth is what leads us to being, the only being is that of becoming, the only being is that of the labyrinth itself. (NP: 188)

According to Deleuze, Nietzsche's labyrinth works on several levels: first, it is an image of the unconscious and its exploration; second, in its circularity and infinite wanderings it denotes the eternal return; and third, it is the dwelling place of being. But since, in its circularity, the labyrinth offers nothing but eternal turns and returns, the only thing that can be said to be is precisely becoming. The labyrinth is thus a synonym of unconscious becoming. And since the labyrinth 'contains many folds', the fold in effect being 'the smallest element of the labyrinth', 'folding, unfolding and refolding' (TF: 3, 6, 158) effectively name the process of becoming. If we come back to the allegory of the baroque house, we can then say that it denotes the becoming of matter and soul. It is my contention that we are confronted with such a baroque house in *House of Leaves*, but it is a strangely twisted baroque house, a house where matter and soul permeate both levels and where the levels do not correspond to a clear distinction between matter and soul. Thus, *House of Leaves* incessantly both emphasises the materiality of the labyrinth, most tangibly when the explorers take samples of the walls, *and* points out that the labyrinth is but a mere projection or manifestation of psyche (21, 165). In fact, the house and labyrinth on Ash Tree Lane do not constitute two levels at all – they are located on one and the same level, matter and soul irreducibly folded into one another. This fold between the two levels is vividly manifested in the notorious anomaly with the house's interior exceeding its exterior by a ¼ inch. It is this in-between, this heterotopia, this difference that constitutes the fold: the outside (matter) folded within and the inside (soul) unfolding outside itself. The novel makes this more than apparent in a number of ways. It is no coincidence that Jonathan Lethem, in his endorsement of the novel, warns the reader that they might find him there 'reduced in size like Vincent Price in *The Fly*, still trapped in the web of its malicious, beautiful pages' (Danielewski 2000a: endorsements). This refers to a reading experience intimating the infinite both due to the novel's massive volume and its excessive circularity that makes the reader go back, or forth, to passages they have already read or will read time and again, and also due to the very fact that the novel makes the reader part of its telling by making them constantly decide which section to continue reading – Zampanò's manuscript? The footnote? Or the footnote within the footnote? Johnny's tale or his mother's letters? The manuscript or 'The Pelican Poems'? One could, then, say that the reader forms a fold with the novel, that they are folded into the novel. At the same time and by the same token, the novel unfolds outside itself within every singular reader and their reading experience.[3] But one can understand Lethem's endorsement in yet another way: namely, with reference to the reader's body. By making the reader turn the book upside down, making them use a mirror to decipher mirror writing, and a host of other, similar demands, the novel basically puts the body back into reading. Reading, traditionally conceived of as contemplative, thus becomes a very physical, bodily experience in terms of both the reader's body and the book as body.[4] What is being engaged here, then, already on this surface level are body and soul, spirit and matter: reading as a psychosomatic experience, body and soul folded into one another. This engagement is true not just with respect to the reader but also, more importantly, with respect to the novel itself, which constantly folds its materiality qua book into its narrative soul and vice versa. *House of Leaves* is thus a paradigmatic exemplar of Deleuze and Guattari's saying that '[t]here is no difference between what a book talks about and how it is made' (ATP: 4). *House of Leaves* is not just a narrative folding story into story into story (metanarrative), or grafting story upon story (palimpsest), but primarily constitutes folds between the material and the immaterial, body and soul, matter and spirit, the given and the transcendental, ecumenon and planomenon, the actual and the virtual, laying them out on a single plane. However, note that while the terms of these dualisms become stretched out on a single plane, their relation is asymmetrical. In all the couplings above the second term determines the first term, while at the same time it cannot exist apart from it: pure immanence.

The labyrinth on Ash Tree Lane, then, denotes precisely the virtual, the site of a 'transcendental principle' acting within, 'a plastic, anarchic and nomadic principle' (DR: 47). This principle is plastic because, even though it never achieves a concrete form, it is also no utter formlessness; it is nomadic because it is constantly shifting, displacing, and in movement; and it is anarchic because it is in fact a non-principle, abyssal groundlessness. Accordingly, the more the labyrinth is penetrated, the emptier it gets, until Navidson in Exploration # 5 finally finds himself floating in utter emptiness. Since the virtual does not just inhere in the actual but is also its determinant, it follows that the cold, dark void of the virtual labyrinth must permeate and determine the actual house standing on Ash Tree Lane. The following excerpt just before Tom, Navidson's brother, vanishes in darkness makes this unmistakably clear:

> The whole place keeps shuddering and shaking, walls cracking only to melt back together again, floors fragmenting and buckling, the ceiling suddenly rent by invisible claws, causing moldings to splinter, water pipes to rupture, electrical wires to spit and short out. Worse, the black ash of below, spreads like printer's ink over everything, transforming each corner, closet, and corridor into that awful dark. (345)

This passage vividly renders how the virtual violently erupts into the actual, transforming it. The virtual is cast as the dwelling place of the animating principle that acts within the actual, the dark, cold emptiness and nothingness of the underground labyrinthine depths that determine the surface house on Ash Tree Lane. It is noteworthy that this passage, by means of simile, explicitly casts the rupturing, transformative underground force as 'printer's ink', thus directly linking the activity of the virtual with that of writing, a link that is established more than once (for example, 334). Writing thus becomes synonymous with violent transformation, a relation that is also manifest in Johnny's job as a (wannabe) tattoo artist. In addition, the force that spreads like 'printer's ink' – what is written and inscribed – is 'the black ash of below'. Ash here takes on its double signification as both the remnants of something burnt and that of the ash tree. The significance of the ash tree, which gives its name to the street the house is located on, is revealed on the novel's very last page when Yggdrasil, the ash tree of Norse cosmology, is invoked (709). The passage quoted above runs together this Norse foundation and principle of the world as embodied by the ash tree and the act of burning, thus suggesting the cosmic tree's consummation by fire resulting in the destruction of the *axis mundi*.[5] This is confirmed in the novel's final words: 'What miracle is this? This giant tree / It stands ten thousand feet high / *But doesn't reach the ground*. Still it stands. / Its roots must hold the sky' (709; my emphasis). Note that while the tree is literally ungrounded, this ungrounding does not amount to absolute nullification. What is destroyed is the tree's stability and centredness qua *axis mundi*, its pivotal positionality around which the world revolves. Ungrounding does not entail negation but inversion: the roots now hold the sky. *Anarchē* is inverted not negated *archē*, difference instead of identity. Similarly, the burnt tree is not absolutely eliminated. Its destruction pertains to its grounding function as the tree is reduced to ashes – being shorn of its grounding function, it is dispersed as cosmic dust. Destruction thus amounts to transformation rather than absolute eradication. Indeed, incessant morphosis and metamorphosis make up the quintessence of this book, both thematically and formally. Casting this transformative inversion and ungrounding as an act of writing, the novel metanarratively and self-consciously enacts what it preaches and preaches what it enacts. It is by means of such a differential narrato-cosmogony that *House of Leaves* ungrounds being, inverts its traditional identitarian principle, and casts it as differential. But what kind of dark, cold being is this? How can darkness and blackness be synonyms of being?[6]

Swarming Cosmos

For an answer, let us turn to Eugene Thacker's essay 'After Life', where he proposes the demonic swarm as an adequate means of conceptualising life. Thacker's notion of the demonic swarm seems apt to grasp the principle according to which *House of Leaves* functions, precisely because it presents a principle that combines elusiveness and emptiness with the horror of underworld darkness. This is what Thacker has to say about life and the swarm:

> The swarm is distributed and horizontal, but also driven by an invisible, intangible life force – 'life' is at once transcendent and immanent to its particular manifestations. Something drives the swarm, but this something is also nothing – at least nothing that stands above and apart from the singular phenomenon of the swarm itself. (Thacker 2011a: 182)

Thacker conjoins this notion of swarming life with an understanding of demonic possession as it is to be found in Dante's *Inferno*:

> [D]emonic possession is not just the possession of the living, but a sort of plasticity of the living to include the non-living. Demons possess not only human beings and animals, but the very landscape, the very terrain of the underworld. Demonic possession is geological and climatological, as well as teratological. (186)

Life as demonic swarm, then, denotes an inherently empty concept of life, since there is literally nothing at its core – this is its swarm aspect; and it goes beyond the living to include the non-living – this is its demonic aspect. In short, life is the monstrosity of swarming emptiness, the 'contradiction of an expressive void' (189), as Thacker writes. He finds this 'vitalist antinomy' (192) most adequately expressed in the cosmic horror of Lovecraftian weird fiction populated by non-creatures – the nameless thing at the limit of thought itself. This nameless thing is precisely 'formless and yet all shapes; it is so ancient it is alien; it is alive only insofar as all human concepts of "life" are irrelevant' (192). *House of Leaves*, however, while clearly belonging – at least partly – to this tradition of writing, is not concerned with the concept of life but with ontology as such; it does not address questions of life but those of being. We can nevertheless revert to Thacker's analysis of life and use it analogously for our purposes, even more so if one considers that Thacker's demonic inclusion of the non-living in the living brings his concept of life very close to that of being (obviously, what Thacker's concept of life does not address and what would have to be included in a concept of being is the non-living in-itself – in Thacker's account the non-living merely figures as the demonic other). In this vein, what swarms in *House of Leaves* is the dark emptiness of being. Everything here hinges on the conceptualisation of this darkness and emptiness, however.

When Iain Hamilton Grant discusses Deleuze's Schellingian notion of the unground or groundlessness in his aptly titled paper 'The Chemistry of Darkness', he reminds us of the following passage from *Difference and Repetition* (Grant 2000: 38):

> Hegel criticized Schelling for having surrounded himself with an indifferent night in which all cows are black. What a presentiment of the differences swarming behind us, however, when in the weariness and despair of our thought without image we murmur 'the cows', 'they exaggerate', etc.; how differenciated and differenciating is this blackness [. . .] The ultimate, external illusion of representation is this illusion that results from all its internal illusion – namely, that groundlessness should lack differences, when in fact it swarms with them. (DR: 347)

Groundlessness, blackness swarms with differences! Thus, Thacker's contradictions of the 'expressive void' and 'vitalist antinomy' have to be made differential; there is no contradiction in being, only difference. Deleuze is adamant about this early on in *Difference and Repetition*:

> Being (what Plato calls the Idea) 'corresponds' to the essence of the problem or the question as such. It is as though there were an 'opening', a 'gap', an ontological 'fold' which relates being and the question to one another. In this relation, being is difference itself. Being is also non-being, *but non-being is not the being of the negative*; rather, it is the being of the problematic, the being of problem and question. Difference is not the negative; on the contrary, non-being is Difference: *heteron*, not *enantion*.

For this reason non-being should rather be written (non)-being or, better still, ?-being. [. . .] Beyond contradiction, difference – beyond *non*-being, (non)-being; beyond the negative, problems and questions. (DR: 76–7)

What the labyrinth on Ash Tree Lane manifests is precisely Deleuzian (non)-being or ?-being. Rather than constituting the house's negative, it corresponds to its underlying Idea, its subterranean problematic structure, and Navidson and his crew immerse themselves in this problem in order to explore it.[7] The unground is thus not a mere void but is rather problematic, labyrinthine: in short, differential. The darkness incessantly shifts and moves, folding and refolding, becoming. As the examination of the samples taken shows, the labyrinth is made of 'magma' (Danielewski 2000a: 383) and other ancestral matter (374). This is indeed a veritable chemistry of darkness and a geology of the unground. It is important to note the ancestrality of the material since this opens the scope well beyond human concerns. In fact, this is one of the passages where the novel explicitly attains cosmic scope. In relation to the 'interplanetary' and even 'interstellar' (378) provenance of the material, the human becomes quite insignificant. This unfolding of time and space beyond the scope of the human is also stressed in the list of architectural styles, which moves back in history from postmodernism to well beyond pre-historic times (120–34) just as in the ensuing list of architects and patrons, again starting in the twentieth century and going back to 'myth, and finally time' itself (135–21). Of course, the non-human is also a significant aspect of the novel's central motif, the twisted house and labyrinth on Ash Tree Lane. Ultimately, what the novel, by way of myth (again in the double sense of narrative indicated above), excavates from the ground (geology) in order to analyse in its constitution (chemistry) is indeed the unfolding of time itself, the formative and transformative powers of becoming.

In this context, one should also remember that it is precisely the notion of ancestrality on which Meillassoux bases his critique of the correlation of being and thought, which posits that everything is always already for us (Meillassoux 2009: 1–27). In *House of Leaves*, nothing is for us. Already the novel's dedication – 'This is not for you' – makes this clear. In this respect it is the epitome of horror, with horror being understood according to what Thacker, in *In the Dust of this Planet*, makes out to be its single most significant aspect: namely, that it tries to think 'the "dark intelligible abyss"' of a 'world-without-us', thereby alluding to the utterly intangible nothingness of the 'world-in-itself' (Thacker 2011b: 8). It is noteworthy how Thacker's threefold of for-us, without-us, and in-itself resonates with Deleuze's tripartite ontology comprising actuality, intensity, and virtuality. Their incompatibility ultimately hinges on their different evaluations of the negative. In contrast to Thacker's emphasis on the negative – he even writes of horror as a kind of 'negative philosophy [...] akin to negative theology' (Thacker 2011b: 9) – both Deleuze and *House of Leaves* emphasise the differential. Horror and the philosophy of difference converge here in what amounts to the horror of dark differentials, the imperceptible and intransigent unfolding of time.

The depth of the unground is 'the matrix of all extensity' (DR: 288), as Deleuze remarks. The unground inheres in the (un)grounded – tectonics in architectonics, the rumblings[8] of the earth in the homeliness of the house – and brings about a 'universal ungrounding' (DR: 80, 114, 252, 289, 344). But a universal ungrounding also denotes the ungrounding of the universe. When, early on in the novel, we read that '[p]hysics depends on a universe infinitely centered on an equal sign' and that 'the universe adds up' (32), the unfolding narrative unmistakably shows that the universe does not add up at all: it is not centred on an equal sign but absolutely decentred and differential. And sure enough, later on, one commentator asserts that the house 'adds up to nothing' (361). This is a monstrous house, a monstrous universe, contingent on the 'dark, stochastic glinting of swarming multiplicity' (Grant 2000: 39). Thus, when Johnny lets us know that

> [o]f course there always will be darkness but I realize now something inhabits it [...] something much more akin to a Voice, which though invisible to the eye and frequently unheard by even the ear still continues, day and night, year after year, to sweep through us all (518),

this Voice is none other than the voice of being, the swarming of univocal being. It is thus only fitting that *House of Leaves* ends with a final evocation of Yggdrasil (709), the ash tree of Norse cosmology, the groundless house of being. What lies at the heart of *House of Leaves* is indeed cosmic horror, a monsterfold: absolute difference.

Unfolding

Due to the asymmetrical relation between the (non)principle and the (un)principled, the (un)ground and the (un)grounded, *House of Leaves*' depiction of an ungrounded universe necessarily is itself abyssal. Indeed, *House of Leaves* vividly manifests the universal ungrounding it presents also on the level of its presentation. We are now in a position to scrutinise this abyssal presentation with a view to how it brings about this ungrounding *and* determines the ungrounded.

'I have no idea whether it's on purpose or not. Sometimes I'm certain it is. Other times I'm sure it's just one big fucking train wreck' (149). What Johnny says with respect to Zampanò's potential fallacies in his analysis of *The Navidson Record*, Navidson's film that attempts to document the occurrences on Ash Tree Lane, must be slightly reformulated when it comes to narrative in Danielewski's novel: *House of Leaves* is *a big fucking train wreck on purpose*. It affirmatively disintegrates and dissolves narrative as we know it. For this end it takes recourse to a host of strategies: the incorporation of an index and heterogeneous, multiple appendices differentiated into diverse media (graphic novel, photography, painting, and so on), genres (epistolary writing, poetry, aphorisms, and so on), and disciplinary discourses (philosophy, psychoanalysis, natural sciences, and so on); diverse narrative strands and voices folded into one another (*The Navidson Record*, Zampanò's manuscript, Johnny's story, the editors' additions, the Whalestoe letters, and so on); extensive reoccurring lists of names and things interrupting the narrative flow; a page layout and typography (space) accelerating or decelerating (time) the reading process and putting the body back into the reading experience, therefore implicating the reader explicitly in the narrative progression while at the same time and by the same token amounting to a spatialisation of narrative, thus manifesting the very spatiotemporal dynamics of narrative; and the irreducible fold between its materiality qua book and its narrative soul, thereby implicating its bookness in its narrative: the book does not merely function as the negligible material container for its transcendent all-important narrative soul.[9]

House of Leaves effectively turns narrative into a 'labyrinth without a thread' where 'Ariadne has hung herself' (DR: 68). By undertaking all these foldings and refoldings, *House of Leaves* literally com-*pli*-cates and essentially problematises narrative. 'Problem' here has to be understood in the Deleuzian sense: as underlying problematic structure. Problematising narrative thus means approaching the Idea of narrative, unearthing narrative virtuality. Narrative is thus split in two, always torn asunder between Narrative (Idea, problematic structure, virtuality) and *n*arrative (expression, individual solution, actuality), the former always inhering in and constituting the latter. What *House of Leaves* suggests is that there is a ¼ inch anomaly peculiar to narrative, a fissure in narratives where Narrative resides, a fold between transcendental and universal Narrative and empirical and specific narratives.

Of course, one cannot explore the depths of *House of Leaves* without taking into account one of the novel's most salient features: namely, its use of the colour blue for the word *house*. Most critics have associated the use of blue print with the blue of hyperlink, and *House of Leaves* indeed seems to be a 'networked novel' (Pressman 2006). In line with this interpretation, Mark Hansen writes:

> Making pseudoserious reference to the blue highlighting of hyperlinks on Web pages, the blue ink of the word 'house' in the work's title transforms this keyword into something like a portal to information located elsewhere, both within and beyond the novel's frame. (Hansen 2004: 598)

Joining Hansen's assertion with Martin Brick's recourse to the medieval art of rubrication in his reading of the novel, where he determines the blue print as a sort of anti-rubric defying authority (Brick 2004: n. p.), an analysis in terms of network becomes more than plausible: decentred and non-hierarchical, the novel weaves a web of interconnections of narrative strands, events, and voices within and extra-textual instances without (on the latter, see note 3). However, there is more to the picture than a mere network. One has to take at face value Hansen's point that the blue print constitutes a portal to something *beyond* the novel.[10] Against Hansen's focus on information, this beyond has to be understood as the transcendental field of Narrative or narrative virtuality. The beyond differs in kind from the within: while the within might indeed be conceptualised as information, the beyond has nothing to do with it. It all boils down to the question of representation. While Hansen emphasises that *House of Leaves* essentially problematises what, with recourse to Bernard Stiegler, he calls the orthographic function of media, he exempts the digital from this critique, effectively equating it with 'the very force of fiction itself' (Hansen 2004: 611). Even though the digital might indeed threaten orthography, Hansen's focus on 'productive imagination' (fiction) versus 'registration of the real' (orthography) (610) misses the point. It is no coincidence that Johnny's remark concerning Zampanò's fallacious analysis quoted earlier refers to the very beginning of the manuscript where Zampanò indeed states that a general problem surfaces with *The Navidson Record*: namely, 'whether or not, with the advent of digital technology, image has forsaken its once unimpeachable hold on the truth' (Danielewski 2000a: 3), thus seemingly inviting Hansen's take on the novel. But just two paragraphs further on, Zampanò claims that analyses of Navidson's film that focus on the 'antinomies of fact or fiction, representation or artifice, document or prank' (3) produce the less interesting material. Instead, he suggests turning to the 'interpretation of events within the film' (3). In this vein, I suggest that a reading of *House of Leaves* along the lines of fact versus fiction, representation versus artifice, document versus prank, or, in Hansen's terms, orthography versus the digital is misleading. Such a reading focuses on the *epistemology* of representation, on whether representation makes a truth claim or not. This is basically the old Platonic distinction between good and bad mimesis, and all of the above-mentioned couplings work according to this distinction.[11] But that does not make them less representational as to their *ontological* status. Thus the digital might indeed contest the truth claim of representation by finally executing what, in this line of reasoning, literature and the arts have always been threatening to do: namely, overthrowing good mimesis. However, what *House of Leaves* problematises is precisely the *ontological* status of representation *as such*. What *House of Leaves* comes to express is not the impossibility of representation as good mimesis, as an adequate instrument to capture the real, as Hansen has it, but rather the inadequacy of conceiving of the real in terms of representation in the first place. *House of Leaves* contests that the relation between appearances and the real (Plato), between the given and the transcendental (Kant), the actual and the virtual (Deleuze) is one of representation. Instead, it suggests that appearances, the given, the actual are precisely *not* to be conceived *in the image of* the real, the transcendental, and the virtual. Of course, Deleuze's virtual–actual relation is explicitly formulated along these lines. It is precisely this critique which drives Deleuze to formulate his virtual–actual relation and to pit it against Plato–Kant. Deleuze's virtual–actual relation cuts through the Platonian–Kantian verticality of representation. The virtual–actual relation is not representational but expressive and genetic, with the real amounting to the absolute immanence of this expressive and genetic relation. Or, rather, representation has to be reconceived along these lines instead of being conceived in terms of image and copy. Conceiving representation in terms of expression in fact amounts to the injunction of *not* to conceive of it in terms of image and copy. In this vein, representations do not resemble the represented; representations and the represented differ in kind, not merely in degree. This is why Deleuze's take on the problem–solution relation is so illuminating in this respect: solutions simply do not resemble their problems. They express problems and they grow out of problems, but they do not 'look like' their problems. They differ in kind. It is in this sense that *House of Leaves* is essentially concerned with a problematisation of representation (which, of course, as we will see shortly, goes hand in hand with its problematisation of narrative). The novel unearths its sub-representative domain, the domain of its underlying problem, the depths of the virtual. The deficiency of representation as copy and image is made explicit numerous times throughout the novel, as when Zampanò points out the labyrinth's '[r]esistance to representation' (90), or when he inserts a footnote in his account of Navidson's rendition of Tom's death, pointing out that Navidson 'draws attention once again to the question of inadequacies in representation, no matter the medium, no matter how flawless' (346),[12] or when Navidson attests that his cameras do not adequately render the events they record: '[T]hat darkness doesn't seem dark at all. You can't see the hollowness in it, the cold. Funny how incompetent images can sometimes be' (344). Most strikingly, perhaps, the inadequacy of representation is embodied in Zampanò's blindness; a blind man writes in detail about occurrences presented on film – a visual medium. This paradox is further accentuated by the fact that the film depicts impossible events.

In this context, the extensive discussion of the phenomenon of echo early on in the novel serves as a programmatic propaedeutic. Not only do echoes manifest auditory perception at the expense of the visible, with vision being the sense impression to which discussions of representation revert almost by default, but also they couple auditory perception with repetition and transformation – there is a reason that the myth of Echo and Narcissus is an episode in Ovid's *Metamorphoses* – for an echo is never identical to the echoed and only ever repeats differentially, a point that is both stressed in and responsible for driving the very myth itself. Echo is governed by difference. The discussion is programmatic because the entire novel ultimately functions as an echo chamber, a laboratory of repetitious transformation (on this latter point, see also Chapter 3); and it is propaedeutic since it establishes the criteria according to which the narrative works. This becomes clear in the respective section's mythological discussion of echo (which is complemented by a scientific discussion). The novel picks up echo's mythological–

theological genealogy in a discussion of John Hollander's *The Figure of Echo*, explicitly stating that Echo[13] 'live[s] in metaphors, puns and the suffix', and, quoting Hollander quoting Henry Reynolds's *Mythomystes* (1632), asserting that she is *'the daughter of the divine voice'* (44). The novel thus showcases that myth, the dwelling place of Echo, fundamentally encapsulates rhetoric and narrative technique while at the same time being an offspring of God's voice. God is thus projected as the grand narrator composing and telling the story of being. Indeed, the passage emphatically associates echo with literature when Johnny asserts in a footnote that the dwelling place of Echo, those metaphors, puns, and suffixes, is to be found in 'literature's rocky caves' (44nΩ). Literature (or myth) then becomes the expression of the Creator, the transformed and transformative incarnation of the creative powers of God.

Against my protestations to the contrary, this seems to confirm Taylor's onto-theological reading of the novel. However, this is not all there is to the picture. *House of Leaves*, unsurprisingly, adds another layer, produces yet another echo. For the novel, by quoting Hollander quoting Reynolds and couching these quotations in Johnny's presentation of Zampanò's writings, merely presents faint echoes and thus repetitious transformations of the 'original' Reynolds utterance, which itself already is but an echo of earlier treatments of the myth going all the way back to the *Metamorphoses*.[14] This is made explicit in yet another detail: namely, in the novel's anonymous editors' correction of Johnny's rendering of echo as literature's rocky caves in another footnote to Johnny's footnote (yet another echo). Since Johnny's footnote is ostensibly a translation of a Latin phrase in Zampanò's text, a translation, however, that is incorrect, the editors' explicit intervention serves to highlight Johnny's transformative work. Of course, such transformative work, the work of echoing, is exactly what *House of Leaves* in its entirety undertakes and embodies, as it is itself replete with metaphors and puns, and by means of the appendices and index which are suffixed to the main story line, gives form to the suffix as such. Ultimately, *House of Leaves* emphasises that it is constituted by echoes all the way down. In this vein, the divine voice whose daughter is Echo is dispersed as the fractured immanent principle of echo rather than a transcendent commanding higher source. There is no narrator–God located outside the narrative orchestrating the spinning of the tale. Rather, narrative voice, multiplied and diffracted, while generating the story always remains immanent to it. Indeed, there is nothing but the unfolding of narration – morphosis and metamorphosis. Accordingly, the above relation between God and Echo is explicitly reversed two pages further on: while the *Mythomystes* characterises echo as the offspring of and thus as determined by the divine voice, 'divinity' now 'seems defined by echo' (46). It is in this fashion that *House of Leaves* explicitly projects narrative as metaphysical while avoiding the lapse into onto-theology. Thus, when, in the course of his discussion of echo, Zampanò quotes John 1: 1, '"In the beginning was the Word, and the Word was with God, and the Word was God"' (45), the novel, in Spinozistic fashion, naturalises this verse – the naturalisation being also manifested in the fact that Echo is a nymph, a nature spirit; it then remakes it to express the singular unfolding of nature, the dispersal of cosmic echo, the 'single voice' that 'raises the clamour of being' (DR: 44) precisely by decentring and dispersing any notion of authority, be it authorial or narratorial.

This naturalisation is then picked up in the ensuing scientific discourse on echo and particularly echolocation in both human technology and nature, culminating in the presentation of a formula that 'describes the resonance frequencies [f] in a room with a length of L, width of W, and height of H, where the velocity of sound equals c:

$$f = {}^c/_2 \left[({}^n/_L)^2 + ({}^m/_W)^2 + ({}^p/_H)^2 \right]^{1/2} \text{Hz.}'$$

To this, Zampanò adds: 'Notice that if L, W, and H all equal ∞, f will equal zero' (49–50). This latter addendum is important in so far as it makes clear that only where there is something rather than nothing is there echo (or, more correct technically, resonance), and conversely, only where there is echo is there something. Infinite space without any obstruction whatsoever – that is, absolutely empty space, nothingness – produces no resonance. The only other conceivable alternative would be an absolutely static and immobile world, but since there *is* resonance we can safely discard this latter option. Physics is thus drawn upon to show that echo (resonance) indeed indicates the unfolding of nature.

This exploration of echo in scientific terms not only is presented in narrative form, but also is undercut by the narrative *exemplification* of echo at work, as a long footnote by Johnny spanning pages 48–9 extracts another account from the discussion in the manuscript; in doing so, it precisely enacts what is being theorised in the very same pages. Johnny provides ever more distant echoes to a passage from the manuscript, thus testifying to the creative and transformative powers of repetition as Zampanò's 'word' – 'empty hallways

Real Folds

long past midnight' – 'ring[s] inside [him] like some awful dream, over and over again, modulating slightly [...] until the music of that recurrence [draws] into relief [his] own scars drawn long ago' (48). Narration is thus figured as recursive resonant modulation. Accordingly, the discussion of echo ends with the superimposition of mythical (that is, narrative) and scientific echo:

> Myth makes Echo the subject of longing and desire. Physics makes echo the subject of distance and design. Where emotion and reason are concerned both claims are accurate. And where there is no Echo there is no description of space or love. There is only silence. (50)

Repetition, resonance, modulation, and transformation are thus figured as the condition of both narration and creation as such. Where there is no repetition, no resonance, no modulation, no transformation, there is simply nothing.

As this brief foray into *House of Leaves*' negotiation of echo shows, the novel does not merely verbalise a critique of representation, but also, more profoundly, enacts this critique. Thus, if we heed Zampanò's advice and focus on the events within the novel, we can now flesh out in more detail *how* the novel does so.

In this vein and coming back to the discussion of the novel's use of blue print for the word *house* and the word's function as a portal of sorts, the word *house* in blue print first of all simply works for the fictional house like a *blueprint* does for a real house: it is an abstract representation. Yet at the same time and by the same token – the colour blue – it points to a beyond of representation: something strange is going on; something uncanny – *unheimlich* – stirs underneath the apparent representation. There is more to this word than meets the eye. It is both house and unhomely, *unheimisch* – non-house, other than house. It could be said that the word house printed in blue is thus this narrative's ¼ inch anomaly precisely in *terms of narrative*; it opens up the space of a problem, which, as we are about to discover, will turn out to be a shifting labyrinth of immeasurable dimensions. This function as portal, as entryway to a beyond, also becomes manifest in the reading experience since the blue print is in fact the first anomaly the reader encounters. While it is not really disturbing on the book's cover, it becomes gradually more unsettling when moving along to flap, endorsements, title page, copyright page, editors' foreword, and finally the first few pages of Johnny's introduction (xi; xiii). It thus doubles on the discourse level the ¼ inch anomaly of the story level as it appears in *The Navidson Record* and Zampanò's account. It functions as entryway, as the portal to the narrative labyrinth unfolding beyond it. This short word in blue thus cracks up the representational surface of the narrative. And it is through this ¼ inch crack that Narrative starts to seep in and disseminate, at first slowly and stealthily until it erupts with violence and sweeps along the narrative at hand, shattering it in a big fucking train wreck, to use Johnny's expression. Thus, when the Navidson crew starts exploring the depths of the uncanny labyrinth, we as readers simultaneously start exploring the depths of the ever-shifting caverns of Narrative: we descend into a dense web of redundant footnotes; we pass through 'tunnels' burrowing into the 'main' text (framed text inserted in the main body continuing over several pages); we follow footnotes-become-circular-hallways (footnotes running along the set-off margin for several pages then 'turning' – one actually has to turn the book upside down – and leading back to the page they started on); we stumble into text-become-empty-halls (blank pages). In all this the novel presents us with an oscillation between the overspilling of narrative and its vanishing, the white and black noise of narrative. Both cases, the too much and the not enough, effectively disintegrate narrative as we know it, making it differential.[15] One could say that in *House of Leaves* narrative undergoes its very own nuclear fission, leaving us with nothing but the dark night of radiating narrative differentials. It is no coincidence that the last four chapters of Zampanò's manuscript (one of them actually being a chapter written entirely by Johnny and inserted into the manuscript) invariably end with dissolution, thus doubling the overall narrative trajectory. Accordingly, Chapter XX ends with the very compelling image of Navidson, lost and disoriented in pitch darkness, reading *House of Leaves* by burning page after page in order to have some reading light, thus dissolving the very narrative in which he features. This instance of metalepsis forcefully drives home how the novel consumes itself, how *House of Leaves* decomposes its very own narrative. Once Navidson is done reading, he has nothing left but himself, as he states (471). But this self is also dissolving. Thus, when he counters his own utterance '"Don't be"' (481) with a reaffirming '"I am"' (482), this is immediately belied on the following page: 'Navidson is forgetting. Navidson is dying' (483). And turning the page once more we read that '[v]ery soon he will vanish completely in the wings of his own wordless stanza' (484).[16] The next chapter, which consists of a series of Johnny's diary entries, ends with an entry in which Johnny recounts a story he has heard about the death of a new-born baby that

Real Folds

ends in the observation that 'the EKG flatlines. Asystole. The child is gone' (521). The following chapter concludes with a short interview of Karen, who silently insists that the house on Ash Tree Lane 'dissolved' (524). And finally, absolute zero seems to be attained when the respective endings of Zampanò's manuscript and Navidson's film converge to constitute the ending of *House of Leaves*' story:

> Navidson does not close with the caramel covered face of a Casper the friendly ghost. He ends instead on what he knows is true and always will be true. Letting the parade pass from sight, he focuses on the empty road beyond, a pale curve vanishing into the woods where nothing moves and a street lamp flickers on and off until at last it flickers out and darkness sweeps in like a hand. (528)

This passage, of course, like everything else in the novel, does not just simply represent. It is not merely a representation of Zampanò's representation of Navidson's film. More profoundly, this passage condenses the overall narrative trajectory of the novel: narrative as a vanishing curve, the becoming-zero of narrative. In this vein, it tells us this: the parade of stories *House of Leaves* has set in motion passes from sight into the empty darkness beyond. The narrative flatlines: asystolic narrative. But we have learned our lesson, we do not believe any more in an 'indifferent night where all cows are black' (DR: 347). Like Navidson, we know the truth. We know that blackness swarms with differences. And indeed, the above-mentioned chapter endings propose that utter dissolution does not coincide with absolute nothingness. To each of the dissolutions there is a remainder, however minimal. Thus, in Chapter XX, immediately after the premonition that Navidson is about to vanish 'in the wings of his own wordless stanza', which is juxtaposed with a page featuring several lines of square brackets arranged so that they carve out a blank space – emptiness – we read that 'this stanza does not remain entirely empty' (486). Accordingly, the blank space constituted by square brackets is reproduced with a difference: a small asterisk appears in the upper right corner (487). Similarly, the interview with Karen questions that dissolution is absolute when the interviewer sceptically surmises that the house is 'still there' (525). Even in Johnny's account of child death, we are not confronted with nothingness; 'the child is gone' (521) essentially means that a body remains. And finally, when we are confronted with utter darkness in what constitutes the ending of the novel's story, this dissolution in darkness is not the last word. Something still stirs in it; the ending of *House of Leaves*' story does not coincide with the ending of its discourse. The novel does not end here at all. In fact, we are just about to delve into narrative darkness.

Swarming Narrative

Indeed, what lies beyond the story's ending is the flickering of the remnants of narrative until it flickers out for good. The whole array of the novel's narrative strategies, from the sheer overkill of the multiplicity of voices to the typographic dismantlings, from the implication of its materiality to the complication of its narrative strands, find their apex in the multiple appendices and index. It is here that *House of Leaves*' already highly differentiated narrative is finally torn to 'Bits' '. . . and Pieces', as two of the entries in the appendices are tellingly entitled (541, 548). This section of the book presents us with a mass of heterogeneous, incoherent, and fragmented material, with the '[e]ndless snarls of words' (xvii) Johnny evokes in his introduction. These snarls of words manifest Deleuzian different/ciation, the repetitious gathering of differential elements in differential relations to be expressed in actuality. This is made explicit by Johnny in his introduction in the passage just mentioned:

> Endless snarls of words, sometimes twisting into meaning, sometimes into nothing at all, frequently breaking apart, always branching off into other pieces I'd come across later – on old napkins, the tattered edges of an envelope, once even on the back of a postage stamp; everything and anything but empty; each fragment completely covered with the creep of years and years of ink pronouncements; layered, crossed out, amended; handwritten, typed; legible, illegible; impenetrable, lucid; torn, stained, scotch taped; some bits crisp and clean, others faded, burnt or folded and refolded so many times the creases have obliterated whole passages of god knows what – sense? truth? deceit? a legacy of prophecy and lunacy or nothing of the kind?, and in the end achieving, designating, describing, recreating – find your own words; I have no more; or plenty more but why? And all to tell – what? (xvii)

Johnny's rant vividly conveys not only the genesis of Zampanò's manuscript as assembled by Johnny, and even not just, in metanarrative fashion, the genesis of Danielewski's novel, but also, most profoundly, the genesis of any narrative *as such*: the assembling and gathering of endless snarls of words, of a heterogeneous multiplicity of divergent series, into form – order out of chaos.[17] Ricœur suggested the term *emplotment* to convey this work of ordering. In this vein, we could say that *House of Leaves* is fundamentally a novel of *deplotment*. *House of Leaves*, in its narrative trajectory, does not plot an order but deplots it: chaos out of order instead of order out of chaos. *House of Leaves* burrows into plot in order to unearth the depth of its virtual genesis. Here, we should remember that plot also means 'parcel of land' or 'area of ground' as well as a graphic representation of such a ground. And in correlation with the noun, the verb 'to plot' designates the division of this ground. Thus, we could say that *House of Leaves* presents us with a geology of narrative, ungrounding the ground of narrative, immersing itself in narrative tectonics underlying the narrative architectonic. It uncovers the shifting tectonic plates of narrative and the 'magma' (383) of which they are made. Rather than envisioning narrative as grounded, as 'plotted' by events and existents, it casts narrative as the spreading-out of the unground, as a nomadic distribution of the differentials of narrative productive of events and existents. In its most compelling form, this work is presented to us in the novel's index.

What *House of Leaves* suggests is that the more you dig, the closer you come to the building blocks (of the house, of the cosmos, of narrative). But at the same time, the more you dig, the more these building blocks tend to vanish until one is surrounded by nothing but empty darkness. In terms of narrative, the index thus manifests *House of Leaves*' ultimate disintegration before it dissipates entirely. The index is as close as the novel gets to its vanishing building blocks; it precisely *indicates* the antecedent different/ciation process with its selection of differentials, the gathering of bits and pieces as the appendix has it, and their actualisation in the novel at hand (*House of Leaves*). In analogy with genetics one could speak of narremes (differential elements) forming a narrome (virtual multiplicity), which is then actualised in the actual narrative. It is by incorporating words that *do not* feature in the story – marked as DNE (presumably meaning 'does not exist') – that the index intimates this narrome, the Idea of narrative, underlying every actual narrative and comprising the ever-shifting totality of differential elements and relations of narrative *in-itself*. In terms of the genetics analogy, one could, then, say that DNE is for narrative what DNA is for genetics: the molecules of narrative, or narrative's differential elements different/ciating themselves, to be actualised in actual narratives. Note that this analogy is not arbitrary since Deleuze's philosophy of difference essentially provides a genetic account of the given – it theorises the genesis of the given.

Still, the genetics analogy might sound somewhat far-fetched or too creative. Also, it does not explain how something essentially non-existent can form the basis for something that is. Such an explanation seems to fall back on the very nihilism it wanted to counter. In that case, it would have to face Parmenides' old assertion that *ex nihilo nihil fit*. But we have to remember what Deleuze said about non-being: namely, that non-being has to be conceived in terms of the problematic rather than the negative. Accordingly, that which does not exist does not necessarily amount to nothingness. On the contrary, even though it does not exist, it *in*sists. It is the very limit of the descent into darkness. This comes to the fore if we consider that DNE is an abbreviation used in calculus to designate that a limit does not exist.[18] The function is boundless. In our case, ever approaching zero, narrative does not converge to any defined limit value. Rather, it amounts to a mad dance of infinitely small differentials.[19]

Overall, *House of Leaves* can be said to present a *mathesis*, a calculus of narrative with its two inverse operations. On the one hand, narrative as a vanishing curve, a differential function approaching zero, flickering on and off, the limit of which is precisely the boundlessness of Narrative's 'dark, stochastic glinting of swarming multiplicity' (Grant 2000: 39). This is narrative as a veritable becoming-zero: from the actuality of the subjective 'I' of Johnny's 'I still get nightmares' (xi) to the virtuality and neutrality of limitless Narrative as intimated by the novel's index; from the diversity of subjective voices the novel casts to the objective 'Voice [. . .] sweep[ing] through [them] all' (518); from actual, emplotted narrative to its deplotted, virtual unground; from the integrality of narrative to the differentials of Narrative; in short, narrative as a process of fission. On the other hand, narrative as a summation of differentials, the outcome of a process of integration; narrative as the emergence of plot from the depths of Narrative's unground; in short, narrative as a process of fusion, or, as *House of Leaves* has it, 'nucleosynthesis' (383). What *House of Leaves* detects in its search for its very own conditions are precisely its vanishing building blocks: the ever-shifting dark caverns of swarming Narrative, the growling of the univocity of narrative, the rumblings of '"the fourth-person singular"' (LS: 118; on this notion, see my Introduction and Chapter 1).

In order to counter the deficiencies of narrative as representation, *House of Leaves* parades before our eyes these very deficiencies *and* maps the realm of narrative virtuality. This novel is a matter of cartography (mapping the unknown), of geology (exploration of depth), and of chemistry (experiments in darkness) – not of tracing and representation. In the way of Deleuze and Guattari's (in)famous orchid–wasp example in *A Thousand Plateaus*, we have to say that *House of Leaves* does not mimic, does not represent a labyrinth, the snapping of a rope (293–6), or the spatial permutations of the place, but that it plunges into a veritable becoming-labyrinth, becoming-rope, becoming-space.[20] In doing so, it indeed 'becomes a new kind of form and artifact', as Hayles asserts (Hayles 2002a: 781), but this new kind of artefact denotes neither 'the rebirth of the novel' nor 'the beginning of the novel's displacement by a hybrid discourse that as yet has no name' (Hayles 2002a: 781). On the contrary, *House of Leaves* manifests what literary narrative (and not just the novel) can do and always could do: produce volcanic eruptions of the new.[21] Thus it amounts to a paradigmatic example of literary narrative and an exemplary presentation of narrative *in essence*.

Refolding: Cosmos Legōn

This chapter has traced how *House of Leaves* monumentalises (in the Deleuzian sense) the correlation between a differential cosmology and a differential narratology. It has done so purely from the point of view of narratology, however, as it has drawn out how *House of Leaves* shows that becoming underlies narrative, how narrative has to be conceptualised in light of becoming. In this, it synecdochically stands in for the entirety of *Narrative and Becoming*. But *House of Leaves* seems to go farther than that. It seems to suggest that narrative and becoming are related in yet another way.

In a recent essay on the relation between life and non-life, Timothy Morton asserts the following: 'When you look at a daffodil, you are seeing the story of how an algorithm was plotted in some kind of phase space. A flower is not an image, but a map' (Morton 2001: n. p.). A little further on, he notes: 'Lifeforms [sic] are maps, plots, graphs.' The interest of these statements lies in the way Morton combines and interweaves the concepts of life, mathematics, science, and narratology in order to think life forms *as stories*. In its insistence on cartography, algorithms, and the non-representational, his account is indeed not very far from my account of differential narrative. Hijacking Morton for the purposes of *Narrative and Becoming* and – analogously to the discussion of Thacker's work – moving from his conceptualisation of life to general ontology, an account of beings as narratives and, concomitantly, of becoming as Narrative suggests itself. This indeed seems to be what the final evocation of Yggdrasil in *House of Leaves* ultimately expresses: that the cosmos plots stories, that it essentially *is* its very own telling. *House of Leaves* thus intimates a much more subterranean, hidden, demonic alliance than has hitherto been unearthed. What dawns at the darkest limit of *House of Leaves* is the incessant folding, unfolding, and refolding of ontology and narratology, the folding of the two realms into one another. What lingers in this darkness is the irreducible implication of the becoming of narrative on the one hand, and the narrativity of becoming on the other: the folds of a narr-on-tology.[22] This, indeed, seems to be the imperceptible zero point that announces itself in the novel's dark depths. The fundus animae, the dark ground, is the swarming multiplicity of the univocal growling of becoming and narrative. *House of Leaves* sketches a veritable cosmo-logia in the strict sense of a cosmos *legōn*: a cosmos that speaks; or, more succinctly, a cosmos that tells.

Notes

1. Taylor, too, argues that difference is the novel's guiding principle. However, Taylor's difference is that of Derrida. For Taylor, the novel thus constantly defers: the real, meaning, signification, the centre, and so on. In his reading, *House of Leaves* instantiates elusiveness as such, thus merely intimating what remains essentially unrepresentable. Difference here comes to mark the fundamental gap between human representation and the impenetrable, divine other. In the final run, Taylor's reading is thoroughly anti-metaphysical, cementing the gap between physics and metaphysics, a gap that can only be bridged by a leap of faith. He thus willingly cedes the space of metaphysics to theology. In what follows, I will show that nothing of this sort can be attributed to *House of Leaves*. Rather than cementing the gap between the two realms, it folds physics and metaphysics into one another, thus thoroughly eradicating God. *House of Leaves* is an atheist's house.
2. For a very similar assessment of the novel in terms of topology and metaphysics, see Beressem 2012. While Beressem's account is likewise Deleuze-inspired and thus presents many overlaps with the present chapter, our respective analyses diverge on a crucial point: Beressem makes mention neither of cosmology nor of mythology and restricts his analysis to mathematics and, particularly, geometry. While he thus downplays the novel's larger ontological and narratological ramifications, his article comes with the added value of (1) addressing Danielewski's overall poetic programme by incorporating a discussion of *Only Revolutions*, and (2) situating Danielewski's work in relation

to literary history (postmodernism, 1950s pulp science fiction, metaphysical poetry). Our two texts thus make for good complementary reading, illuminating one another.

3. The reader is, of course, not the only site of the novel's external unfolding, which ranges from its intertextuality to the separate publication of *The Whalestoe Letters*, from its implication in various internet forums to the interplay with Danielewski's sister Poe's music album, *Haunted*.

4. For a detailed and sophisticated discussion of *House of Leaves* in terms of the materiality of the book and the physicality of the reading process, see Starre 2015: 128–66.

5. The notion of the mythological tree as *axis mundi* is explicitly discussed in *House of Leaves* in a quotation from Christian Norberg-Schulz's *Existence, Space and Architecture* that appears in the novel's central (if one can say that) labyrinth chapter in a passage that discusses and enacts decentring. For a similar assessment of this issue, see Taylor's reading of the novel's last page (Taylor 2013: 153–4).

6. By means of a first hint, it is no coincidence that this darkness is reminiscent of both Baumgarten's *fundus animae* and Schelling's dark ground (see Chapter 3).

7. I should note here that Thacker, even though he does not refer to him in his essay, discusses Deleuze at length in *After Life* (the monograph), with a particular focus on the notions of univocity and immanence (Thacker 2010). He is too quick, however, in dismissing Deleuze as propagating a generous and overflowing vitalism predicated on full life and full being. He basically reads difference as not going far enough and proposes an ontology predicated on nothingness instead (meontology as primary to ontology). Passages such as the one quoted above, however, make it quite clear that, for Deleuze, being (and life) are essentially fractured *from the outset*. The fracture is just not modelled according to the rules of contradiction. Rather, it is differential. In fact, from Deleuze's standpoint, it is negativity that does not go far enough. In showing that *House of Leaves* pushes difference rather than negativity my analysis also diverges markedly from Will Slocombe's nihilist reading of the novel (Slocombe 2005). Even though Slocombe identifies the labyrinth as the house's underlying structure, he remains attached to a reading of non-being as being of the negative.

8. These tectonic rumblings are figured in the strange growl that haunts the depths of the labyrinth. The growl is even once explicitly linked to tectonic (or at least geological) movement when likened to 'calving glaciers, far off in the distance' (123).

9. On this final point, see again Starre 2015, particularly 133–47.

10. Also, one has to take into account that there are different editions of the novel and that, even though the word *house* is markedly set off in all existing editions, not all of them use the colour blue. The hyperlink

analogy is contingent on those editions that do use the colour blue. My reading of the novel is based on the 'Remastered Full-Color Edition'.
11. This includes representation versus artifice, where representation is narrowed to mean good mimesis only.
12. This not only emphasises the novel's act of problematisation (drawing attention to *questions*), but, against Hansen, also emphasises that *no medium* can be exempt from this critique.
13. In what follows, instances that predominantly refer to the mythological figure are capitalised – I say predominantly, as obviously evoking the mythological also necessarily evokes the scientific connotation. Echo is thus always already duplicitous, echoing itself.
14. Of course, the fact that the *Metamorphoses* are the source of this discourse already posits transformation and thus difference rather than identity as the principle.
15. Let me emphasise that the mathematical connotations are not coincidental. As we will see, narrative's dis-integration *is* a differentiation: the process of differentiating narrative (integral) towards its vanishing limit (differential).
16. Contrary to N. Katherine Hayles and Martin Brick, who read the novel as saving the subject (Hayles) and as essentially being about personal experience (Brick), such passages emphasise that *House of Leaves* in fact dissolves the subject. This is fundamentally a novel of *de*personalisation and *im*personal experience.
17. It is important to note that Johnny is by no means the mastermind behind this process, no more than Danielewski or the reader is. As has been pointed out, there is no authoritative centre to the novel, no centripetal force around which the novel (r)evolves. In addition to all the various strategies already mentioned, the novel makes this clear with its incorporation of *anonymous* editors and by claiming to be the second edition. This is not to suggest that Johnny has not compiled Zampanò's material, but rather that Johnny, and Danielewski by proxy, have to be viewed as just *another set of differential elements* entering into relation with all other elements complicit in constituting the novel's narrative.
18. My reading of 'DNE' is indebted to the respective discussion thread on the MZD forums, which also mentions its use in calculus.
19. On the mathematical origins of Deleuze's philosophy of difference, see Duffy 2006, particularly Chapters 2 and 3 (43–93). Suffice here to say that Deleuze's use of calculus fundamentally builds on the traditional notion of differentials as infinitesimals.
20. It is no coincidence that Brick asserts that 'Danielewski's novel *has* rooms' (Brick 2004: n. p.; my emphasis).
21. See also Danielewski's own assertion in an early online interview with Sophie Cottrell that books were always able to do what *House*

of Leaves does (Cottrell 2000: n. p.). Unfortunately, as of September 2015, the respective interview seems to have been removed.
22. Due credit for the coinage of this term goes to my friend, Andreas Hägler.

Conclusion:
From the Becoming of Narrative to the Narrativity of Becoming

> The task of the narrator is not an easy one, he said. He appears to be required to choose his tale from among the many that are possible. But of course that is not the case. The case is rather to make many of the one. Always the teller must be at pains to devise against his listener's claim – perhaps spoken, perhaps not – that he has heard the tale before. He sets forth the categories into which the listener will wish to fit the narrative as he hears it. But he understands that the narrative is itself in fact no category but is rather the category of all categories for there is nothing which falls outside its purview. All is telling. Do not doubt it.
> Cormac McCarthy, *The Crossing*[1]

To rehearse: what has been established under the heading of differential narratology is becoming as it pertains to narrative, narrativity in constant variation generating ever new variants of narrative; the virtual dance of narrative differentials producing actual, numerically differentiated narratives; the intensive sensations and forces of transcendental Narrative (affects, percepts, forces) bringing about the extensive states of affairs and networks of empirical narratives (events, existents, plots). In short, becoming, the dynamic and continuous process of selecting and gathering heterogeneous elements to be expressed, has been revealed as the ontologically primary virtual realm of any given actual narrative. But this has been possible only by following the reverse movement of the speculative becoming-virtual of actual narratives as they crack open their representational surface and burrow ever deeper towards their conditioning differentials. For this end, *Narrative and Becoming* has resorted to four *literary* narratives as its tutor texts. This does not mean that literature and narrative are synonymous, however. Even though a plethora of related terms have been employed throughout this book, terms such as narrative, literature, fiction, legend, myth, and writing, these concepts, despite considerable overlaps, remain distinct. Already in the Introduction, I noted in passing how I conceive of the distinction between literariness, narrativity, fictionality, and the activity of fiction-making: while fictionality denotes a state of non-existence (or non-actuality),

Conclusion

fiction-making emphasises the creative and constructive work of narrative. Literature, in turn, is a designator for the respective quantitative and qualitative use of rhetorical and narratological devices and their effects. Narrativity, finally, as expounded throughout this book, is the concept grounding all the other concepts. The ensuing chapters have both explicated and complicated – that is, unfolded and refolded – the conceptual terrain staked out by these terms. They have done so by multiplying and adding to the available conceptual arsenal and introducing concepts such as fabulation, the faculty of speculation (Chapter 1), figuration and, importantly, disfiguration, the forming and deforming of figures (Chapter 2), speculative constructivism, the facilitation of events (Chapter 3), narreme and narrome, the constituents of Narrative, and emplotment and deplotment, their respective putting together and taking apart (Chapter 4). All these notions, in their specific functionality, serve to construct the general function of narrative. In this vein, what *Narrative and Becoming* has shown is that narrative captures how literature captures sensations: that the Deleuzian monumentalising function of literature rests on its narrativity (virtual Narrative, Idea of narrative). If this is the case, given that according to Deleuze all the arts are engaged in erecting such monuments, then narrativisation, fiction-making, and emplotment denominate the gathering, selection, and distribution of singularities as they occur in all the arts. It is narrativity that is responsible for art's 'enterprise of co-creation' (WIP: 173). This is so because narrativity and narrative not only pervade all the arts, but also already permeate the everyday and all of life. Narrativity (Idea) and narrativisation (actualisation of Idea) thus emerge as genuinely *metaphysical* terms; they adequately capture and describe Deleuze's 'indi-drama-different/ciation' (DR: 308). Accordingly, the bond between becoming and narrative is not exhausted by the twofold *becoming of narrative* as elaborated throughout the present pages. It also entails the *narrativity of becoming* as becoming in the first sense is precisely the process of *configuring, composing, emplotting*, while in the second sense it is that of *disfiguring, decomposing*, and *deplotting* revelatory of becoming in the first sense. Deleuze's 'movement of dramatization' (Deleuze 2004d: 94) has thus to be recast as a *process of narrativisation*, the process that names *the way* anything comes into being. If, according to Brian Massumi's Deleuzo-Whiteheadian conceptualisation, ecology – the logic of the house; that is, the cosmos – is tantamount to 'relational-qualitative goings on' (Massumi 2011: 28), then narrative is the name for the very way these goings on go on. And since within the framework of Deleuzian metaphysics, any relation on the level of the actual is established by means of virtual differentials and the nomadicity of differential elements, narrative and narrativisation ultimately name *the machinery of relation as such*.

Interestingly and somewhat surprisingly, given its de-emphasis on relations and relationality, and the emphasis on a resurrected notion of substance, it is the recent metaphysical project of object-oriented philosophy and ontology (OOP/OOO) that provides leverage for theorising this narrativity of becoming. I am thinking here of Graham Harman's, Ian Bogost's, and Tim Morton's recent theorisations of tropes, particularly metaphor (Harman 2005: 101–24; Bogost 2012: 61–84; Morton 2011: n. p.; Morton 2013b: 70–87), as the primary means of relation with the withdrawn being of objects.[2] According to these three thinkers, the proper being of objects can never be fully disclosed to any other object nor even the object in question itself, but only alluded to, pointed towards. While OOP/OOO's non-human turn is laudable, its emphasis on just one type of rhetorical figure, trope as opposed to scheme, and even only one specific figure, metaphor, at the expense of all the others is lamentable. The privilege granted to one (type of) rhetorical figure supposedly doing all the work is untenable in the face of a whole array of figures doing it.[3] More importantly and as has been shown, these figures are employed within the larger framework of narrative and in combination with more specifically narrative strategies (for example, employment of voice, mood, and tense). The work of fostering connections, of building bridges into and with the withdrawn, is precisely the speculative work of narrative as manifested in the narratives discussed throughout *Narrative and Becoming*. By focusing on metaphor, OOP/OOO largely neglects the syntactic domain in favour of the semantic; it occupies itself with transformations of content, disregarding the permutations of form (this is why Deleuze favours anamorphic images over metaphoric ones, as elaborated in Chapter 1). It operates with isolated metaphor-objects at the expense of taking into account the involvement of these objects within a larger framework and process, on both the molar and the molecular levels. It is narration, not merely metaphor, by way of which things become related. There is even an etymological point to this: after all, to relate something also means to tell something. OOP/OOO thus needlessly reduces the arsenal of tools available for any speculative endeavour to unearth the being of things. In fact, speculative realism in general

Conclusion

(and not just OOP/OOO) provides evidence to the contrary, as one cannot fail to notice a certain penchant for telling stories (and not just for creating images). This is most visibly so in Graham Harman's *Circus Philosophicus*, a collection of little narratives in the vein of Platonic myth, and, particularly, Reza Negarestani's *Cyclonopedia*, a monstrous hybrid of theory–fiction (Harman 2011a; Negarestani 2008). But even an otherwise science-oriented and technical thinker such as Ray Brassier reverts to narrative form at his most speculative moments, as is the case in his fascinating account of the death of the universe in *Nihil Unbound*.[4] One might even be tempted to surmise that speculation and narrative constitute conjoined twins: from Platonic to Harmanian myth, from Nietzsche's *Thus Spoke Zarathustra* to Deleuze's 'science fiction' and 'psychological novel' (DR: xix; LS: x),[5] speculation seems to enjoy a particular relation with narrativity. Speculative philosophy might just be conceived as a particular genre of narrative dedicated to relating the adventures of ideas, as the title of Alfred North Whitehead's eponymous book so beautifully indicates. Indeed, it is in this vein that Lyotard decries speculation as 'the name given the discourse on the legitimation of scientific discourse', in which '[t]he subject of knowledge' is precisely 'the speculative spirit' (Lyotard 1984: 33). One should note here that Lyotard's aversion to metanarratives lies not in their narrativity (after all, he is all for small narratives), but in their totalising nature. This is why he particularly zooms in on Hegel (though he thinks Hegel is prefigured in Fichte and Schelling) when discussing speculative philosophy as metanarrative: for Lyotard, the problem is that the speculative narrative needs to be anchored in a narrator-as-metasubject – for example, Hegelian spirit – and that everything comes to be explained by finding a place for it within the overarching story this metasubject 'tells' (Lyotard 1984: 34–5). In other words, the problem is 'speculative unity' or totality (Lyotard 1984: 35). Lyotard seems unable to envision speculation without unity or totality. This is why, for him, Hegel's account is indeed paradigmatic and why he is allergic to any kind of speculative metaphysics. In contrast, Deleuze's life-long project was precisely devoted to devising a speculative system without unity or totality, thus safeguarding it from being conflated with totalisation; the result is his philosophy of difference with its constitutive processes of differen*t/c*iation.

The literary narratives scrutinised in the previous chapters confirm the intimate relation between narrative and speculation. The evidence assembled in these pages thus opens up the possibility that wresting oneself from the fallacious correlation of being and thought might mean to acknowledge the correlation of becoming and narrative. The famous beginning of Nietzsche's 'On Truth and Lies in a Nonmoral Sense', which Brassier quotes as an epigraph to one of the chapters in *Nihil Unbound*, is quite telling in this sense:

> Once upon a time, in some out of the way corner of that universe which is dispersed into numberless twinkling solar systems, there was a star upon which clever beasts invented knowing. That was the most arrogant and mendacious minute of 'world history', but nevertheless, it was only a minute. After nature had drawn a few breaths, the star cooled and congealed, and the clever beasts had to die. – One might invent such a fable, and yet he still would not have adequately illustrated how miserable, how shadowy and transient, how aimless and arbitrary the human intellect looks within nature. There were eternities during which it did not exist. And when it is all over with the human intellect, nothing will have happened. (qtd in Brassier 2007: 205)

While Brassier uses this quotation as a starting point to argue against what he perceives to be a wrongly postulated superabundant life in the philosophical tradition of vitalism, I simply wish to indicate that this passage casts the life and death of human consciousness as an utterly inconsequential and unimportant event within the much larger story of nature. Thought indeed will have been just a minor episode in the relentless story of being unfolding. In this vein, Deleuze's univocity and clamour of being are the very voice and noise of being's telling. Or, in the words of *The Crossing*, 'narrative is [. . .] the category of all categories [. . .] All is telling' (McCarthy 1994: 155). What the efforts of *Narrative and Becoming* ultimately point to is that this proposition has to be taken at its word.

In closing, let me emphasise that this is not yet another anthropomorphism crafted to humanise the non-human. Having sketched my reasons for rejecting the static substance ontological metaphorisms of OOO/OOP in favour of a process metaphysical account of narrativity,[6] I likewise wish to disown the anthropomorphism inherent in much process metaphysics. For an illustrative example of such anthropomorphism, let me quote from Steven Shaviro's introduction to *Cognition and Decision in Non-Human Biological Organisms*, a recent collection of essays that Shaviro edited for Open Humanities Press's Living Books about Life series:

> [B]oth cognition based on acquired data, and spontaneous decision and action, presuppose other sorts of mental stances – what we would

describe, in human terms, as feelings, expectations, attitudes, and moods. I would argue, philosophically, that this has to do with the affective basis of all cognition and all decision. Understanding and willing are cognitive activities, but they have their necessary basis on some pre-cognitive level of affect or feeling. And this is true of bacteria, slime molds, and insects, just as it is true of human beings. (Shaviro 2011: n. p.)

While I agree with the general thrust of Shaviro's statement, I also think that in its anthropomorphisation of the non-human, this passage is symptomatic of much of current anti-anthropocentric thought. Rather than projecting anthropomorphic features such as 'feelings, expectations, attitudes, and moods' on to non-human entities, I suggest we have to rid these features of their anthropomorphic qualities first. This is what I believe we can gain from Deleuze's philosophy in so far as it thoroughly dehumanises a term such as affect. Deleuze helps us to extract the non-human from the human. Whereas thinkers like Shaviro, Harman, and most recently N. Katherine Hayles (Hayles 2014) place their bets on the value of anthropomorphic as against anthropocentric thought, I think this contrast does not hold.[7] Rather than anthropomorphise nature, we need to naturalise the *anthropos* thoroughly. Deleuze's unwavering insistence on becoming-imperceptible, depersonalisation, dissipation, and de-formation is precisely aimed at de-morphing and thus undoing the anthropomorphic. Thus, while, with Shaviro, Harman, and Hayles, I would insist on the metaphysically fundamental status of *aisthesis*, I part with them with regard to their understanding of this process. In my book, *aisthesis* is a general activity in nature because it is a thoroughly *natural* process *and thus warrants to be treated as such*. Treating nature as thoughtful or proto-thoughtful does not achieve this. Shaviro's and Harman's respective metaphysical systems tend toward such a panpsychism because they ultimately still envision *aisthesis* in human terms: that is, as a modality of thought – note that in the quotation above Shaviro refers to sub- or pre-cognitive states as 'mental'. I think this is why Meillassoux's recently voiced subjectalism charge, the charge that such positions amount to a post-Berkeleyan anti-materialist speculative absolutisation of thought, is to the point (Meillassoux 2016: 121–33). I would just add that it also holds for Meillassoux himself. For Harman, the respective operative term here is Husserlian intentionality, which he hypostatises to a general feature beyond the human sphere. Shaviro relies on a similar hypostatisation in so far as he adopts Whitehead's cosmologically enhanced notion of feeling. Meillassoux himself can only posit his principle of unreason due to his absolutisation of the reaches of mathematical thought: there simply are no limits to mathematics, as it gets us to the absolute itself. In turn, I do not believe that the same charge of hypostatising (a feature of) human thought can be brought against my employment of the term narrative. The reason for this lies in the directionality of the respective operations: while both Harman and Shaviro try to recuperate non-human activity (such as, say, a supernova) with human terms, I have tried to expose the non-human basis of a human activity (namely, literary narrative). While the first option leads directly into panpsychism – in the sense of a mentalisation of nature – my approach results in the naturalisation of mentality. Basically, I think Harman's and Shaviro's concepts, in order to properly function as non-anthropocentric, ontological descriptors, would have to be shorn of their anthropomorphism first. Both Harman's and Shaviro's concepts lack such a propaedeutic. The same holds for Meillassoux's mathematicism, as mathematics is a thoroughly human science and, even if formal, a language devised by humans. In contrast, what I suggest is that we need to envision thought as a (particular) modality, or, more accurately, extension of *aisthesis*. In short, I think we should strive for a pan-aestheticism that is thoroughly devoid of any remnants of *psyche* in the sense of mentality. And I believe that this can be achieved by recasting Deleuze's movement of dramatisation as a movement of narrativisation where the activity of virtual emplotment *is* the way things come to be, the way things occur without needing to revert to a however minimal but universal remnant of thought. In this framework, thought is but one such thing that happens to have been generated. Ultimately, such a stance amounts to just another conceptualisation of the traditional notion of *poiesis*, a conceptualisation that, while being elaborated in the context of poetry in the general sense of literature, is made inflationary and pervasive so as to capture all acts of onto- and morphogenesis. This generalisation is apposite, as the term *poiesis* derives from Greek *poieō*, to make, to produce; it thus is not reducible to a particular field of human practice, but is a general term in origin, a generality to which its employment in the sciences (for example, biology) also testifies.

To recapitulate, then, apart from narrative, the three most important concepts of this book have been *poiesis*, *aisthesis*, and *noesis*. While Chapter 2 explicitly discussed the notions of *aisthesis* and *noesis*, and Chapter 3 briefly touched on all three terms in their interrelation, *aisthesis* and *noesis* mostly surfaced under the headings of aesthetics and thought. *Poiesis* in turn appeared in many guises: crea-

Conclusion

tion, production, generation, emergence, and facilitation, to name but a few. My readings of *The Mixquiahuala Letters*, *The Collected Works of Billy the Kid*, *The Intuitionist*, and *House of Leaves* have all elaborated on the relation between these concepts. This relation has been sketched thus: *aisthesis* reveals *poiesis*. This revelation then is captured and articulated by *noesis*, which in turn, as much as *aisthesis*, is itself the product of *poiesis* (through the intermediary of *aisthesis*). While actual narratives are *aisthetic* and thus reveal their very own *poiesis*, this revelatory activity has been captured in the *noetic* work of the present project: it has created a new concept of narrative. This work of creation is contingent on the previous work of *poiesis* and *aisthesis* as it is directly grafted on to the revelatory *aisthetic* work performed by the respective literary narratives. This is the case in a strong, genetic sense: it is not just that these narratives give food for thought, as the saying goes, thus presupposing a thought to be fed. Rather, these narratives provide an encounter that forces one to think, an encounter that *generates* thought. My encounters with Castillo's, Ondaatje's, Whitehead's, and Danielewski's blocs of sensation affected me such that they elicited a response – they made me think. Ultimately, the new concept of narrative presented here is the result of being propelled to think by the bombardment with sensations that these narratives provided.

In conclusion, while I take it that the work of formulating a new concept of narrative has been accomplished here, what still awaits its proper formulation, even though it already necessarily formed a subterranean undercurrent in the present book, is the corresponding new concept of becoming. Having established the becoming of narrative, the narrativity of becoming has yet to be elaborated. While part of my argument in this book was indeed that such a narrativity of becoming constitutes the speculative wager of literary (or artistic) narrative as exemplified by the four narratives scrutinised in detail here, this in itself clearly does not suffice to establish it. In order to do so, the present enquiries in the field of literature (or art more generally) have to be supplemented with enquiries in the fields of philosophy and – crucially – science. Thus, in Deleuzian fashion, this book, rather than concluding its task and wrapping up its results so that they can be safely shelved away, ends by posing a new problem. Let me then clearly and unmistakably state the task that has yet to be undertaken: the *differential narratology* presented here needs to be supplemented with a proper *narrative ontology* – the black box that still awaits its invention.

Notes

1. I would like to thank Johannes Fehrle for drawing my attention to this passage from McCarthy's novel.
2. 'Withdrawn' and 'withdrawal' are technical terms in OOP/OOO designating the elusiveness and occlusion of the inner real core of objects (substance). The withdrawn real object as such never surfaces and never directly enters any relation – hence Harman's reworking of medieval occasionalism (Harman 2007). My usage here, while alluding to OOP/OOO's *terminus technicus*, is in the broader sense of designating the non-experiential realm without necessarily entailing a substance ontology.
3. Admittedly, Morton discusses the import of rhetoric as a discipline for OOO in *Realist Magic* (Morton 2013b: 78–87). However, when it comes to rhetorical figures, to tropes and schemes, he decidedly favours and zooms in on metaphor.
4. This is the relevant passage (which mixes the simple future of prophecy with the future perfect of fictional narrative as elaborated in my Chapter 3):

   > But this is only to postpone the day of reckoning, because sooner or later both life and mind will have to reckon with the disintegration of the ultimate horizon, when, roughly one trillion, trillion, trillion (10^{1728}) years from now, the accelerating expansion of the universe will have disintegrated the fabric of matter itself, terminating the possibility of embodiment. Every star in the universe will have burnt out, plunging the cosmos into a state of absolute darkness and leaving behind nothing but spent husks of collapsed matter. All free matter, whether on planetary surfaces or in interstellar space, will have decayed, eradicating any remnants of life based in protons and chemistry, and erasing every vestige of sentience – irrespective of its physical basis. Finally, in a state cosmologists call 'asymptopia', the stellar corpses littering the empty universe will evaporate into a brief hailstorm of elementary particles. Atoms themselves will cease to exist. Only the implacable gravitational expansion will continue, driven by the currently inexplicable force called 'dark energy', which will keep pushing the extinguished universe deeper and deeper into an eternal and unfathomable blackness. (Brassier 2007: 228)

5. These are the terms in which Deleuze asks his readers to conceive of *Difference and Repetition* and *Logic of Sense* respectively.
6. Of course, the reasons given for my rejection are only those that bear directly on the project undertaken here. This is not to say that there is not a plethora of other reasons, not the least of which is that the status quo of contemporary scientific knowledge seems to favour process ontological explanations:

   > The perhaps most powerful argument for process philosophy is its wide descriptive or explanatory scope. If we admit that the basic entities of our

Conclusion

world are processes, we can generate better philosophical descriptions of all the kinds of entities and relationships we are committed to when we reason about our world in common sense and in science: from quantum entanglement to consciousness, from computation to feelings, from things to institutions, from organisms to societies, from traffic jams to climate change, from spacetime to beauty. Moreover, results in cognitive science, some philosophers have claimed, show that we need a process metaphysics in order to develop a naturalist theory of the mind and of normativity. (Seibt 2012: n. p.)

For a veritable takedown of OOP/OOO's philosophical programme, particularly Harman's, see Wolfendale 2014.

7. On Harman's anthropomorphism, see the scathing review by Nathan Brown, in which he draws attention to the fact that, apart from the theorisations of metaphor already mentioned, Harman bases his account of causation on discussions of humour – both elements being clearly imported from a decidedly human world (Brown 2013: 63).

Works Cited

'... DNE', *MZD Forums*, <http://forums.markzdanielewski.com/forum/house-of-leaves/house-of-leaves-aa/2204–dne> (last accessed 21 September 2015).

Aarseth, Espen J. (1997), *Cybertext: Perspectives on Ergodic Literature*, Baltimore: Johns Hopkins University Press.

Abbot, H. Porter (2011/2014), 'Narrativity', in Peter Hühn, Jan Christoph Meister, John Pier, and Wolf Schmid (eds), *The Living Handbook of Narratology*, Hamburg: Hamburg University Press, <http://www.lhn.uni-hamburg.de/> (last accessed 21 September 2015).

Aghoro, Nathalie (2012), 'Textual Transformations: Experience, Mediation, and Reception in *House of Leaves*', in Sascha Pöhlmann (ed.), *Revolutionary Leaves: The Fiction of Mark Z. Danielewski*, Newcastle: Cambridge Scholars, pp. 63–75.

Alber, Jan (2016), *Unnatural Narrative: Impossible Worlds in Fiction and Drama*, Lincoln: University of Nebraska Press.

Alber, Jan (2013), 'Unnatural Narratology: Developments and Perspectives', *Germanisch-Romanische Monatsschrift* 63.1: pp. 69–84.

Alber, Jan (2009), 'Impossible Storyworlds – And What to Do with Them', *Storyworlds: A Journal of Narrative Study* 1.1: pp. 79–96.

Alber, Jan and Monika Fludernik (eds) (2010), *Postclassical Narratology: Approaches and Analyses*, Columbus: Ohio State University Press.

Alber, Jan and Rüdiger Heinze (eds) (2011), *Unnatural Narratives – Unnatural Narratology*, Berlin: De Gruyter.

Alber, Jan, Stefan Iversen, Henrik Skov Nielsen, and Brian Richardson (2012), 'What Is Unnatural About Unnatural Narratology? A Response to Monika Fludernik', *Narrative* 20.3: pp. 371–82.

Alber, Jan, Stefan Iversen, Henrik Skov Nielsen, and Brian Richardson (2010), 'Unnatural Narratives, Unnatural Narratology: Beyond Mimetic Models', *Narrative* 18.2: pp. 113–36.

Alber, Jan, Henrik Skov Nielsen, and Brian Richardson (eds) (2013), *A Poetics of Unnatural Narrative*, Columbus: Ohio State University Press.

Anzaldúa, Gloria (1987), *Borderlands/La Frontera: The New Mestiza*, San Francisco: Aunt Lute Books.

Aristotle (1987), *The Poetics of Aristotle*, trans. and comment. Stephen Halliwell, Chapel Hill: University of North Carolina Press.

Works Cited

Arteaga, Alfred (1997), *Chicano Poetics: Heterotexts and Hybridities*, Cambridge: Cambridge University Press.
Askin, Ridvan (2015), 'Prolegomenon to a Differential Theory of Narrative', *SubStance* 44.3: pp. 155–70.
Askin, Ridvan (2012), 'Difference and Identity in Richard Powers' *The Echo Maker*: A Deleuzian Reading', in Antje Kley and Jan Kucharzewski (eds), *Ideas of Order: Narrative Patterns in the Novels of Richard Powers*, Heidelberg: Winter, pp. 217–38.
Askin, Ridvan, Paul J. Ennis, Andreas Hägler, and Philipp Schweighauser (eds) (2014), *Aesthetics in the 21st Century*, spec. issue, *Speculations: A Journal of Speculative Realism* 5.
Austin, Michael (2011), 'Unthinking Nature: Transcendental Realism, Neo-Vitalism and the Metaphysical Unconscious in Outline', *Thinking Nature: A Journal on the Concept of Nature* 1, <https://thinkingnature-journal.wordpress.com/volume-1/> (last accessed 21 September 2015).
Avanessian, Armen and Anke Hennig (2012), *Präsens: Poetik eines Tempus*, Zürich: Diaphanes.
Barbour, Douglas (1993), *Michael Ondaatje*, New York: Twayne Publishers.
Barthes, Roland (1978) [1966], 'Introduction to the Structural Analysis of Narratives', in Roland Barthes, *Image, Music, Text*, trans. Stephen Heath, New York: Wang & Hill, pp. 79–124.
Baumgarten, Alexander Gottlieb (1963) [1739], *Metaphysica*, 7th edn, Hildesheim: Georg Olms.
Bell, Alice (2011), 'Ontological Boundaries and Methodological Leaps: The Importance of Possible Worlds Theory for Hypertext Fiction (and Beyond)', in Ruth Page and Bronwen Thomas (eds), *New Narratives: Stories and Storytelling in the Digital Age*, Lincoln: University of Nebraska Press, pp. 63–82.
Bennett, John M. (ed.) (2008), *Visual Poetry in the Avant Writing Collection*, Columbus: Ohio State University Libraries.
Bennett, Tanya Long (1996), 'No Country to Call Home: A Study of Castillo's *Mixquiahuala Letters*', *Style* 30.3: pp. 462–78.
Beressem, Hanjo (2012), 'The Surface of Sense, the Surface of Sensation and the Surface of Reference: Geometry and Topology in the Works of Mark Z. Danielewski', in Sascha Pöhlmann (ed.), *Revolutionary Leaves: The Fiction of Mark Z. Danielewski*, Newcastle: Cambridge Scholars, pp. 199–221.
Bergson, Henri (1954) [1932], *The Two Sources of Morality and Religion*, trans. R. Ashley Audra and Cloudsley Brereton, Garden City, NY: Doubleday Anchor.
Berlant, Lauren (2008), 'Intuitionists: History and the Affective Event', *American Literary History* 20.4: pp. 845–60.
Bérubé, Michael (2004), 'Race and Modernity in Colson Whitehead's *The Intuitionist*', in Peter Freese and Charles B. Harris (eds), *The Holodeck in*

the Garden: Science and Technology in Contemporary American Fiction, Champaign: Dalkey Archive Press, pp. 163–78.

Bethell, Kathleen I. (2003), 'Reading Billy: Memory, Time, and Subjectivity in *The Collected Works of Billy the Kid*', SCL/ÉLC 28.1: pp. 71–89.

Bhabha, Homi (2004) [1994], *The Location of Culture*, Abingdon: Routledge.

Bilsky, Brianne (2012), '(Im)Possible Spaces: Technology and Narrative in *House of Leaves*', in Sascha Pöhlmann (ed.), *Revolutionary Leaves: The Fiction of Mark Z. Danielewski*, Newcastle: Cambridge Scholars, pp. 137–65.

Bogost, Ian (2012), *Alien Phenomenology, or What It's Like to Be a Thing*, Minneapolis: University of Minnesota Press.

Brassier, Ray (2011), 'Concepts and Objects', in Levi Bryant, Nick Srnicek, and Graham Harman (eds), *The Speculative Turn: Continental Materialism and Realism*, Melbourne: Repress, pp. 47–65.

Brassier, Ray (2007), *Nihil Unbound: Enlightenment and Extinction*, Basingstoke: Palgrave Macmillan.

Bray, Joe (2003), *The Epistolary Novel: Representations of Consciousness*, London: Routledge.

Brick, Martin (2004), 'Blueprint(s): Rubric for a Deconstructed Age in *House of Leaves*', *Philament: An Online Journal of the Arts and Culture* 2, <http://sydney.edu.au/arts/publications/philament/issue2_Critique_Brick.htm> (last accessed 21 September 2015).

Brown, Charles Brockden (1986) [1801], *Clara Howard: In a Series of Letters; Jane Talbot: A Novel*, Kent: Kent State University Press.

Brown, Nathan (2013), 'The Nadir of OOO: From Graham Harman's *Tool-Being* to Timothy Morton's *Realist Magic: Objects, Ontology, Causality* (Open Humanities Press, 2013)', *Parrhesia: A Journal of Critical Philosophy* 17: pp. 62–71.

Bruns, Gerald L. (2012), review of Richard Eldridge and Bernard Rhie (eds), *Stanley Cavell and Literary Studies: Consequences of Skepticism*, *Notre Dame Philosophical Reviews*, <http://ndpr.nd.edu/news/32075–stanley-cavell-and-literary-studies-consequences-of-skepticism/> (last accessed 21 September 2015).

Bryant, Levi R. (2011), *The Democracy of Objects*, Ann Arbor: Open Humanities Press.

Bryant, Levi R. (2008), *Difference and Givenness: Deleuze's Transcendental Empiricism and the Ontology of Immanence*, Evanston: Northwestern University Press.

Buchanan, Ian (2001a), 'Deleuze and American (Mythopoeic) Literature', *Southern Review* 34.2: pp. 72–85.

Buchanan, Ian (2001b), 'Deleuze's "Immanent Historicism"', *Parallax* 7.4: pp. 29–39.

Works Cited

Burns, Walter Noble (1999) [1925], *The Saga of Billy the Kid*, Albuquerque: University of New Mexico Press.

Calvin, Ritch (2007), 'Writing the Xicanista: Ana Castillo and the Articulation of Chicana Feminist Aesthetics', in Christa Davis Acampora and Angela L. Cotton (eds), *Unmaking Race, Remaking Soul: Transformative Aesthetics and the Practice of Freedom*, Albany: SUNY Press, pp. 21–45.

Campbell, Neil (2008), *The Rhizomatic West: Representing the American West in a Transnational, Global, Media Age*, Lincoln: University of Nebraska Press.

Casati, Roberto and Achille C. Varzi (1999), *Parts and Places: The Structures of Spatial Representation*, Cambridge: MIT Press.

Castillo, Ana (1995), *Massacre of the Dreamers: Essays on Xicanisma*, New York: Plume.

Castillo, Ana (1992) [1986], *The Mixquiahuala Letters*, New York: Doubleday.

Castillo, Ana (1975), 'I Close My Eyes ... to See', Ana Castillo Papers, California Ethnic and Multicultural Archives 2, Special Collections, Santa Barbara: University of California.

Cervantes Saavedra, Miguel de (2003) [1605/1615], *The History and Adventures of the Renowned Don Quixote*, trans. Tobias Smollett, Athens: University of Georgia Press.

Chanen, Brian W. (2007), 'Surfing the Text: The Digital Environment in Mark Z. Danielewski's *House of Leaves*', *European Journal of English Studies* 11.2: pp. 163–76.

Clark, Matthew (2012), 'Narratological Rhetoric', Paper presented at the International Conference on Narrative, Las Vegas, 15–17 March.

Cogburn, Jon and Mark Allan Ohm (2014), 'Actual Qualities of Imaginative Things: Notes towards an Object-Oriented Literary Theory', *Speculations: A Journal of Speculative Realism* 5: pp. 180–224.

Colebrook, Claire (2014), 'Not Kant, Not Now: Another Sublime', *Speculations: A Journal of Speculative Realism* 5: pp. 127–57.

Colebrook, Claire (2012), 'Feminist Extinction', in Henriette Gunkel, Chrysanthi Nigianni, and Fanny Söderbäck (eds), *Undutiful Daughters: New Directions in Feminist Thought and Practice*, New York: Palgrave Macmillan, pp. 71–84.

Colebrook, Claire (2010), *Deleuze and the Meaning of Life*, London: Continuum.

Coover, Robert (1982), *Spanking the Maid*, New York: Grove Press.

Cottrell, Sophie (2000), 'A Conversation with Mark Danielewski', *Bold Type* 3.12: n. p. Web interview now removed (last accessed 20 November 2013).

Danielewski, Mark Z. (2000a), *House of Leaves*, Remastered Full-Colour Edition, New York: Pantheon Books.

Danielewski, Mark Z. (2000b), *The Whalestoe Letters*, New York: Pantheon Books.
Deleuze, Gilles (2008) [1985], *Cinema 2: The Time-Image*, trans. Hugh Tomlinson and Robert Galeta, London: Continuum.
Deleuze, Gilles (2007a) [1999], Interview by Arnaud Villani, 'Responses to a Series of Questions', *Collapse: Philosophical Research and Development* 3: pp. 39–43.
Deleuze, Gilles (2007b) [1946], 'Mathesis, Science and Philosophy', trans. Robin Mackay, *Collapse: Philosophical Research and Development* 3: pp. 141–55.
Deleuze, Gilles (2006a) [1988], *The Fold: Leibniz and the Baroque*, trans. Tom Conley, London: Continuum.
Deleuze, Gilles (2006b) [1962], *Nietzsche and Philosophy*, trans. Hugh Tomlinson, New York: Columbia University Press.
Deleuze, Gilles (2004a) [1956], 'Bergson, 1859–1941', trans. Christopher Bush, in Gilles Deleuze, *Desert Islands and Other Texts 1953–1974*, New York: Semiotext(e), pp. 22–31.
Deleuze, Gilles (2004b) [1968], *Difference and Repetition*, trans. Paul Patton, London: Continuum.
Deleuze, Gilles (2004c) [1969], *Logic of Sense*, trans. Mark Lester, London: Continuum.
Deleuze, Gilles (2004d) [1967], 'The Method of Dramatization', trans. Michael Taormina, in Gilles Deleuze, *Desert Islands and Other Texts 1953–1974*, New York: Semiotext(e), pp. 94–116.
Deleuze, Gilles (2003a), 'Cours Vincennes: 21/12/1980 – Ontology-Ethics', trans. Simon Duffy, <http://www.webdeleuze.com/php/texte.php?cle=190&groupe=Spinoza&langue=2> (last accessed 21 September 2015).
Deleuze, Gilles (2003b) [1981], *Francis Bacon: The Logic of Sensation*, trans. Daniel W. Smith, Minneapolis: University of Minnesota Press.
Deleuze, Gilles (1997) [1993], 'Literature and Life', in Gilles Deleuze, *Essays Critical and Clinical*, trans. Daniel W. Smith and Michael A. Greco, Minneapolis: University of Minnesota Press, pp. 1–6.
Deleuze, Gilles (1995) [1990], 'Letter to a Harsh Critic', in Gilles Deleuze, *Negotiations, 1972–1990*, trans. Martin Joughin, New York: Columbia University Press, pp. 3–12.
Deleuze, Gilles and Félix Guattari (2007) [1980], *A Thousand Plateaus*, vol. 2 of *Capitalism and Schizophrenia*, trans. Brian Massumi, London: Continuum.
Deleuze, Gilles and Félix Guattari (1994) [1991], *What Is Philosophy?*, trans. Hugh Tomlinson and Graham Burchell, New York: Columbia University Press.
Deleuze, Gilles and Félix Guattari (1986) [1972], *Anti-Oedipus*, vol. 1 of *Capitalism and Schizophrenia*, trans. Robert Hurley, Mark Seem, and Helen R. Lane, Minneapolis: University of Minnesota Press.

Works Cited

Deleuze, Gilles and Claire Parnet (2006) [1977], *Dialogues II*, trans. Hugh Tomlinson and Barbara Habberjam, London: Continuum.
Delgadillo, Theresa (2011), *Spiritual Mestizaje: Religion, Gender, Race, and Nation in Contemporary Chicana Narrative*, Durham, NC: Duke University Press.
Dery, Mark (1993), 'Black to the Future: Interviews with Samuel R. Delany, Greg Tate, and Tricia Rose', *South Atlantic Quarterly* 92.4: pp. 735–78.
Duffy, Simon (2006), *The Logic of Expression: Quality, Quantity and Intensity in Spinoza, Hegel and Deleuze*, Aldershot: Ashgate.
Dunham, Jeremy, Iain Hamilton Grant, and Sean Watson (2011), *Idealism: The History of a Philosophy*, Durham: Acumen.
Elam, Michele (2011), *The Souls of Mixed Folk: Race, Politics, and Aesthetics in the New Millennium*, Stanford: Stanford University Press.
Ellison, Ralph (1963) [1948], *Invisible Man*, New York: Modern Library.
Ennis, Paul J. (2011), *Continental Realism*, Winchester: Zero.
'Enter Sandman', in *Metallica*, CD, composed by Metallica. Los Angeles: Elektra Records, 1991.
'Es gibt Wiederholungen', in *Song*, LP, composed by Attwenger. Munich: Trikont Musikverlag, 1997.
Eskelinen, Markku (2012), *Cybertext Poetics: The Critical Landscape of New Media Literary Theory*, London: Continuum.
Evans, Mel (2011), 'This Haunted House: Intertextuality and Interpretation in Mark Z. Danielewski's *House of Leaves* (2000) and Poe's *Haunted* (2000)', in Joe Bray and Alison Gibbons (eds), *Mark Z. Danielewski*, Manchester: Manchester University Press, pp. 68–85.
Fludernik, Monika (2012), 'How Natural Is "Unnatural Narratology"; or, What Is Unnatural about Unnatural Narratology?', *Narrative* 20.3: pp. 357–70.
Fludernik, Monika (2010), 'Narratology in the 21st Century: The Cognitive Approach to Narrative', *PMLA* 125.4: pp. 924–30.
Fludernik, Monika (2005), 'Histories of Narrative Theory (II): From Structuralism to the Present', in James Phelan and Peter J. Rabinowitz (eds), *A Companion to Narrative Theory*, Malden: Blackwell, pp. 36–59.
Fludernik, Monika (1996), *Towards a 'Natural' Narratology*, London: Routledge.
Freud, Sigmund (2001) [1914], 'Remembering, Repeating and Working-Through (Further Recommendations on the Technique of Psycho-Analysis II)', trans. James Strachey, in Sigmund Freud, *The Case of Schreber, Papers on Technique and Other Works*, Standard Edition of the Complete Psychological Works of Sigmund Freud, vol. 12, London: Vintage, pp. 145–56.
Freud, Sigmund (1977) [1916/1917], *Introductory Lectures on Psychoanalysis*, trans. James Strachey, Standard Edition of the Complete

Psychological Works of Sigmund Freud, vol. 15, New York: W. W. Norton.

Garcia, Tristan (2014) [2011], *Form and Object: A Treatise on Things*, trans. Mark Allan Ohm and Jon Cogburn, Edinburgh: Edinburgh University Press.

Gibbons, Alison (2012), 'Altermodernist Fiction', in Joe Bray, Alison Gibbons, and Brian McHale (eds), *The Routledge Companion to Experimental Literature*, London: Routledge, pp. 238–52.

González, Marcial (2009), *Chicano Novels and the Politics of Form: Race, Class, and Reification*, Ann Arbor: University of Michigan Press.

González, María C. (1996), *Contemporary Mexican–American Women Novelists: Toward a Feminist Identity*, New York: Peter Lang.

Grace, Dominic M. (1992), 'Ondaatje and Charlton Comics' "Billy the Kid"', *Canadian Literature* 133: pp. 199–203.

Grant, Iain Hamilton (2011), 'Does Nature Stay What-it-is?: Dynamics and the Antecedence Criterion', in Levi Bryant, Nick Srnicek, and Graham Harman (eds), *The Speculative Turn: Continental Materialism and Realism*, Melbourne: Repress, pp. 66–83.

Grant, Iain Hamilton (2008) [2006], *Philosophies of Nature after Schelling*, London: Continuum.

Grant, Iain Hamilton (2000), 'The Chemistry of Darkness', *Pli* 9: pp. 36–52.

Gratton, Peter (2014), *Speculative Realism: Problems and Prospects*, London: Bloomsbury.

Hansen, Mark B. N. (2004), 'The Digital Topography of Mark Z. Danielewski's *House of Leaves*', *Contemporary Literature* 45.4: pp. 597–636.

Harman, Graham (2011a), *Circus Philosophicus*, Winchester: Zero.

Harman, Graham (2011b), *Quentin Meillassoux: Philosophy in the Making*, Edinburgh: Edinburgh University Press.

Harman, Graham (2011c), *The Quadruple Object*, Winchester: Zero.

Harman, Graham (2007), 'On Vicarious Causation', *Collapse: Philosophical Research and Development* 2: pp. 187–221.

Harman, Graham (2005), *Guerilla Metaphysics: Phenomenology and the Carpentry of Things*, Chicago: Open Court.

Haunted, CD, composed by Poe. New York: Atlantic Recordings, 2000.

Hayles, N. Katherine (2014), 'Speculative Aesthetics and Object Oriented Inquiry (OOI)', *Speculations: A Journal of Speculative Realism* 5: pp. 158–79.

Hayles, N. Katherine (2008), *Electronic Literature: New Horizons for the Literary*, Notre Dame: University of Notre Dame Press.

Hayles, N. Katherine (2002a), 'Saving the Subject: Remediation in House of Leaves', *American Literature* 74.4: pp. 779–806.

Hayles, N. Katherine (2002b), *Writing Machines*, Cambridge, MA: MIT Press.

Works Cited

Hegel, G. W. F. (1977) [1807], *Hegel's Phenomenology of Spirit*, trans. A. V. Miller, Oxford: Oxford University Press.

Heinze, Rüdiger (2008), 'Violations of Mimetic Epistemology in First-Person Narrative Fiction', *Narrative* 16.3: pp. 279–97.

Herman, David (2012), 'Exploring the Nexus of Narrative and Mind', in David Herman, James Phelan, Peter J. Rabinowitz, Brian Richardson, and Robyn Warhol (eds), *Narrative Theory: Core Concepts and Critical Debates*, Columbus: Ohio State University Press, pp. 14–19.

Herman, David (2009), *Basic Elements of Narrative*, Malden: Wiley–Blackwell.

Herman, David (2005), 'Histories of Narrative Theory (I): A Genealogy of Early Developments', in James Phelan and Peter J. Rabinowitz (eds), *A Companion to Narrative Theory*, Malden: Blackwell, pp. 19–35.

Herman, David (1999), 'Introduction: Narratologies', in David Herman (ed.), *Narratologies: New Perspectives on Narrative Analysis*, Columbus: Ohio State University Press, pp. 1–30.

Herman, David (1997), 'Scripts, Sequences, and Stories: Elements of a Postclassical Narratology', *PMLA* 112.5: pp. 1046–59.

Hillger, Annick (2006), *Not Needing All the Words: Michael Ondaatje's Literature of Silence*, Montreal: McGill–Queen's University Press.

Hochbruck, Wolfgang (1994), 'Michael Ondaatje's *Coming through Slaughter* and *The Collected Works of Billy the Kid*', in Bernd Engler and Kurt Müller (eds), *Historiographic Metafiction in Modern American and Canadian Literature*, Paderborn: Schöningh, pp. 447–63.

Inwood, Michael (1992), *A Hegel Dictionary*, Oxford: Blackwell.

Jameson, Fredric (2013), *The Antinomies of Realism*, London: Verso.

Jameson, Fredric (1981), *The Political Unconscious: Narrative as a Socially Symbolic Act*, Ithaca, NY: Cornell University Press.

Johnson, Kelli Lyon (2004), 'Violence in the Borderlands: Crossing to the Home Space in the Novels of Ana Castillo', *Frontiers* 25.1: pp. 39–58.

Kant, Immanuel (1998) [1781/1787], *Critique of Pure Reason*, trans. Paul Guyer and Allen W. Wood, Cambridge: Cambridge University Press.

Kerslake, Christian (2009), *Immanence and the Vertigo of Philosophy: From Kant to Deleuze*, Edinburgh: Edinburgh University Press.

Kerslake, Christian (2007), *Deleuze and the Unconscious*, London: Continuum.

Landow, George P. (2006), *Hypertext 3.0: Critical Theory and New Media in an Era of Globalization*, 3rd edn, Baltimore: Johns Hopkins University Press.

Lavender, Isiah, III (2007), 'Ethnoscapes: Environment and Language in Ishmael Reed's *Mumbo Jumbo*, Colson Whitehead's *The Intuitionist*, and Samuel R. Delany's *Babel-17*', *Science Fiction Studies* 34.2: pp. 187–200.

Lichtenauer, Fritz (1994), 'Textteppiche', in Christian Steinbacher (ed.), *Linzer Notate: Positionen*, Linz: Blattwerk, pp. 57–60.

Lichtenauer, Fritz (1991), *Buchstäblich: Ein Werkheft*, Linz: Neue Texte.
Liggins, Saundra (2006), 'The Urban Gothic Vision of Colson Whitehead's *The Intuitionist* (1999)', *African American Review* 40.2: pp. 359–69.
Lord, Beth (2011), *Kant and Spinozism: Transcendental Idealism and Immanence from Jacobi to Deleuze*, Basingstoke: Palgrave Macmillan.
Lundy, Craig and Daniela Voss (eds) (2015), *At the Edges of Thought: Deleuze and Post-Kantian Philosophy*, Edinburgh: Edinburgh University Press.
Lyotard, Jean-François (1984) [1979], *The Postmodern Condition: A Report on Knowledge*, trans. Geoff Bennington and Brian Massumi, Minneapolis: University of Minnesota Press.
McCarthy, Cormac (1994), *The Crossing*, New York: Alfred A. Knopf.
McCormick, Paul (2011), 'Houses of Leaves, Cinema and the New Affordances of Old Media', in Joe Bray and Alison Gibbons (eds), *Mark Z. Danielewski*, Manchester: Manchester University Press, pp. 52–67.
McHale, Brian (1987), *Postmodernist Fiction*, London: Routledge.
MacLulich, T. D. (1981), 'Ondaatje's Mechanical Boy: Portrait of the Artist as Photographer', *Mosaic* 14.2: pp. 107–19.
Madsen, Deborah L. (2000), *Understanding Contemporary Chicana Literature*, Columbia: University of South Carolina Press.
Marinkova, Milena (2011), *Michael Ondaatje: Haptic Aesthetics and Micropolitical Writing*, New York: Continuum.
Massumi, Brian (2011), *Semblance and Event: Activist Philosophy and the Occurrent Arts*, Cambridge, MA: MIT Press.
Maszewska, Jadwiga (2008), 'The Quixotic Strain in Ana Castillo's *The Mixquiahuala Letters*', in Tuomas Huttunen, Kaisa Ilmonen, Janne Korkka, and Elina Valovirta (eds), *Seeking the Self – Encountering the Other: Diasporic Narrative and the Ethics of Representation*, Newcastle: Cambridge Scholars, pp. 262–75.
Meillassoux, Quentin (2016), 'Iteration, Reiteration, Repetition: A Speculative Analysis of the Sign Devoid of Meaning', trans. Robin Mackay and Moritz Gansen, in Armen Avanessian and Suhail Malik (eds), *Genealogies of Speculation: Materialism and Subjectivity since Structuralism*, London: Bloomsbury, pp. 117–97.
Meillassoux, Quentin (2009 [2006]), *After Finitude: An Essay on the Necessity of Contingency*, trans. Ray Brassier, London: Continuum.
Meister, Jan Christoph (2011/2014), 'Narratology', in Peter Hühn, Jan Christoph Meister, John Pier, and Wolf Schmid (eds), *The Living Handbook of Narratology*, Hamburg: Hamburg University Press, <http://www.lhn.uni-hamburg.de/> (last accessed 21 September 2015).
Millière, Raphaël (2011), 'Metaphysics Today and Tomorrow', trans. Mark Allan Ohm, *Atelier de métaphysique et d'ontologie contemporaines / Workshop on Contemporary Metaphysics and Ontology at the École Normale Supérieure*, <https://atmoc.files.wordpress.com/2012/06/

milliere_metaphysics_today_and_tomorrow1.pdf> (last accessed 21 September 2015).
Moody, Rick (2002) [1995], 'The Grid', *The Ring of Brightest Angels around Heaven*, Boston: Little, Brown & Company, pp. 29–37.
Moore, Adrian William (2012), *The Evolution of Modern Metaphysics: Making Sense of Things*, Cambridge: Cambridge University Press.
Morelle, Louis (2012), 'Speculative Realism: After Finitude, and Beyond? A Vade Mecum', trans. Leah Orth, *Speculations: A Journal of Speculative Realism* 3: pp. 241–72.
Morton, Timothy (2013a), *Hyperobjects: Philosophy and Ecology after the End of the World*, Minneapolis: University of Minnesota Press.
Morton, Timothy (2013b), *Realist Magic: Objects, Ontology, Causality*, Ann Arbor: Open Humanities Press.
Morton, Timothy (2011), 'Some Notes towards a Philosophy of Non-Life', *Thinking Nature: A Journal on the Concept of Nature* 1, <https://thinkingnaturejournal.wordpress.com/volume-1/> (last accessed 21 September 2015).
Mujčinović, Fatima (2004), *Postmodern Cross-Culturalism and Politicization in U.S. Latina Literature: From Ana Castillo to Julia Alvarez*, New York: Peter Lang.
Mullarkey, John (2006), *Post-Continental Philosophy: An Outline*, London: Continuum.
Nancy, Jean Luc (2009) [2007], *The Fall of Sleep*, trans. Charlotte Mandell, New York: Fordham University Press.
Negarestani, Reza (2008), *Cyclonopedia: Complicity with Anonymous Materials*, Melbourne: Repress.
Nielsen, Henrik Skov (2004), 'The Impersonal Voice in First-Person Narrative Fiction', *Narrative* 12.2: pp. 133–50.
Nodelman, Perry M. (1980), 'The Collected Photographs of Billy the Kid', *Canadian Literature* 87: pp. 68–79.
Ondaatje, Michael (1996) [1970], *The Collected Works of Billy the Kid*, New York: Vintage.
Powers, Richard (2007) [2006], *The Echo Maker*, London: Vintage.
Pressman, Jessica (2006), '*House of Leaves*: Reading the Networked Novel', *Studies in American Fiction* 34.1: pp. 107–28.
Priest, Graham (2002), *Beyond the Limits of Thought*, 2nd edn, Oxford: Oxford University Press.
Priest, Graham (1997), 'Sylvan's Box: A Short Story and Ten Morals', *Notre Dame Journal of Formal Logic* 38.4: pp. 573–82.
Pynchon, Thomas (1985 [1984]), 'Introduction', in Thomas Pynchon, *Slow Learner: Early Stories*, London: Jonathan Cape, pp. 1–23.
Ramachandran, Vilanayur S. and Sandra Blakeslee (1988), *Phantoms in the Brain: Probing the Mysteries of the Human Mind*, New York: William Morrow.

Ramey, Joshua (2012), *The Hermetic Deleuze: Philosophy and Spiritual Ordeal*, Durham, NC: Duke University Press.
Richardson, Brian (2015), *Unnatural Narrative: Theory, History, and Practice*, Columbus: Ohio State University Press.
Richardson, Brian (2006), *Unnatural Voices: Extreme Narration in Modern and Contemporary Fiction*, Columbus: Ohio State University Press.
Ricœur, Paul (1984/1985/1988) [1983/1984/1985], *Time and Narrative*, 3 vols, trans. Kathleen McLaughlin and David Pellauer, Chicago: University of Chicago Press.
Rölli, Marc (2003), *Gilles Deleuze: Philosophie des Transzendentalen Empirismus*, Vienna: Turia + Kant.
Rudrum, David (2006), 'On the Very Idea of a Definition of Narrative: A Reply to Marie-Laure Ryan', *Narrative* 14.2: pp. 197–204.
Rudrum, David (2005), 'From Narrative Representation to Narrative Use: Towards the Limits of Definition', *Narrative* 13.2: pp. 195–204.
Russell, Alison (2007), 'Recalibrating the Past: Colson Whitehead's *The Intuitionist*', *Critique: Studies in Contemporary Fiction* 49.1: pp. 46–60.
Ryan, Marie-Laure (2006), 'Semantics, Pragmatics, and Narrativity: A Response to David Rudrum', *Narrative* 14.2: pp. 188–96.
Saldívar, Ramón (2013), 'The Second Elevation of the Novel: Race, Form, and the Postrace Aesthetic in Contemporary Narrative', *Narrative* 21.1: pp. 1–18.
Saldívar, Ramón (1990), *Chicano Narrative: The Dialectics of Difference*, Madison: University of Wisconsin Press.
Schelling, F. W. J. (2006) [1809], *Philosophical Investigations into the Essence of Human Freedom*, trans. Jeff Love and Johannes Schmidt, Albany, NY: SUNY Press.
Schweighauser, Philipp (2016), *Beautiful Deceptions: European Aesthetics, the Early American Novel, and Illusionist Art*, Charlottesville: University of Virginia Press.
Seibt, Johanna (2012), 'Process Philosophy', *The Stanford Encyclopedia of Philosophy* (Fall 2013 edn), <http://plato.stanford.edu/archives/fall2013/entries/process-philosophy/> (last accessed 21 September 2015).
Seibt, Johanna (2009), 'Forms of Emergent Interaction in General Process Theory', *Synthese* 166: pp. 479–512.
Serres, Michel (2008) [1985], *The Five Senses: A Philosophy of Mingled Bodies*, trans. Margaret Sankey and Peter Cowley, London: Continuum.
Shaviro, Steven (2014), *The Universe of Things: On Speculative Realism*, Minneapolis: University of Minnesota Press.
Shaviro, Steven (ed.) (2011), *Cognition and Decision in Non-Human Biological Organisms*, Ann Arbor: Open Humanities Press.
Shaviro, Steven (2009), *Without Criteria: Kant, Whitehead, Deleuze, and Aesthetics*, Cambridge, MA: MIT Press.
Shklovsky, Viktor (1998) [1917/1929], 'Art as Device', in Viktor Shklovsky,

Works Cited

Theory of Prose, trans. Benjamin Sher, Normal: Dalkey Archive Press, pp. 1–14.

Sistiaga, Sergey (2012), 'Der Satz vom Grund', MA thesis, University of Freiburg.

Skrbina, David (ed.) (2009), *Mind that Abides: Panpsychism in the New Millennium*, Amsterdam: John Benjamins.

Slocombe, Will (2005), '"This Is Not For You": Nihilism and the House that Jacques Built', *Modern Fiction Studies* 51.1: pp. 88–109.

Slotkin, Richard (1998) [1992], *Gunfighter Nation: The Myth of the Frontier in Twentieth-Century America*, Norman: University of Oklahoma Press.

Slotkin, Richard (1994) [1985], *The Fatal Environment: The Myth of the Frontier in the Age of Industrialization, 1800–1890*, New York: Harper Perennial.

Slotkin, Richard (1973), *Regeneration through Violence: The Mythology of the American Frontier, 1600–1860*, Middletown, CT: Wesleyan University Press.

Smith, Daniel W. (2013), review of James Williams, *Gilles Deleuze's Philosophy of Time: A Critical Introduction and Guide*, *Notre Dame Philosophical Reviews*, <http://ndpr.nd.edu/news/42146–gilles-deleuze-s-philosophy-of-time-a-critical-introduction-and-guide/> (last accessed 21 September 2015).

Smith, Daniel W. (2012), *Essays on Deleuze*, Edinburgh: Edinburgh University Press.

Smith, Daniel W. (2006), 'Deleuze, Kant, and the Theory of Immanent Ideas', in Constantin V. Boundas (ed.), *Deleuze and Philosophy*, Edinburgh: Edinburgh University Press, pp. 43–61.

Solecki, Sam (2003), *Ragas of Longing: The Poetry of Michael Ondaatje*, Toronto: University of Toronto Press.

Somers-Hall, Henry (2012), *Hegel, Deleuze, and the Critique of Representation: Dialectics of Negation and Difference*, Albany, NY: SUNY Press.

Speculations: A Journal of Speculative Realism 4 (2013).

Spinks, Lee (2009), *Michael Ondaatje*, Manchester: Manchester University Press.

Spinoza, Baruch (1985) [1677], 'Ethics', in Edwin Curley (ed. and trans.), *The Collected Works of Spinoza, Volume 1*, Princeton: Princeton University Press, pp. 408–617.

Starre, Alexander (2015), *Metamedia: American Book Fictions and Literary Print Culture after Digitization*, Iowa City: University of Iowa Press.

Stengers, Isabelle (2008), *Spekulativer Konstruktivismus*, trans. Gabriele Ricke, Henning Schmidgen, and Ronald Voullié, Berlin: Merve.

Sternberg, Meir (2003a), 'Universals of Narrative and Their Cognitivist Fortunes (I)', *Poetics Today* 24.2: pp. 297–395.

Sternberg, Meir (2003b), 'Universals of Narrative and Their Cognitivist Fortunes (II)', *Poetics Today* 24.3: pp. 517–638.
Sternberg, Meir (2001), 'How Narrativity Makes a Difference', *Narrative* 9.2: pp. 115–22.
Taylor, Mark C. (2013), *Rewiring the Real: In Conversation with William Gaddis, Richard Powers, Mark Danielewski, and Don DeLillo*, New York: Columbia University Press.
Thacker, Eugene (2011a), 'After Life: Swarms, Demons, and the Antinomies of Immanence', in Derek Attridge and Jane Elliott (eds), *Theory after 'Theory'*, London: Routledge, pp. 181–93.
Thacker, Eugene (2011b), *In the Dust of this Planet*, vol. 1 of *Horror of Philosophy*, Winchester: Zero.
Thacker, Eugene (2010), *After Life*, Chicago: University of Chicago Press.
The Man Who Shot Liberty Valance, DVD, directed by John Ford. USA: Paramount Home Entertainment, 2005 [1962].
Thomas, Bronwen (2011), 'Trickster Authors and Tricky Readers on the MZD Forums', in Joe Bray and Alison Gibbons (eds), *Mark Z. Danielewski*, Manchester: Manchester University Press, pp. 86–102.
Tucker, Jeffrey Allen (2010), '"Verticality Is Such a Risky Enterprise": The Literary and Paraliterary Antecedents of Colson Whitehead's *The Intuitionist*', *Novel: A Forum on Fiction* 43.1: pp. 148–56.
Turner, Frederick Jackson (1986) [1920], *The Frontier in American History*, Tucson: University of Arizona Press.
Tynan, Aidan (2012), *Deleuze's Literary Clinic: Criticism and the Politics of Symptoms*, Edinburgh: Edinburgh University Press.
Van Tuinen, Sjoerd (forthcoming), *Matter, Manner, Idea: Deleuze and Mannerism*.
Van Tuinen, Sjoerd (2014a), 'Difference and Speculation: Heidegger, Meillassoux and Deleuze on Sufficient Reason', in Alain Beaulieu, Edward Kazarian, and Julia Sushytska (eds), *Deleuze and Metaphysics*, Lanham: Lexington Books, pp. 63–90.
Van Tuinen, Sjoerd (2014b), '*Disegno*: A Speculative Constructivist Interpretation', *Speculations: A Journal of Speculative Realism* 5: pp. 434–73.
Vattimo, Gianni (1987), '*Verwindung*: Nihilism and the Postmodern in Philosophy', *SubStance* 16.2: pp. 7–17.
Voss, Daniela (2013), *Conditions of Thought: Deleuze and Transcendental Ideas*, Edinburgh: Edinburgh University Press.
Walsh, Richard (2007), *The Rhetoric of Fictionality: Narrative Theory and the Idea of Fiction*, Columbus: Ohio State University Press.
Walter, Roland (1998), 'The Cultural Politics of Dislocation and Relocation in the Novels of Ana Castillo', *MELUS* 23.1: pp. 81–97.
Wart, Alice van (1985), 'The Evolution of Form in Machael [sic] Ondaatje's

Works Cited

The Collected Works of Billy the Kid and *Coming through Slaughter*', *Canadian Poetry: Studies, Documents, Reviews* 17, <http://www.uwo.ca/english/canadianpoetry/cpjrn/vol17/Van%20wart.htm> (last accessed 21 September 2015).

Welchman, Alistair (2009), 'Deleuze's Post-Critical Metaphysics', *Symposium: Canadian Journal of Continental Philosophy* 13.2: pp. 25–54.

Whitehead, Colson (2000) [1999], *The Intuitionist*, New York: Anchor Books.

Williamson, Timothy (2014), 'How Did We Get Here From There? The Transformation of Analytic Philosophy', *Belgrade Philosophical Annual* 27: pp. 7–37.

Wittgenstein, Ludwig (1981) [1953], *Philosophical Investigations*, trans. G. E. Anscombe, Oxford: Basil Blackwell.

Wolfendale, Peter (2014), *Object-Oriented Philosophy: The Noumenon's New Clothes*, Falmouth: Urbanomic.

Wolfendale, Peter (2012), 'Ariadne's Thread: Temporality, Modality, and Individuation in Deleuze's Metaphysics', Paper presented at MMU Deleuze Workshop, 24–25 March, *Deontologistics: Researching the Demands of Thought*, <https://deontologistics.files.wordpress.com/2011/03/deleuze-mmu.pdf> (last accessed 21 September 2015).

Yarbro-Bejarano, Yvonne (1996), 'Chicana Literature from a Chicana Feminist Perspective', in María Herrera-Sobek and Helena María Viramontes (eds), *Chicana Creativity and Criticism: New Frontiers in American Literature*, 2nd edn, Albuquerque: University of New Mexico Press, pp. 213–18.

Yaszek, Lisa (2005), 'An Afrofuturist Reading of Ralph Ellison's *Invisible Man*', *Rethinking History* 9.2/3: pp. 297–313.

Index

Aarseth, Espen, 46, 48, 72n8
Abbott, H. Porter, 37n15
abyss *see* ungrounding
active synthesis, 50–2, 96–7
actor-network-theory, 6
actual, the, 16–17, 21–4, 29, 44–5, 61–2, 73n10, 88–9, 110–11, 165
aesthetics
 correlationism and, 6–7
 epistemology and, 32–3, 94–100, 149n15
 expression and, 78–80
 ontology and, 41–5
 politics and, 72n3
 rendering and, 78–80
 sensation and, 4–5, 102–11, 112nn6–7
 speculation and, 124–34, 146–7
affects, 25–7, 31, 39n25, 96, 107–8, 180, 185–9
Afrofuturism, 141–2, 151n23
After Life (Thacker), 177n7
'After Life' (Thacker), 159–62
Aion, 68–70, 109–10
aisthesis, 5, 104, 106–7, 115n21, 185–7
Alber, Jan, 13–14, 28, 35nn8–9
altermodern, 118–19, 134–6, 148nn3–4
American West, 77–89, 114n9
amor fati, 140, 145–7
analepsis, 119–20
analytic philosophy, 19–20, 37n18
anarchē see ungrounding
animals, 90–100
anthropocentrism
 animality and, 90–100
 correlationism and, 6–7, 9, 35n6, 40n28, 125–7, 149n10, 161, 184

fourth-person singular and, 29–32, 70–2
Kant's metaphysics and, 14–16
in narratology, 1–3, 6, 184–9
sensations' relation to, 25–7
speculative realism and, 184–9
anti-metaphysics, 19–20
Anzaldúa, Gloria, 58
Aristotle, 13–14, 36n12
'Art as Device' (Shklovsky), 4–5
Arteaga, Alfred, 72n1
Austin, J. L., 19
Avanessian, Armen, 118, 132, 134, 148n4, 150n16

Bacon, Francis, 26, 112nn6–7
Badiou, Alain, 147n1
Bal, Mieke, 10
Barbour, Douglas, 83–6, 111n2, 114n11
Barthes, Roland, 1, 3–4
becoming
 Barthes on, 1, 3
 expression and, 78–80
 imperceptibility and, 55–6, 90–100, 104–5, 112n6, 133–4, 138–42, 150n18
 impersonality and, 25–6
 metalepsis and, 82–9
 narratives and, 28–9, 180, 187–9
 as principle, 54–5, 68, 128–34, 175–6
 process philosophy and, 3–4, 22–4
 sensation and, 39n26, 101–11
 speculation and, 23–4, 88–100, 110, 112n7
 unconsciousness and, 3–4
 ungrounding and, 39n23, 57–70, 155–72
 see also fourth-person singular;

Index

morphogenesis; ontology; processes
being
  correlationism and, 6–7, 35n6, 40n28, 125–7, 161
  Deleuze on, 7
  difference and, 160–2
  expression and, 5–6, 16–17, 21
  fourth-person singular and, 29–32, 70–2
  sensation and, 7–8, 127–34
  univocity of, 23, 27, 31, 70–1, 91, 116n26, 162, 174–6, 177n7, 184
Beressem, Hanjo, 176n2
Bergson, Henri, 20, 32, 39n26, 52, 66, 69
Berlant, Lauren, 148n4
Bérubé, Michael, 148n4
Beyond the Limits of Thought (Priest), 32
black boxes, 123, 130–4, 141–7, 187
'Black to the Future' (Dery), 151n23
Blakeslee, Sandra, 149n13
bodies
  mingling of, 92–3, 115n20
  souls and, 110, 114n14, 120, 128, 155–7, 162–72
  territoriality and, 70, 95, 105–7
  without organs, 103–4, 106–7
Bogost, Ian, 182
Borderlands (Anzaldúa), 58
Bourriaud, Nicolas, 118
Brassier, Ray, 9, 183–4, 188n4
Bray, Joe, 50
Brick, Martin, 164, 178n16
Brown, Charles Brockden, 50
Brown, Nathan, 189n7
Bruns, Gerald L., 72n3
Burns, Walter Noble, 77

Calvin, Ritch, 72n2
Capitalism and Schizophrenia (Deleuze), 111n3
Carnap, Rudolf, 19
Casati, Roberto, 150n19
Castillo, Ana, 33, 41–72, 118, 187
Cervantes, Miguel de, 53–4, 73n11
Chanen, Brian W., 153

'The Chemistry of Darkness' (Grant), 160
Chicano movement, 66–70
Chicano Narrative (Saldívar), 72n1
Chicano Novels and the Politics of Form (González), 72n1
Chronos, 68–70
Circus Philosophicus (Harman), 183
Clark, Matthew, 40n28
Cogburn, Jon, 38n20, 137
Cognition and Decision in Non-Human Biological Organisms (Shaviro), 184–5
cognitive narratology, 8–9
Colebrook, Claire, 70, 76n21, 115nn20–1
The Collected Works of Billy the Kid (Ondaatje), 33, 77–111, 118, 187
communication, 1–31; *see also* expression; narrative
A Companion to Narrative Theory (Herman and Fludernik), 2
comparative textual media, 153–5
congeries, 23, 103
consciousness
  Cartesian dualism and, 90–1, 93, 156–7
  correlationism and, 6–7, 35n6, 40n28, 125–7, 161, 184
  Deleuze's circumvention of, 7, 94–100, 115n20
  Kant and, 5, 8, 13–14
  the unconscious and, 3–4, 25–7, 33n1, 50–1
  see also anthropocentrism; Copernican Revolution (of Kant); epistemology; speculation
Continental Realism (Ennis), 149n10
Coover, Robert, 47–9
Copernican Revolution (of Kant), 5, 8, 15, 20, 32, 125, 128, 133, 148n9
correlationism, 6–7, 9, 35n6, 40n28, 125–7, 149n10, 161, 184
cosmology, 153, 159–62, 172–6, 176n2, 181–2
counterfactuals, 137–8
cracks (in surfaces), 21–4, 30–1, 42–5, 55–6, 60, 165–6, 177n7

The Crossing (McCarthy), 180
cybertextuality, 47–9, 72n8
Cyclonopedia (Negarestani), 183

Danielewski, Mark Z., 33, 153–72, 177n3, 178n16, 187
Dante Alighieri, 159
death, 80, 82–9, 104–5
Deleuze, Gilles
 the actual and, 16–17, 21–4, 29, 44–5, 61–2, 73n10, 110–11, 165
 animality and, 90–100
 anti-anthropocentrism of, 184–9
 diagrammatology of, 40n31, 108–9
 difference and, 4, 23, 27, 39n25, 44–5, 62, 88–9, 111, 114n16, 127–8, 141–7, 160–2, 172–5
 the event and, 73n10, 84, 122–5, 140, 143–7
 folding and, 154–9, 162–72
 idealism of, 7–8, 14–15, 21–2, 27, 29, 59–60, 84–5, 125, 165
 immanence and, 15–16, 21–3, 32, 45
 Kant and, 21, 26–7, 32, 36n13, 37n14, 94, 127–8
 Leibniz and, 83–4, 155
 literary studies' use of, 111n3
 metaphysics of, 16, 18–27, 32, 33n1, 34n4, 37n18, 39n25, 61–2, 65–6, 72n6, 78–80, 91–2, 95, 103–4, 111n3, 161–2, 165–72, 177n7, 181–2
 monism of, 109–10, 114n14, 116n26
 problem-solution matrix and, 78, 112n5
 sensation and, 7–8, 101–11
 spiritualism of, 59, 73n14
 temporality and, 36n13, 50–2, 54–6, 68–70, 82, 97, 121–2, 124–5, 131–43, 150n16
 the virtual and, 16–17
 see also specific works
Deleuze and the Unconscious (Kerslake), 57, 75n20
Delgadillo, Theresa, 58
Derrida, Jacques, 19, 40n31, 72n6, 108, 176n1
Dery, Mark, 151n23

Descartes, René, 62–3, 90, 156–7
deterritorialisation, 106–7, 130
diagrammatology, 31, 40n30, 108–10, 112n6, 116n25
dialetheism, 32–3
difference
 cosmology and, 153–5
 Deleuze's concept of, 4, 23, 27, 39n25, 44–5, 59–60, 62, 72n6, 88–9, 110–11, 114n16, 127–8, 141–7, 160–2, 172–5
 Derrida's, 176n1
 folding and, 55, 61–2, 154–9
 identity politics and, 41–5, 66–70
 kinds of, 59–60
 philosophers of, 72n6
 ungrounding and, 39n23, 57–70, 155–72
Difference and Repetition (Deleuze), 7, 34n4, 36n13, 39n24, 44–5, 50–1, 112n5, 112n7, 114n16, 124, 160
different/ciation, 23, 39n25, 81, 88, 172–5, 183–4
differential narratology, 1, 4, 21–31, 81–2, 153–5, 162–72, 175–6, 180–9
disfiguration, 26, 81, 88–9, 101, 110, 112n7, 114n17, 145–6, 181
dissolution, 42–5, 50, 61–2, 87–9, 103–4, 112n7, 162–72
DNE, 173–5, 178n18
Don Quixote (Cervantes), 53–4, 73n11
dreaming, 43–4, 55–72, 75n16

Echo, 166–72, 178n13
The Echo Maker (Powers), 25–7
ecology, 181–2
ecumenon, 154, 181
Elam, Michele, 121
electronic literature, 46–7
Electronic Literature (Hayles), 72n8
eliminative neuroscience, 6
Ellison, Ralph, 138–9, 151n21, 151n23
empiricism
 intuitionism and, 118–34, 143–7
 Kant's, 8, 14–15
 spiritualism and, 56–70
 see also transcendental empiricism

Index

emplotment, 35, 47–9, 100, 138–9, 154–5, 172–3, 186
encounter, the, 7–8, 45, 114n16
Ennis, Paul, 149n10
enstrangement, 4–5, 24, 87
epistemology
  aesthetics and, 32–3, 94–100, 149n15
  correlationism and, 6–7, 9, 35n6, 40n28, 125–7, 149n10, 161, 184
  ignorance and, 123–4
  Intuitionism and, 123–34
  narratology and, 1, 3, 5, 34n3
  ontology and, 5–6, 130–1, 165
  representation and, 165
epistolary form, 43–56, 71
Eskelinen, Markku, 47–8, 72n8
esotericism, 56–70, 73n14
Essays on Deleuze (Smith), 111n3
eternal return, 54, 110–11, 156
event, the, 73n10, 84, 122–5, 140, 143–7, 180
Existence, Space and Architecture (Norberg-Schulz), 177n5
experientiality, 1–9, 15, 23–7, 34n5, 47, 72n2, 75n20, 188n2; *see also* empiricism; metaphysics; representationalism; sensation
expression
  aesthetics and, 78–80
  being and, 5–6, 16–17, 21
  narrative and, 21, 23, 25–6, 163–4
  sensation and, 4–5, 7–8, 77–82, 84–5, 94–100, 102–11
  unground and, 160–2

fabulation, 66, 69
The Fall of Sleep (Nancy), 61
Fehrle, Johannes, 188n1
feminism, 45, 54–5, 63–4, 72n2, 76n21
'Feminist Extinction' (Colebrook), 76n21
Ferlinghetti, Lawrence, 29, 70
Fichte, Johann Gottlieb, 14–15, 183
fiction, 18–19, 33n2, 36n11, 41–5, 69–70, 118–23, 130–4, 137, 180–1; *see also specific authors and works*

The Figure of Echo (Hollander), 167
figures, 101–3, 108, 112n7, 114n17; *see also* tropes; *specific narratological elements*
first-person narrative fiction, 31–2
Five Senses (Serres), 93
Fludernik, Monika, 2, 6, 13–14, 34n5
The Fly, 156
focalisation, 28, 119–20
The Fold (Deleuze), 154
folding, 21–2, 55, 61–2, 154–9, 175–6; *see also* infolding; topology; unfolding
Ford, John, 77
forms *see* idealisms; morphogenesis
fourth-person singular, 29–32, 70–2
fracturing, 21–4, 30–1, 42–5, 55–6, 60, 165–6, 177n7
Francis Bacon (Deleuze), 26, 109, 112n6
Freud, Sigmund, 44, 140, 151n22
Freytag, Gustav, 89
'From Narrative Representation to Narrative Use' (Rudrum), 10–11
frontier thesis, 116n24
Fulton, James, 119, 125, 127–30, 134, 140, 149n14, 150n18
futurity, 28, 38n19, 51, 55, 69, 121–3, 130–47, 150n16, 188n4; *see also* speculation; temporality

gender, 45–55, 63–4, 72n2, 76n21
General Process Theory, 37n18
genesis (philosophical), 3–4, 15–16, 23–4, 34n4, 44–5, 88–9, 94, 110, 116n25, 173, 181; *see also* becoming; Deleuze, Gilles; different/ciation; DNE
Genette, Gérard, 10, 28
González, Marcial, 72n1
grammatology, 40n31, 108–9
Grant, Iain Hamilton, 14–15, 147n1, 160
Gratton, Peter, 38n19
'The Grid' (Moody), 27–8, 30–2
Guattari, Félix, 30–1, 57, 66, 69, 95, 101, 104–5, 112n6, 114n9, 154, 157, 175; *see also specific works*

Habermas, Jürgen, 19
Hägler, Andreas, 179n22
Hamburger, Käte, 36n11
Hansen, Mark B. N., 153, 164–5
Harman, Graham, 21, 147n1, 182–3, 185–6
Hayles, N. Katherine, 73n8, 153, 178n16, 185
Hegel, G. W. F., 34n3, 61, 147n1, 160, 183
Heidegger, Martin, 19, 72n6, 96, 126, 145, 149n14
Heinze, Rüdiger, 28, 31
Hennig, Anke, 118, 132, 134, 148n4, 150n16
Herman, David, 2, 37n17
Hollander, John, 167
House of Leaves (Danielewski), 33, 153–62, 177n3, 178n16, 187
Huffman, L. A., 77, 80
human, the *see* anthropocentrism
Husserl, Edmund, 185
hybridity, 41–5, 99
hypertextuality, 43–56, 71, 156–7, 164

idealisms
  Deleuze's, 14–16, 21, 23, 27, 29, 59–60, 84–5, 165, 175–6, 180–1
  Hegel's, 147n1
  Intuitionism and, 125
  Kant's, 8, 37n14, 165
  Plato's, 13, 160, 165
identitarianism, 18–19, 45, 136, 159; *see also* representationalism
imagination, 96–7
immanence, 15–16, 21–4, 32, 45
imperceptibility, 55–6, 90–100, 104–5, 112n6, 133–4, 138–42, 150n18
In the Dust of this Planet (Thacker), 161–2
Inferno (Dante), 159
infolding, 21–2; *see also* folding; unfolding
intensity, 22, 29–31, 44–5, 71–2, 98–9, 103–4, 108–9, 143–7, 161–2; *see also* Deleuze, Gilles; metaphysics; ontology

'Introduction to the Structural Analysis of Narratives' (Barthes), 1
Intuitionism, 118–34, 143–7, 149n14
The Intuitionist (Whitehead), 33, 118–43, 151n21, 187
Invisible Man (Ellison), 138–9, 151n21, 151n23
Iversen, Stefan, 13, 35n8

Jameson, Fredric, 39n25, 42
Jane Talbot (Brown), 50

Kant, Immanuel
  Copernican Revolution of, 5, 8–9, 13–15, 20, 32, 125, 128, 133, 148n9
  Deleuze on, 21, 26–7, 36n13, 37n14, 94, 127–8
  Nancy on, 61
  Rimbaud and, 38n22
Kermode, Frank, 121
Kerslake, Christian, 57, 73n14, 75n20
Klee, Paul, 79, 112n6
knowledge *see* epistemology

labyrinths, 114n13, 154–72, 175, 177n5
Lavender, Isiah, 151n23
legends, 77–82, 106, 154–5
Leibniz, Gottfried Wilhelm, 83–4, 155
Lethem, Jonathan, 156–7
Lichtenauer, Fritz, 112n7
liminality, 82–9, 99
literature (as subset of narrative), 4, 33n2, 36n11, 41–5, 130, 180–1
'Literature and Life' (Deleuze), 112n6
The Living Handbook of Narratology, 2, 37n15
logic, 32–3, 130
Logic of Sense (Deleuze), 68
Lord, Beth, 36n13
Lyotard, Jean-François, 34n3, 72n6, 183

McCarthy, Cormac, 180, 188n1
McHale, Brian, 18–19, 37n16
machines, 24, 182
Malfatti, Johann, 57

Index

The Man Who Shot Liberty Valance (Ford), 77
Massacre of the Dreamers (Castillo), 57
Massumi, Brian, 181
mathematics, 175–6, 176n2, 185–6
matter, 47, 139, 142, 153–7, 162–72; *see also* bodies
Matter, Manner, Idea (Van Tuinen), 149n15
mechatronics, 24–5
Meillassoux, Quentin, 6–7, 9, 21, 35n6, 125, 143–4, 152n25, 161, 185–6
Meister, Jan Christoph, 2
memory, 50–2
mereotopology, 135–6
mestizaje see hybridity
metalepsis, 23, 84–5, 87–9
Metamedia (Starre), 153
Metamorphoses (Ovid), 166, 178n14
metaphor, 23, 71–2, 167–9, 182, 189n7
metaphysics
  anti-metaphysicians and, 19–20
  correlationism and, 6–7, 35n6, 40n28, 125–7, 161, 184
  Deleuze's, 14–16, 18–27, 32, 33n1, 34n4, 37n18, 39n25, 61–2, 65–6, 111n3, 165–72, 177n7, 181–2
  grammar and, 107–8
  Kant and, 5, 8–9, 13–16
  narratology and, 3, 7, 14–17
  spiritualism and, 56–70
  unground of, 39n23, 57–70, 155–72
'Metaphysics Today and Tomorrow' (Millière), 19
milieu, 143–4
Millière, Raphaël, 19, 37n18, 38n19
mimesis, 1–2, 11–14, 165, 178n11; *see also* representationalism
The Mixquiahuala Letters (Castillo), 33, 41–72, 118, 187
monism, 90–1, 109–10, 114n14, 116n26; *see also* Spinoza, Baruch
monuments, 30, 79, 101, 105, 175, 181
Moody, Rick, 27–32
Moore, A. W., 33n1
Morelle, Louis, 20, 38n19
morphogenesis, 3–4, 15–16, 24, 34n4, 58, 70–1, 97, 110, 186; *see also* becoming
Morton, Timothy, 175, 182, 188n3
motion, 80, 92–4, 181
Mullarkey, John, 108
multiplicities *see* Deleuze, Gilles; difference
myth, 154–5, 166–72, 176n2
Mythomystes (Reynolds), 167–8

Nancy, Jean-Luc, 61–2, 64, 75n16
narrative
  becoming and, 17, 21–3, 27–9, 163–4, 170, 174–6, 180–1, 187–9
  correlationism and, 1–3, 6–7, 184–9
  definitions of, 2–4
  dissolution of, 162–72
  expression and, 25–6
  first-person perspective and, 31–2
  hypertextuality and, 43–56, 71, 156–7, 164
  intensity and, 22–3, 25–6, 44–5, 49, 71–2
  the non-human and, 184–9
  ontological accounts of, 5–6, 9
  poetics and, 18–19
  representation and, 1–2, 9–10, 14–15, 18, 21, 24–6, 34n5, 35n7
  sensation and, 101–11
  speculation and, 4, 23–4, 28–9, 118–23, 183–9
  temporality and, 28, 36n13, 82, 123–43
  unfolding and, 162–72
  see also aesthetics; speculative constructivism; speculative realism
Narrative (journal), 10
narrativity, 17–18, 33–9, 110, 118, 131, 153, 175–6, 180–4, 187; *see also* idealisms; metaphysics
narratology
  anthropocentrism and, 1–3, 6, 184–9
  correlationism and, 1–3, 6–7, 9, 184–9
  cosmology and, 153–5, 159–62
  differential, 1, 4, 21–31, 81–2, 153–5, 162–73, 175–6, 180–9

narratology (cont.)
  epistemology and, 1, 34n3
  experience and, 23–4, 34n5
  fiction and, 69–70
  focalisation and, 119–20
  pragmatic versions of, 10–11
  representationalism and, 1–2, 8–10, 14–15, 17–18, 21, 24, 34n5, 35n7
  story matter and, 34n5, 44–7
  unnatural, 11–14, 27–8, 31, 34n5, 35n7, 35n9, 36n10, 71
  see also metaphysics; ontology; speculation
narr-on-tology, 176
Negarestani, Reza, 183
Nelson, Theodor H., 45–6, 48–9
new materialisms, 6
Nielsen, Henrik Skov, 13, 31–2, 35n8, 70–1
Nietzsche, Friedrich, 110–11, 183–4
Nietzsche and Philosophy (Deleuze), 155–6
Nihil Unbound (Brassier), 183–4
Nin, Anaïs, 53, 63
noesis, 94, 186
nomadicity, 54, 105–6, 112n6, 128, 157, 173, 182
Norberg-Schulz, Christian, 177n5
Notre Dame Journal of Formal Logic, 32
noumenon, 16, 78, 149n11; see also Deleuze, Gilles; difference; immanence; Kant, Immanuel; metaphysics; phenomenon; virtual, the

object-oriented ontology, 147n1, 182–5, 188nn2–3
objects
  correlationism and, 6–7, 9, 35n6, 40n28, 125–7, 149n10, 161, 184
  Deleuze on, 127–8
  poetic, 41–5
Ohm, Mark Allan, 38n20, 137
'On Truth and Lies in a Nonmoral Sense' (Nietzsche), 184
Ondaatje, Michael, 33, 77–111, 118, 187

ontology
  aesthetics and, 41–5
  Deleuzian metaphysics and, 21–3, 44–5, 161–2
  difference and, 42–5
  epistemology and, 5–6, 130–1, 165
  expression and, 5, 16–17
  the fold and, 155–72, 175–6
  genesis and, 3–4, 15–16, 23–4, 34n4, 44–5, 88–9, 94, 110, 116n26, 173–5, 181
  Heideggerian, 125–6
  narratives and, 187–9
  objectivity and, 25–6
  the ontic and, 78
  OOO/OOP and, 147n1, 182–3, 188n2
  process ontology and, 1–3, 14–15, 21–2, 184–9, 188n6
  sensation and, 39n26, 85–6, 90–111
onto-theology, 58, 153, 167
orchid-wasp encounter, 34n4, 175
Ovid, 166, 178n14

panpsychism, 93, 114n15, 126, 185–6
paralepsis, 23, 28–9, 31–2
Parmenides, 174
passing, 133–4, 148n6, 150n18
passive synthesis, 36n13, 50–1, 97, 112n6, 150n16
past, the, 28; see also memory; temporality
perceptibility, 55–6, 90–100, 104–5, 112n6, 127–34, 138–42, 150n18
percepts, 25–7, 31, 96, 180
phantom limb sensation, 127, 143–4, 149n13
Phantoms in the Brain (Ramachandran and Blakeslee), 149n13
phenomenon
  empiricism and, 123–5
  Nancy on, 61–2, 75n16
  problem-solution matrix and, 78
  unnatural narratology and, 12–13
  see also Copernican Revolution (of Kant); speculative realism
Philosophical Investigations (Wittgenstein), 10

Index

photography, 77, 109
planomenon, 154, 157
Plato, 13, 37n14, 160
plot *see* emplotment
pluralism, 110–11; *see also* monism
poetics, 18–19, 41–5, 70–2
poiesis, 186–7
The Political Unconscious (Jameson), 42
The Postmodern Condition (Lyotard), 34n3
postmodernism, 18–19, 34n3, 118
Powers, Richard, 25–7
Pressman, Jessica, 153
Priest, Graham, 32–3
Prince, Gerald, 10
principle of unreason, 143–4, 152n25, 185–6
problem-solution matrix, 78, 112n5, 160, 165–6
processes, 1–3, 14–15, 21–2, 37n18, 184–9, 188n6; *see also* becoming; morphogenesis; *specific philosophers*
production, 22, 108–9; *see also* genesis (philosophical)
pure past, 51–5
Putnam, Hilary, 19
Pynchon, Thomas, 124

race, 118, 123, 137–40, 150n18, 151n24; *see also* Afrofuturism; difference; passing
Ragas of Longing (Ondaatje), 83
Ramachandran, Vilanayur, 149n13
Ramey, Joshua, 57
rationality, 87–100, 115n20, 145–6; *see also* anthropocentrism; consciousness
real, the, 12–15, 67–8, 118–23; *see also* idealisms; metaphysics; ontology; speculative realism
Realist Magic (Morton), 188n3
recognition, 4, 7–8, 114n16, 123, 127
'Remembering, Repeating, and Working-Through' (Freud), 151n22

representationalism
  Deleuze on, 7–8, 78–80, 84–6, 165–6
  echoing and, 165–72
  fiction and, 77–82, 84, 137
  Kantian metaphysics and, 8–9, 145–6
  memory and, 50–1
  mereology and, 135–6
  mimesis and, 1–2, 11–12, 178n11
  narratology and, 1–2, 9–10, 14–15, 18, 21, 24–6, 34n5, 35n7
  photography and, 77
  sensation and, 99–100
  spatiality and, 131–4, 150n19
  see also Copernican Revolution (of Kant); epistemology
reterritorialisation, 105–7
Revolutionary Leaves, 153
Reynolds, Henry, 167
The Rhetoric of Fictionality (Walsh), 33n2
Richardson, Brian, 13, 35n8
Ricœur, Paul, 110–11, 172–3
Rimbaud, Arthur, 30, 38n22
Rorty, Richard, 19
Rudrum, David, 10–11
Ryan, Marie-Laure, 10–11
Ryle, Gilbert, 19

The Saga of Billy the Kid (Burns), 77
Saldívar, Ramón, 72n1, 118, 147n1, 148n6, 151n23
Schelling, Friedrich, 14–15, 32, 75n19, 160, 183
Scholes, Robert, 10
sensation
  aesthetics and, 4–5, 77–82, 84–5, 94–100, 102–11
  becoming and, 39n26, 85–6, 99–111
  being and, 7–8, 127–34
  disfiguration and, 26, 81, 88–9, 101, 110, 112n7, 145–6, 181
  monuments and, 79, 101, 105, 175, 181
  narratives and, 4–5, 7, 25–6, 175, 181
  representationalism and, 99–100
  speculation and, 124–34

sensation (*cont.*)
  violence and, 19, 81, 85, 101–11, 113n8, 144, 170
Serres, Michel, 93
Shaviro, Steven, 184–6
Shklovsky, Viktor, 4–7, 24, 102
singularities, 29–32, 70, 83–4, 121–4, 142–7, 181
sleeping, 59–70, 75n16
Slotkin, Richard, 81
Slow Learner (Pynchon), 124
Smith, Daniel W., 111n3
Solecki, Sam, 82–3
Somers-Hall, Henry, 34n4
souls, 91–3, 110, 114n14, 120, 128, 155–7, 162–72; *see also* spiritualism
Spanking the Maid (Coover), 47–9
spatiality, 70, 95, 105–7, 131–4, 150n19, 162–72
speculation
  aesthetics and, 101–11, 127–8, 146–7
  becoming and, 23–4, 88–100, 110, 112n7, 128–34
  fabulation and, 66–70
  narrative and, 4–5, 20–1, 183–9
  political movements and, 66–70
  temporality and, 28, 38n19, 51, 55, 68–70, 121–5, 131–2, 137–46
Speculations (journal), 38n19
speculative constructivism, 69–70, 122–5, 131–43, 148n7
speculative realism, 20–1, 32, 147n1, 151n23, 182–9
Speculative Realism (Gratton), 38n19
Spinks, Lee, 83, 111nn2–3
Spinoza, Baruch, 90–2, 94–5, 98–9, 110, 114n14, 116n26, 168
Spiritual Mestizaje (Delgadillo), 58
spiritualism, 56, 58–70, 107
Starre, Alexander, 153
Stengers, Isabelle, 122–3, 148n7
Sternberg, Meir, 17
Stiegler, Bernard, 164
story matter, 34n5, 44–7
subject, the
  Descartes on, 62–3
  dissolution of, 42–5, 50, 61–2, 87–9, 103–4, 112n7, 163
  epistolary form and, 50–1
  grounding of, 59–60
  Kant's version of, 15
swarms, 159–62, 172–5
System of Transcendental Idealism (Schelling), 75n19

Taylor, Mark C., 153, 167, 176n1
temporality, 28, 36n13, 50–6, 68–70, 82, 97, 118–25, 131–43, 150n16
tense (grammatical), 28, 118–19
territoriality, 70, 95, 105–7
Thacker, Eugene, 159–62, 175–6, 177n7
Theoretical Elevators (Fulton), 119, 125, 128–30, 140, 149n14
A Thousand Plateaus (Deleuze and Guattari), 34n4, 50, 57, 75n20, 109–10, 112n6, 114n9, 154, 157, 175
Thus Spoke Zarathustra (Nietzsche), 183
topology, 21–3, 61–2, 135, 176n2; *see also* folding; immanence; virtual, the
Towards a 'Natural' Narratology (Fludernik), 2, 34n5
transcendental empiricism, 7–8, 14–16, 26–7, 33n1, 36n13, 45, 122, 127–8
tropes, 23, 109, 182; *see also* anthropocentrism; metaphor
Turner, Frederick Jackson, 116n24

uncanny, the, 169–70
unconscious, the, 3–4, 17, 26, 50–1, 75n19, 156; *see also* anthropocentrism; consciousness
unfolding, 55, 68, 101–2, 108, 121–2, 124–5, 135–6, 162–72; *see also* folding; infolding
ungrounding, 39n23, 57–70, 155–72
universals, 24–5, 70–1
univocity, 23, 27, 31, 70–1, 91, 116n26, 162, 174–6, 177n7, 184; *see also* immanence

Index

unnatural narratology, 11–14, 27–8, 31, 34n5, 35n7, 35n9, 36n10, 71

Van Tuinen, Sjoerd, 125, 146–7, 149n15
Varzi, Achille C., 150n19
Vattimo, Gianni, 21
vice-diction, 83–4
'Violations of Mimetic Epistemology in First-Person Narrative Fiction' (Heinze), 31
virtual, the, 16, 21–9, 44–5, 52–68, 78–82, 88–9, 108–11, 130–43, 164–5; *see also* Deleuze, Gilles; idealisms; narrative
vitalism, 184
Voss, Daniela, 36n13

Walsh, Richard, 33n2
Welchman, Alistair, 38n21
What Is Philosophy? (Deleuze and Guattari), 30–1, 39n26, 57
Whitehead, Alfred North, 20, 32, 183, 185–6
Whitehead, Colson, 33, 118–43, 151n21, 187
Wittgenstein, Ludwig, 10, 19
Wolfendale, Peter, 38n21, 116n26
Wright, Richard, 151n24
Writing Machines (Hayles), 72n8
'Writing the Xicanista' (Calvin), 72n2

Yaszek, Lisa, 151n23